Lest We Forget

INDIRA VARMA

Lest We Forget

HOW THREE SISTERS
BRAVED THE PARTITION

First published by Westland Books, a division of Nasadiya Technologies Private Limited, in 2023

No. 269/2B, First Floor, 'Irai Arul', Vimalraj Street, Nethaji Nagar, Alapakkam Main Road, Maduravoyal, Chennai 600095

Westland and the Westland logo are the trademarks of Nasadiya Technologies Private Limited, or its affiliates.

ISBN: 9789357768559

10 9 8 7 6 5 4 3 2 1

Typeset by SÜRYA, New Delhi

Printed at Thomson Press India Ltd

For
Uma (Didi) and Roopy,
my two sisters, my lifelines

For
our beloved children and grandchildren
who have carried the closeness further

In memory of

Ramesro Devi and Sardar Manmohan Singh, my Nana and Nani

Satwant Kaur and Sardar Anoop Singh, my parents

Shrimati Shakuntla Varma and H.L. Varma, my parents-in-law

Baldev Varma, my husband

Sushil Dhand and Brijesh Mathur, my sisters' husbands

My Mami Anoop and my Mama Sardar Amrik Singh-ji

My Minnie Maasi and her husband Sardar Gurdip Singh-ji

Contents

Foreword

MUCH HAS BEEN WRITTEN ABOUT THE PARTITION OF INDIA THAT claimed the lives of approximately one million people and rendered over 12 million people refugees. This unprecedented exchange of population caused untold trauma and unimaginable horrors. Some of these have been rendered as black-and-white facts by professional historians. Some have been recounted by creative writers in the vast amounts of partition literature in the languages of the people most affected by this human tragedy, namely, Urdu, Hindi, Punjabi and Bangla. Translations into English as well as original writings in English find their fair share amongst these attempts by a generation of survivors who lived through this horrific time. These can be seen as a form of 'narrativising history', that is, providing a supplementary way of understanding history through literature. These forms have an increasing validity at a time when the professional historian is bringing into question the traditional form of telling history.

First-person accounts have a special resonance, an attention to the small, everyday details, an interest in the minutiae of real lives that is often missing in dry, factual chronicles. They contain stories of suffering and endurance, pain and misery, even anger and guilt, as well as vignettes of hope and renewal, of courage and conviction, of rising above the constraints of time and circumstance. These first-person accounts can help make the partition human and palatable, or grotesque and hateful. Sometimes the lingering pain and trauma of those times seep through these accounts even when these experiences are narrated fifty, sixty or even seventy years later.

While the majority of writers make a conscious effort to hold up the tattered fabric of secularism in the face of communalism, bitter and painful memories also find expression, especially in the first-person accounts, diaries, reportages, etc.

While there is a general agreement in much of partition-related writings that the murder and mayhem that accompanied the partition was a human tragedy of epic proportions, there is far more ambivalence in the ways of dealing with or accepting the consequences of partition. Two worlds—the lost and the emergent—fused and merged after 1947. While most writers are in agreement that countless innocent lives were lost due to the political decisions of a mere handful, many are left grappling with mixed feelings: should they feel sorrow that the *annus horribilis* had brought *batwara* (literally meaning division but commonly referred to as partition or *taqseem*) in its wake? Or should they feel joyful because the year also marked the beginning of *azadi* (freedom) and the birth of two new nations, namely India and Pakistan? Should they constantly hearken back to what they had lost in their old land? Or should they look forward with courage and conviction towards new horizons?

Like the writers, the inhabitants of these new lands didn't know whether to celebrate their hard-won independence or mourn the passing of an age. Should one celebrate the birth of a new nation? Should one rejoice at gaining independence at the end of a fierce and prolonged struggle that had come at such a heavy price? Or should one mourn the loss of an age and an end of pluralism and syncretism? Should one search for new directions? Or, were all routes to regeneration irrevocably closed for this weary generation? These questions, and many others, jostle for answers in the outpourings of partition chroniclers.

Seldom, if ever, there is a stoic acceptance and a gentle, but determined attempt to look beyond the loss, such a genuine demonstration of grace under pressure as in this first-person account of *Lest We Forget: How Three Sisters Braved the Partition*. Indira Varma takes the reader by the hand and delicately, deftly draws us into her story and the story of her two sisters. And she does so with a guileless innocence, a genuine heartwarming large-heartedness and humanity:

> 'India is being divided,' Didi tried to explain.
>
> 'Like a cookie? Whoever gets the smaller half will be upset,' I nodded wisely.

And:

> Unlike us, Papa knew when he left Peshawar that he would never be going back. And so, in his meagre bag, he carried his most treasured belongings, small booklets of what to feed the pigeons to keep them healthy. Written in Urdu and well-thumbed, my grandfather kept them till the end, my mother after him, Didi after her, and now I keep them with me.

Emerging from a cocoon of love, warmth and safety, the partition rendered Indira-ji and her family—comprising her mother, her maternal grandparents (Papa and Badi Mummy) and her two sisters—not merely homeless but destitute. There is the occasional flash of anger at having to leave behind the fabulous house, horses, cars, in fact, an entire way of life in Peshawar to live as paupers in India. But that is only to be expected from a child who is just seven years old in 1947:

> I would also have preferred to be in independent India in Peshawar. I missed home. The trees, the sky, the feel of the air, the smell. Not just of the city but of our house. Oh, how I craved the smells of home.

Soon the family begins to put down new roots in new soil: for the first three years in Naintial as homeless refugees, briefly in Delhi in a house allotted by the Resettlement Commission, then Kanpur in 1950 which would be home for the next decade or so and thence a life shuttling between Aligarh, Dehradun and finally Delhi. 'Reality,'

Indira-ji writes, 'was too sharp and in its teeth, it carried hunger and poverty.' But help came from unexpected sources as this family of six learns to make do with very little, to do odd jobs such as making candles and pasting labels on bottles to earn a meagre living. But still, the family lived on the edge of poverty often going without a proper meal till Mian-ji, a kindly Muslim, ensured every morning when the family opened its door, they would find small packets left at the doorstep. This memory, like so many others, comes laced with humanity: 'We were a Sikh Hindu family and maybe ten or more Muslim families were cutting into their children's food of the day to feed us.'

Marriage, motherhood, the loss of her dearly beloved grandparents, prolonged and persistent shortage of funds, a busy working life juggling the demands of a career and family—everything is recounted with grace and good humour. With time, each of the three sisters goes on to carve new trajectories for themselves through the grit and dedication that the partition generation is justly famous for: Didi would spend her entire life working at the Cottage Industries Emporium; Indira-ji would have various stints in banking, travel and tourism; and the youngest Roopy in the fledgling airline industry. All three—the Singh Sisters as they were called in their convent school—would carry bits and pieces of their past, wear their suffering and sorrows like a badge of courage and honour, and walk through life with their head held high. More importantly, all three would be pillars of support to each other, filling the vacuum in their lives with an abundance of support and nurturing. What is more, the husbands of the three sisters get along fabulously well with many shared interests—as do the children—making this an ecosystem that shelters, nourishes and shores up those who need help at any given time.

Like friendship and family, food is a recurring motif throughout this book. There are delightful vignettes of times well spent with friends who are like family, bonding over food, drink, music and singing. Despite being very young at the time of partition, all three sisters remained proud of their Pishori Sikh heritage. Didi would bring gifts of jalebas (a larger version of the doodle-like jalebis) and yellow meethey chawal every year without fail on Baisakhi. She would also make the achaars that were once famous in Peshawar, such as the paani-wala achaar, the gobi-shalgam-gajar achaar, the distinctive pashlara saag eaten with makki ki roti, thus keeping alive a tenuous link with the past for future generations. Pishori traditions find a mention in an entire chapter devoted to Indira-ji's roots. But ultimately, it is not just Peshawar and its neighbourhood but all of Punjab, with its glorious multicultural, multi-religious social fabric that comes alive in Indira-ji's retelling of a life well lived.

Knowing Indira-ji as I do, I know she sees the good in human beings, choosing to ignore their faults and shortcomings. For her, the glass is always half full, not half empty. Friendships never fade. Family comes first. But all along music is a constant, as is Urdu poetry. In fact, Indira-ji ends several chapters in this book with a selection of her own Urdu verses, the choice of verse serving as a summary of sorts for each chapter. Having written two collections of Urdu poetry, *Hum-Umr Khayal* and *Shafaq ke Rang* and a third comprising translations of Tagore's poetry into Urdu, she describes her poetic journey thus: 'Sometimes a ghazal danced in my blood. I could see it in my mind's eye. When I was able to read what the words were saying to me, I put them down on paper. The ghazal never left me even for a day or even for an hour. We were one. My heartbeat was the ghazal.'

Despite the many blessings and gains that Indira-ji fulsomely acknowledges, there is also a lingering feeling of loss:

> The loss of home was the loss of identity, the loss of roots, a way of living, a language, food, culture, traditions. For people like my grandparents, it was the loss of self. Who they were was wiped out and they struggled throughout the rest of their lives, not able to accept the new selves created by the act of partition.

But in the final analysis, the thanksgiving outweighs the loss. *Lest We Forget* should be read for its overwhelming message of compassion, of the triumph of positivity, goodness and optimism: 'Six of us conquered the Partition together. We are now just two left. I think on a scale of one to ten we have all triumphed.'

Dr Rakhshanda Jalil

1

Childhood in Peshawar

WE WERE THREE DAUGHTERS OF A BEAUTIFUL EVE.

My mother was to the manor born. The only child of an aristocratic, land-owning Sikh family of Peshawar, Satwant Kaur was brought up like a princess.

She travelled in a Rolls Royce, had many admirers, many houses and immense wealth.

In her dowry she is said to have brought to my father's house five maids, called golees, who catered to her every need, including bathing, dressing, and drying her hair over the harmal dhuan, an essence-filled herb lighted over coal.

She smelled divine.

She was a beauty.

Nothing local appealed to her. Evening in Paris was her preferred perfume, her blanket was pure white mohair.

There were cut glass bottles and powder puffs on her dresser. The dresser itself felt like something from the silver screen. Her sarees were hand-embroidered chiffons and georgettes. Her idols were Princess Elizabeth and Princess Margaret. Their portraits held pride of place in her bedroom, in gilded frames, hung on walls hand-painted with roses.

I can close my eyes and recall every inch of the room, its intricately carved bay windows at one end, the geometric, floral designs of the frames highlighted with blue, green, yellow and red stained-glass pieces, the sun's journey through the day bathing the room in a kaleidoscope of hues. The large four poster bed, the dresser, its three mirrors in a semi-circle, silver-backed brushes fanned out, a cluster of imported perfumes in fancy crystal bottles and a huge crystal chandelier hanging from her ceiling.

The diamond-shaped, cobalt blue bottle of Evening in Paris was her favourite. It was one of the most famous perfumes of the twentieth century, created by Ernest Beaux, the same man who had crafted Chanel No. 5. Seeing her spray it was like watching a sound and light show: the pump whooshed softly, the tassels danced, the spray shimmered, and the room was filled with the sweet smells of vanilla, rose and musk mixed with the glamour and beauty that was my mother. A vision in hand-embroidered chiffons and georgettes, worn ulta palla, a slim, fair young girl, so young we considered her our elder sister and even referred to our father as Jija-ji.

I don't think Mummy ever had formal or school education. Teachers and ustads came to the house and taught her, some in purdah. She wrote Gurmukhi and read romantic tomes like *Heer Ranjha*. At home, she spoke Urdu and Pishori. My father would write her letters in Gurmukhi. I have some letters from the early days of their marriage. They had married in 1937, a beautiful couple. My father, Sardar Anoop Singh, the child of an old Pishori family, was still a law student then, but much was expected of his future.

But first came three daughters, produced at regular intervals, Didi in 1938, I followed in 1940, and Roopy in 1944. My parents separated before Roopy's birth and if my father ever sent my mother any letters after, I neither heard about them nor found them.

My sister and I were brought up by our grandparents, Sardar and Sardarni Manmohan Singh. We called my grandfather Papa, my grandmother Badi Mummy and my mother Mummy. My grandfather's visiting card read 'Banker and Landlord'.

The wealth came from Badi Mummy, Ramesro Devi. Her father was Lala Balmakand Sahib, who built the Sir Cunningham Clock Tower near the Qissa Khwaani Bazaar in Peshawar, which is popularly known as the Ghantaghar.

My grandmother, as a minor, had been a ward of the then Viceroy due to the immense wealth of her inheritance. She told me that her father was the only Indian allowed on all the roads where the British roamed. He used to have two kitchens: one for the family and the other to entertain the British.

Papa's haveli is the only home I remember in Peshawar. It was supposed to have a hundred rooms, but I remember maybe forty. A grand marbled entrance gave onto the house. On the ground floor were the business areas, the mardana, a large warren of rooms where Munshi Avinashi Singh and Papa used to have meetings. There were people always coming and going and I enjoyed the full house.

It was where Papa sat with piles of coins to distribute to the forty servants, hoping for a grandson when Roopy was being born.

That day, high above, on the terrace, I had snatched a doll from Didi's hands and run away, with our maids and friends Pari and Quadra in hot pursuit. Didi was crying, I was laughing. In the family quarters on the first floor, women scurried about with basins of hot water. Dr Swaroop was there too.

When I ran down, I was overwhelmed by the smell of Dettol. In *Remembrance of Things Past,* Marcel Proust wrote about involuntary memory and how the taste of a madeleine cake transposed him to his childhood. Submerged memories need such triggers. Like summer roses and their fragrance, memory returns to us suddenly like a waft of a forgotten but once dearly loved scent. Even today, just a whiff of Dettol is enough to take me back to the day of Roopy's birth: 20 November 1944.

The first floor held a grand drawing room with its dozen sofas, vases taller than my five-year-old self, and six or seven chandeliers. Bimla Maasi's dowry was decorated here. This was where the women gathered, and the carpets were covered with trays and tokris and the clothes hung on the walls as showpieces. Servants bustled around, sweets were rolled out, saris oohed and aahed over, the silver bowls approved, the jewellery closely examined. First the men were called in to look, and then finally the groom and his family were called to see the dowry and they too would call us to see the wari (what the groom's side gives). There were endless cups of chai, wedding songs being sung to the beat of dholaks, and squeals of laughter.

Little did we know that Bimla Maasi's wedding was the last grand wedding we would see in that house.

I liked to dive in and out of the wedding excitement. Whenever I was bored, I would slip out of the windows to the verandah that ran round the haveli, peeping from its grills at the road below, inhaling the smell of damp earth from the streets freshly sprinkled with water every evening by a maashki, from a mashk of buffalo skin.

Or I would run around and duck into the dining room … and leave it quickly too. It was a formal space; meals were all eaten at the table, Western style with forks, knives and spoons. Dal, sabzi, roti, bhuna gosht, chaap, kofte, naan, seekh kebab, rumali roti.

We ate lots of tinned food too: salmon, anchovies, mackerel, Kraft cheese, sardines, beans, fish cakes and cherries. I realised much later that these could have been war rations. I've never found anything that tasted like them again. These were served as snacks at tea.

I loved food, I loved milk and everything that came from it—paneer, butter, ghee, khoya. The delicacy in our house was khamiri roti, a soft, spongy, yeasty roti that was paired with tandoori chicken, a taste I can never forget and have not been able to recreate. Tandoori chicken, no red colouring, no ready masala, but chicken cooked in the tandoor, just Pishori food. We now know it as North-West Frontier cuisine.

Once I drove to a small town called Pabbi with Papa. I was bewildered at what I saw. Mounds and mounds of dry fruit being strung into garlands to dry by the local women. Till date when I see anjeer and khurmani haars at dry fruit shops I go back in memory to Pabbi.

Another very memorable taste was guchhi, a sort of dried mushroom, which was almost black in colour and was used in rice pulao. It had an amazing aroma.

We ate a pocketful of chilgoza (pine nuts) every day. The Pishoris have a special knack of placing them on the tongue and cracking them into half and eating the kernel. Nowadays they are so expensive, and people struggle to crack open the small shell. My sons and granddaughters use them only in salads. Eating chilgoza in my salad—sacrilege!

We had melons of all kinds. Red watermelon could only be eaten first thing in the morning, right after brushing my teeth. Shareefa or custard apple, all kinds of ber, jamun, faalsa, anjeer, shahtoot, peaches, aadoo and khurmani would all come from our lands. Papa had made a haudi, a pool-like, cemented dugout, which had a zenana and a mardana. Women would take a dip in the water with their shameez on. Later they would sit around and enjoy the fruit.

There were trees all around. The staff would roast choliya, green gram, which we would eat later, sitting on charpais. Sometimes there would be sugarcane or bhutta too.

The hot, sweltering summers of Peshawar were usually spent in Murree, Srinagar, Gulmarg or Pahalgam where a house was rented for a month. I remember in Pahalgam and Srinagar, a basket full of fruit was lowered into the river or stream near our tents and left there to cool for a few hours. How amazing are nature's ways!

On one memorable trip to Gulmarg, I fell five feet down into a canal. I got such a fright! But I was brave and only a few tears escaped, before I was rescued and coddled by Papa and Badi Mummy. Papa even roasted chicken on the campfire for me.

You couldn't escape the heat completely in Peshawar. I didn't mind. Staying home meant spending time in the tehkhana (basement) or the traditional, cool, summer rooms. These large rooms were sectioned off for men and women. Besides the takhts you sat or lay on, they also had wooden cupboards and tables. Wooden ventilators with slanted window shades let in light and threw long shadows on the walls.

Pari, Quadra and I would spend hours together, making up stories about the strange, elongated silhouettes that appeared on the walls as people walked by outside.

'He must be the son of an Afghan chief, stolen away as a baby. He is trying to find his family …' The films played out in our heads.

The terrace was my second favourite place, the first being Mummy's room. There were little cooling vents on the terrace above the public rooms and you could peek into the house through them. Elsewhere on the terrace, you could lie on your back and soak up the sun. Here there were no adults, and I could tease Didi, though I did it rarely, or lead Pari and Quadra into a merry chase. Here I could balance on the inner parapet walls that Pari and Quadra had given up trying to keep me off.

On the terrace one could also hear the tinkling of bells which came from the kabootar khana where Papa kept his pigeons. He had hundreds of pigeons and they fluttered around the room-sized dovecote, each with tiny bells attached to their feet. Every famous flyer had his own designs for the jhanjare; I was fascinated by how light they were, like feathers, their tinkling sound was delicate too. They would bring back an enemy kabootar by encircling it or we would lose one to an enemy flock. Kabootar baazi was a game and big money was involved in it.

The pigeons came from all over the world, from Russia, Iran, Turkey, Afghanistan and various parts of India. More powerful than eagles, pigeons fly faster, have more endurance and greater stamina, and their vision is just as keen.

One of the Afghan chiefs gave me a pair of pigeons called Kutty. Those two white pigeons would fly with lemons on their tails and return without dropping them. Other pigeons could tumble, they could roll, they could race. They were the apple of my grandfather's eye. Papa would whistle his instructions to them: hover, fly, somersault, return. Special food was made for them using dry fruit and ghee, it was called churi, and all of them received tonic for strength.

I copied my Papa as much as I could. We shared not just green eyes but also strength. We were Frontier Sikhs and I was my sisters' protector, after all. He was the most handsome man I've ever seen.

He was a real Pathan, a righteous Pathan, and like them a keeper of promises.

I would follow Papa about. He did fascinating things. He would ride a motorbike and sometimes be gone for days. There was a painting of him on one of the walls in the big drawing room. I would spend hours watching him fly his pigeons. Or watch him feed the horses. He also had five ferocious dogs in the house on one floor, well-guarded.

Unfortunately, my dog, Moti, had not been so well guarded. He bit me in my stomach as he was enthusiastically trying to grab the bones I had brought for him in my frock. Seven painful injections to ward off rabies had followed.

I would go with Papa to the lands we cultivated, that rolled ahead of us as far as the eye could see. 'Zaminon pe ja rahe hain' is what these trips were called. There were gardens with fruit trees: apples, apricots and plums. I would eat sugarcane with him. Pluck corn from the fields, which was browned for us there and then on charcoal fires. Sweet and wholesome.

I would stare at the many guns that were hung on the walls at home. Papa had large guns and pistols. He hunted. My dearest wish was to hold one—just hold, not fire it. But no, I wasn't allowed to so much as lay a finger on them. Too young, I was told. No one listened to my indignant cries. I am five! Almost six! I am a big girl!

So I watched him clean them, the metallic tang of sulphur and gun oil and smoke, the things my dreams were made of. He would clean them once a month, with a cork attached to a string that he would pull slowly through the barrel. I lived for the times he said 'Tel do' or 'Paani do'.

Papa considered me his son and called me Pom beta. 'Because your red cheeks are like pom-poms,' he explained. Later he taught me how to clean my bicycle and how to play hockey. He, too, used to play hockey and football.

He was the first person to quote shairs to me. I heard this couplet throughout my childhood:

Girte hain shahsawar hi maidan-e-jang mein
Wo tifl kyaa girega jo ghutnon ke bal chale

Only the horse rider falls in the battlefield
A child crawling on their knees cannot fall

Then he would tell me to go play sports.

'Hockey by practice, cricket by chance, and football by might. So, choose what you want to play.'

He was the one who made me sports crazy. I learnt how to fly kites; different kinds of kites had names and come Basant we would all be out on terraces flying them.

He used to ride horses to go inspect the land and I think sometimes he would race the horses too. Our horses were as famous as our pigeons.

Papa wore Savile Row suits imported from London. I loved his Pishori chappals, their surface woven like plaits into beautiful designs.

Papa had a very manly smell to him and wore an ittar specially made for him. When we hugged him, we could smell that fragrance from his neck. He was the only male in the family who was clean-shaven and had cut his hair short.

Once I got whacked in school on the calves by a nun with a ruler.

Streaks of black decorated my legs.

Papa saw the streaks on my legs when I got home. 'I'll shut the school down,' he stormed. Unfortunately, Badi Mummy talked him out of it.

She was the most loving human being.

Ramesro Devi came from a family of legends—not just her father, but also the extended family. Most Khatri families in Peshawar were interconnected, either by blood or by marriage. It was the biradari: the Khannas, the Kapoors, the Mehras. Regular visitors to our house were Prithvi Uncle (Prithviraj Kapoor) and Diwan Wazir Chand Mehra, whom we called Nanak Uncle. Mummy tied rakhi to both of them all her life.

Basheswarnath Uncle (the Bollywood legend Prithviraj Kapoor's father) and Shashi Kapoor visited us often and even stayed with us much later in Friends Colony, Kanpur. In fact, Shashi brought the jamni from the Mama's house when Vineet was born. Prithvi Uncle came for the choora on Roopy's wedding and received the baraat real Pishori style where the men dance in circles waving their handkerchiefs. Amrik Mama, Bachittar Mama, Prithvi Uncle, Joginder Mama, Lakhbir Mama and more ... it was a beautiful sight.

Prithvi Uncle's Theatre used to tour everywhere and once in Delhi he put out his jholi to collect money for us. At that time, sweeping his stage was a big honour. Sometimes, Shashi, Raj, Shammi or even the other artistes would do it. Raj would put me on his shoulders while sweeping. 'Raj Uncle! I'll fall down,' I would say.

All the ladies of the family—my mother, grandmother and all the aunts—would go often to the cinema in Peshawar. There were family boxes in the balcony and charpais would be laid for us. We would sit comfortably, eat and watch cinema.

Badi Mummy was very devout. She would sing shabads like *Uthat sukhiya baithat sukhia, Bhau na laage aise bujhiya .../Thir kar baiso har jan pyaare/Satgur tumre kaaj savaare* and lightly blow over us in blessing while putting us to bed.

We had a sunroom on the terrace because of my mother's health, and inside it was a room where the Guru Granth Sahib was kept and where Badi Mummy would have sermons attended by numerous people.

Everywhere she went, she was accompanied by a maid carrying cushions so that whenever Badi Mummy wanted to sit, she would do so on a cushion. Like at the Gurudwara, where Badi Mummy took us for Gurpurab. We travelled in a car with curtained windows, or in a tonga covered from all sides. Didi and, at times, my mother too wore a burqa, which was folded and kept away when in the Gurudwara.

We spent so much time there that the distant sound of a kirtan heard half asleep as I huddled in her shawl on cold winter nights still echoes in my mind.

Gurudwara Bhai Biba Singh is considered to be an architectural masterpiece and is said to have been established at the time of the tenth Sikh Guru, Gobind Singh, who died in 1708. For me, it was a land of treats. Outside, there was the lemony tang from the bunta bottles of Vimto that went pop when flicked open. Inside, there was the karah-parshad that I can still taste, and the pink milky kahwa with cardamom in kaansi ki katoris, the double-layered copper bowls with ghunghru in them that clinked when they were moved; double-layered so that the bottom never got too hot to hold. Every tinkle of the bell was a thrill, the thrill of drinking tea, that grown-up drink that we were never allowed to have in our house. I drew it out as long as I could.

Badi Mummy looked on indulgently, though Didi would tap her feet impatiently to get home. Not because she had finished her tea, but because she only ever took a few sips of any drink ever.

Mashallahs were uttered when Didi ate half a roti; the servants would even get rewards.

Didi was delicate, quiet, feminine, slight. Her weight never crossed 50 kg all her life. She was afraid of the dark and somebody had to accompany her to the bathroom at night. The bathroom was usually in the sehan of the house at the back or across the courtyard. No one had heard of attached washrooms in those days.

I couldn't jump out at her because she cried.

She would spend hours at my mother's dressing table playing with her bangles, trinkets, jewellery and makeup. The two would even wear matching jewellery.

Didi would drag me to Mummy's dresser and pat my cheeks with powder. She would be thrilled to get her hands on the pretty little powder puffs, whose softest down emerged from what looked like a satin potli and had a little satin covered handle or sat in a cameo-decorated octagonal box, its back decorated with little flowers.

'It tickles,' I would protest, but Didi would have none of it, and my face was firmly powdered.

She had scores of dolls, some handmade, and weddings would be celebrated of the dolls and the dulhas (grooms) that her coterie of maids and Pari had made for her.

I was very naughty compared to her. I never played with dolls, I loved football and badminton. My craze for cricket was still to come.

Didi and I were pampered children; Roopy was still a squalling baby. We had our own ponies. Even when I turned sixteen, I used to do a lot of horse riding in Shimla.

My only feminine attribute was my hair. All three of us had inherited the thick tresses from our mother but mine were golden; they touched the ground when I sat on a stool. Only poppy oil especially ordered from London or Paris was considered worthy enough to use on them.

Badi Mummy told me I used to prophesise when I was about four and many people came to our house seeking answers to their problems. Once, when sleeping on the terrace, Guru Nanak-ji appeared in my dream and I woke up with flowers in my hands. When I turned five, I developed a very high fever, and it all stopped.

The Peshawar of my childhood is made up of a few places and mostly memory. That Peshawar is a land where the sun always shone, where everyone wore new clothes on Gurpurab, Diwali, Bhai Duj (a festival celebrated by Sikhs two days after Diwali), and money was something we never thought about. That Peshawar is an emotion, a cocoon of warmth, laughter and safety. It is the fragments of memory of a Sikh girl barely six years old. It is the taste of love and privilege and safety.

It was an idyllic world, this Peshawar, gone too soon.

Kabhi murh ke phir usi raah par Na to aaye tum na to aaye hum
Kabhi faaslon ko samait kar Na to aaye tum na to aaye hum

Jo tumhain hai apni ana pasand To mujhe bhi shart ka paas hai
Ye zidon ke silsiley torh kar Na to aaye tum na to aaye hum

Unhi chahaton mein bandhe huwe Abhi tum bhi ho abhi hum bhi hain
Hai kashish dilon mein bahut magar Na to aaye tum na to aaye hum

Shab-e-wasl bhi shab-e-hijr hai Shab-e-hijr ab to hai mustaqil
Yehi sochne mein hui sehar Na to aaye tum na to aaye hum

Wo jharonkey pardo'n mein band hain Wo tamam galiyan udaas hain
Kabhi khuwaab mein sar-e-rehguzar Na to aaye tum na to aaye hum

Usi shehar ki usi raah par they hamare ghar bhi qareeb tar
Yunhi ghumtey rahe hum umr bhar Na to aaye tum na to aaye hum
Kabhi ittefaaq se mill gaye kisi shehar ke kisi morh par
To yeh keh uthegi nazar nazar Kyon na aaye tum kyon na aaye hum

Turning back on that very road
You did not come, nor did I
Gathering together distances
You did not come, nor did I
If your ego is dear to you
I, too, must heed my oath
Breaking this chain of stubbornness
You did not come, nor did I
Bound in the same bonds of love
You remain, as I do
Despite the pull of our hearts
You did not come, nor did I
The Night of Meeting is the Night
of Separation
The Night of Separation is a
continuum
With these thoughts, morning comes
You did not come, nor did I
Those windows are shut
behind curtains
All those alleys are sad
Even on the pathway of dreams

You did not come, nor did I
On that same road, in the same city
Our homes once stood close beside
Wandering, we spent our lives
You did not come, nor did I
Someday, perchance, if we meet
On a turning in some city
Our glances shall speak up:
Why did you not come, why didn't I

This ghazal has been used in an Indo-Pak Serial called *Partition Ek Safar* as the theme song. It depicts the remorse between our two countries and our two nationalities instead of two persons. Shreya Ghoshal and Udit Narayan have sung it to the music of Vanraj Bhatia. The serial was directed by Rana Shaikh and has been aired on many channels worldwide October 2004 onwards.

2

The Partition and a Long Summer in Nainital

The May of 1947 brought us to Nainital.

I would have preferred the familiar Kashmir or Murree, but I could accept Nainital. It could be an adventure.

'Safer,' I had heard the elders decide at the home of Papa's nephew, Amrik Mama-ji. I was in the courtyard, on one leg, and didn't know what they meant. Would I not fall into a ditch in Nainital, like I had in Gulmarg? But that was a long time ago. Look how I was playing hopscotch, at night, with my cousins, Bholi Didi and Balo Bhapa. They were Raj Maasi's children. They were a little older than me but I was as good as them! They might have had more practice, but I was giving them fierce competition.

Raj Maasi was one of my favourite aunts. She was one of Amrik Mama's two elder sisters. She was married to Iqbal Jija-ji in Jalandhar, and Amrit Maasi was married in Amritsar. Amrik Mama-ji's youngest sister, Mummi Maasi, lived in Delhi. I don't remember where Guchi Mama, his third brother, was. I think Billi Mama-ji, the youngest, went to stay with Raj Maasi to continue his studies.

Amrik Mama-ji's home was in the cantonment. That night the sky was a blaze of red and the men had binoculars glued to their eyes while they considered it. Fragments of conversation drifted towards us. 'Lahore ...', 'burning ...', 'riots ...', Sadar ...', 'train ...', 'Nainital'.

Our next holiday destination had been decided, I understood, as we sat in our Rolls Royce and were driven home towards Hashtnagari Darwaza. I snuggled up to Badi Mummy. I was excited. I liked holidays.

Nainital was also in the hills and there was a big lake, I learnt. It was going to be much cooler than Peshawar.

It would be cooler than the Lahore we passed by on our train journey. Had there been fire all around? Miles and miles of fire, the sky pink … smoke. There had been so many people, crowds, Sikh men with their pagris under their arms and children on their heads. Two men carrying an old woman in their pagri. Were they going to Nainital too?

Our holiday group was larger than usual. From our family, Badi Mummy, Mummy, Didi, Roopy and I. We were accompanied by Amrik Mama-ji's family: his mother Jhayee-ji, his wife Anoop Mami and their two sons, Cuckoo, who was a little younger than me, and Tito, who had just been born (Toni, their third child, was born after Partition), his unmarried sister Mummi Maasi, and his younger brother Bachiter Mama-ji.

Papa was going to join us later. He was looking after Pari and Qadra, Badi Mummy said. And the pigeons and the house, and the zameen and horses.

I could help with that, I thought, like I did when I went with him to survey the lands we owned. Then we could ride his motorcycle to Nainital. That would be such an adventure. I could picture us riding for miles, Papa cooking at campfires and I helping him. I wasn't sure how, but I would definitely help, maybe finally hold his guns?

A beautiful house was rented in Nainital, 3, Temperton Hall. A huge kothi, Temperton Hall had three individual apartments, huge and spacious, with large bedrooms, bathrooms and a cemented terrace. The top floor had two very large fully furnished houses. One was taken by Papa for us, the other by Amrik Mama-ji for his family.

Our apartment had a large hall, three bedrooms, bathrooms, kitchen and a verandah-like room in front that overlooked the hills and the Naini Lake. It was a beautiful house.

Right above us was the Ramsay Hospital, about a mile away, and below was Suffolk Hall, a boutique hotel. Our school—where we would get admission in a few months—was on the opposite hill.

The Culleys occupied the lower half of the house. I played all day with the Culley family kids, especially Jennifer Culley who was Didi's age. The cemented terrace was heaven—we would skate on it all day.

The first month flew by. So many relatives came over from Peshawar to holiday with us. There were picnics, boating, walks down the Mall. I could even get in a little horse riding.

Badi Mummy, Mummy and Amrik Mama-ji listened to the radio every evening. The same people seemed to be speaking every day—Nehru, Jinnah and Gandhi. 'Speeches.' I learnt a new word. I knew what to avoid in the future.

But something was up, I knew. Something I could not understand was happening in the family. I heard the word 'partition'.

'India is being divided,' Didi tried to explain.

'Like a cookie? Whoever gets the smaller half will be upset,' I nodded wisely. But what did it have to do with Papa being away from us, I wondered.

The talk about partition gave us new things to do though. One evening, all the cousins gathered to shout slogans together.

'Tody bachha hai hai!'

'Hindustan hamara hai!'

'What's a Tody bachha?' Cuckoo asked.

I had no idea, I had to admit that to Cuckoo.

I found out later it meant foreigner.

Our holiday came to an end in June.

When Amrik Mama-ji's family left for Delhi, Nainital became quiet. Our family was suddenly smaller, and now I missed Papa even more. Where was he?

We heard that Badi Mummy's side of the family, her sister Rawaila Maasi and her children, had gone to Dehradun.

'Why not Nainital?' I could have played with my cousins. We could have skated, we could have shouted slogans too.

'They already have family there,' said Badi Mummy.

What were we then?

Then the unthinkable happened. Didi and I got temporary admission into Wellesley Girls High School. We were the only two Indian girls in the school.

I protested a lot to Badi Mummy and Mummy. Holidays and school didn't mix.

Neither of them listened to me.

Our walk to school was cold, very cold. We had to go downhill first from 3, Temperton Hall past the Nainital Yacht Club, on to the New Club, then climb a hill again up to school.

I laughed and ran all the way. Didi struggled, tired. She cried. She was thin and delicate. Every night Badi Mummy would rub brandy on her knees.

Badi Mummy started to act strangely. Ever so often I would catch her furtively wiping her eyes.

The evening ritual with the radio continued. Beyond the boring speeches, every day brought with it news about something more sinister.

I heard that there was blood in the trains. I didn't remember any from our journey. Why were they not being cleaned now?

People were being killed, I heard Badi Mummy say one day.

'Are they having sword fights on the trains?' I asked curiously, imagining Fearless Nadia in a sword fight on a moving train. That would explain the blood. That made sense.

'Chup! Go out and play,' Badi Mummy told me angrily.

Later, of course, I would understand all too well. Thousands of books have been written on the massacres. I remember reading that the partition of the Indian subcontinent deserves to rank as one of the ten great tragedies in recorded human history, not only for the loss of human lives and property but the near-fatal blows on culture. People were uprooted, leaving an impoverished culture behind them. Of all the provinces, Punjab suffered the most. The massacre that preceded and followed its partition, along with that of India, was predictable and was indeed predicted.

What did I know or care for these things?

All I knew was that Papa was not home and people were having sword fights on trains. Well, Papa was good with his guns and he would win against a sword, I was sure. But still, what if he didn't, a small voice persisted in my head.

Badi Mummy was wailing softly, openly now, wiping away her tears with her dupatta.

Mummy was always talking about going back home. Home to the haveli, to her room. The bottle of Evening in Paris was empty. There was no harmal to dry her hair.

But she had her Belgian mirror that folded into three and always travelled with her, and a silver filigree shikara from Kashmir, to hold her trinkets. There were a pair of earrings, long dangling baalis, which we would later cut and make into three pairs of earrings as mementos for us three sisters of our mother. Didi and I still watched her get dressed, applying cream after cream, then rouge and lipstick. She looked like a princess and smelled like one too. She was so young, only twenty-eight.

Everyone was thinking the same thing. When would we go back home?

Three months had passed.

Partition had been declared. Did the people who had lived through it thrill at finally gaining independence or mourn the partition and the loss of roots and life, and family, friendship, land and culture?

August 1947.

There was migration. Millions were going to the new Pakistan. Millions were coming to the new India. Why, why, why?

There were killings and rapes and trains full of blood. Night after night I woke up from nightmares soaked in the fear and the blood I heard about.

No news of Papa.

The money depleted; there was hardly any jewellery left to sell. Badi Mummy sold her shawl, then finally she sold her bangles.

One night there was a knock at the door, we all woke up with a fright.

'Don't open, don't open,' Badi Mummy cried.

We heard a beloved voice.

Papa!

A strange looking Papa. Tired and bedraggled. So thin. He must have lost about 30 kg; he looked like a shadow of his former self. There was a rifle clung on each of his shoulders and a pistol in hand.

I hugged him. We all hugged him. Everybody cried.

Mummy fainted.

Papa's friend, the chief of Jamrud, Khan Sahib had managed to get a pass for him.

Khan Sahib was Papa's best friend. In Peshawar, they would go on shikaar together. Khan Sahib had found a box of coins while digging the foundation of his house. These were old coins, some from the Ottoman Empire, some British. There were also around fifty to hundred pre-Independence coins, 2 paisa, taka, which had turned green with time. Khan Sahib had gifted the box to Papa when he was leaving Peshawar.

Papa passed it on to Mummy; she gave it to me.

What do things signify? The box sits in my cupboard, safely locked away with the strange-looking brown card which allowed Papa to travel to Delhi and then onwards to Nainital—a crossing Papa never spoke about.

The coins have value in themselves, though I have never had them evaluated. They are also a legacy of friendship. But to me they are more than that. They are a talisman of Papa's life, a friendship because of which Papa made it safely to Nainital and we could have another two decades together.

They are the gift of Papa's life, from a friend we no longer know.

Unlike us, Papa knew when he left Peshawar that he would never be going back. And so, in his meagre bag, he carried his most treasured belongings, small booklets of what to feed the pigeons to keep them healthy. Written in Urdu and well-thumbed, my grandfather kept them till the end, my mother after him, Didi after her, and now I keep them with me.

Along with the booklets was a box full of cards that read 'Landlord and Banker'. Papa never used them again; we found them among a box of my nephew Siddharth's toys that came from London.

Papa's cards became a memory, history. I have all these treasures, going back three generations. What will happen to them? Even the books my father gave my mother, they all lie together in a cupboard, with my treasured collection of books of poetry.

Dil ke bechain jazeeron mein utar jaiga
Dard aahon ke muqaddar ka pata laiga

Mere bichrey huwe lamhaat sajakar rakhna
Waqt lafzon mein ghazal ban ke thehar jaiga

Alighting on the restless islands
of the heart
Pain will bring news of the fate
of sighs
Keep safe the moments of
my separation
Time, in the guise of a ghazal,
will stand still

3

Beginnings and Endings

I TURNED SEVEN IN OCTOBER 1947.

'You are a citizen of independent India', I heard often. That meant we were no longer ruled by the British, I was told. But I was sad that the Culleys were leaving. Who would I play with?

I would also have preferred to be in independent India in Peshawar. I missed home. The trees, the sky, the feel of the air, the smell. Not just of the city but of our house. Oh, how I craved the smells of home. The smell of cooking from the bawarchi khana. Was it chicken? Was it dal? Was it khamiri roti? I would dream of running through the house where the fragrant dhuan and polish would give way to the mouthwatering smells of food as I would run through the courtyard and towards the kitchen. The general smell of food would separate into its different ingredients, like pyaaz being fried, and then become something new as I would go through the kitchen and onto the verandah on the other side, where the aromas would mix with the smells of the earth and trees.

I also missed the smell of Badi Mummy's toosh that she always covered us with when we slept on her lap, and how Didi and I would vie for that precious spot. Decades later, when my granddaughter Tarika was travelling, as young people do when they pack, she did not keep anything warm except a shawl that I had insisted she take. 'Nani, the whole night I slept with you,' she told me later. That was how I felt with Badi Mummy's shawl.

I missed watching the dogs, keeping my distance, always just a little scared. I missed the terrace. I missed riding ponies. I missed being carried in Papa's arms. I missed the innocence of childhood.

We now had a new name too. We were called refugees. What did it mean?

I did not understand much but I still understood one thing—all hopes of returning to our own home in Peshawar were now dashed.

'Our haveli is in a different country now,' Didi explained to me patiently. 'It's not ours any longer.'

Did Didi think I would fall for that? How could our home no longer be ours? The land of my forefathers, where I was born, was now a new country? And that too not my country? Hah.

Where were we then? Hadn't we always been in India? What was new then? What was our identity? Where were we?

My family was with me, all my loved ones, yet I yearned for Peshawar. For our home, family, friends.

I don't know if I ever stopped yearning for it, only that I got better at putting that yearning aside. And I slowly came to understand what being a citizen of independent India meant. What being a refugee meant.

We were to live in Nainital for almost three years. Three years of limbo, as we waited for the Resettlement Commission to compensate our claims.

We were invited to tea with Governor Sarojini Naidu at Raj Bhawan, which looked like a Scottish castle. Naidu was the first female Governor of a state in independent India.

We were dying to eat but had been strictly coached to say, 'No, thank you,' if offered anything. The table was laid with thin, mouth-watering sandwiches and biscuits, there were delicate teacups in front of us.

And so, we watched hungrily, but oh-so-politely, as the adults drank their tea and spoke about how our transfer certificates and admissions would be sorted out. When Governor Naidu insisted, we finally ate a biscuit each. But the sandwiches stayed on the table. I sneaked a glance at them. Maybe if she insisted enough I could eat one out of politeness. Badi Mummy caught my eye and my hand dropped back into my lap.

Our transfer certificates arrived from Peshawar, and Didi and I moved from Wellesley Girls School to our alma mater St. Mary's Convent, Ramnee Park.

Our first major event after Partition was a drill display. Everyone had to carry the Indian flag. The Indianisation had started to show.

Wellesley and many other schools wound up from Nainital in the next year or two. The British started to leave. Many of the teachers migrated to Australia and New Zealand. Mrs Newington left for Australia and sent me a card from there hoping that my sisters and I were well. The card had a picture of kangaroos on it—that was the first time I had seen kangaroos in my life.

We survived on whatever money we had and sold whatever little jewellery Mummy had.

The numbers piled: 14.5 million people crossed the new borders, or that according to the 1951 census of displaced persons, 72,26,000 Muslims went to Pakistan from India while 72,49,000 Hindus and Sikhs moved to India from Pakistan.

We were six of those numbers. Trying to understand where we should go and what we should do.

The rehabilitation of the refugees began.

Papa was allotted a house, 3, Peeli Kothi in Darya Ganj, Delhi, in place of the haveli we lived in at Peshawar.

He was also given a steel-bucket-making factory. But all this was nothing compared to the vast lands left behind or the money left in the banks of Peshawar. And can you imagine a zamindar from Peshawar, who would sit in a Rolls Royce and travel on a Harley Davidson from Peshawar to Murree, getting a small factory near the railway line? We soon lost the business.

Similarly, Mummy was far too wealthy, and what she got in the rehabilitation was paltry compared to what she had left behind. She was allocated a mango farm of 100 acres near Lucknow called the Malka Zamani Bagh.

We took trips to Dehradun, to explore the possibility of settling there. We lived in Daryaganj for a few weeks. It was a huge three-storey house in one of those tiny lanes. It must have belonged to a very educated family, either barristers or professors, because the house was full of books, English books, law books. Papa tried to find out whose house it was, but to no avail. The rooms were spacious and the kitchen had a fridge. It was the first time I had seen a fridge that ran on oil. What a luxury!

We found some beautiful books of quotations, which Didi kept with her always. A fat, faded, frazzled book. This house was fraudulently taken away from us by a relative. Though I was too little then to understand how, but I assumed that when claims were being laid it was very easy to manipulate a change of name.

Malka Zamani Bagh, an orchard of mangoes near Lucknow, was allocated to my grandmother. Papa went to see it and so did Mummy. They told us it was beautiful and vast. Then what happened to it, the seven-year-old me didn't get to know. We never saw it and we never got anything out of it. I remember hearing later that the people who lived there and looked after the farm created too much of a stir and didn't let it be allocated in my grandmother's name.

A year after we moved from Peshawar, we were in Lucknow. Why? I do not know. The family was invited to dinner. A shiny armoured car came to pick us up. We were in General Nathu Singh's house. Papa and he hugged each other like the good friends they were. He patted the three of us on our heads.

Two tables were laid out, one for the elders and one for the three of us. Liveried waiters served us dinner. I ate heartily but Didi's plate was often removed before she could finish her food because she ate so slowly and took so long, and the next course had to be served. She also placed the fork and knife straight while eating, not crossed, not realising it meant she had finished her meal.

But soon dinner was forgotten.

An aide rushed up to General Nathu Singh. He left immediately and we were sent home.

The date was 30 January 1948.
Gandhi-ji had been shot.

Mere bichre huwe bachpan ke dayaaro aao
Aao maazi key dareechoon ko sanwaroo aao

Doob jai na bhanwar mein kahin kashti meri
Mauj-e-dariya mein sahelee key saharoo aao

O long lost places of my childhood, come
Come and adorn the windows of my past

Lest my boat sinks in the whirlwind
O waves of the river come
To the rescue of your friend

4

Kanpur, the City of Saviours

FINALLY, THE DAY WE HAD BEEN WAITING FOR ARRIVED. BADI Mummy was allotted a house in Kanpur (Cawnpore earlier). It was a small two-room, two-storey house in the newly built Friends Colony.

Kanpur, then, would be our new home. The city had a St. Mary's and our school certificates were easily transferred from Nainital to Kanpur.

It was 1950 and the glory of Kanpur was still undimmed. The war years had been a boom time, as the city became a world hub for cotton, jute and leather goods for armies. It was known as the Manchester of the East. After the First War of Independence in 1857, this little British cantonment town had become India's major manufacturing city. Mills had been set up and railway lines laid. It was one of the biggest stops on two important rail routes—Delhi to Calcutta and Bombay to Calcutta; in fact, it was a competitor to Bombay and Calcutta. Some of the country's richest mills were here and they included Elgin Cotton Spinning & Weaving Company, Muir Mills, Cawnpore Cotton Mills and Lal Imli. The Singhanias' JK Cotton Mills became the first Indian-owned mill. Kanpur was also a big silk centre and trading town.

Some of the best English schools and colleges were there too.

The British were still there, though they all left India by 1960. A significant Parsi community lived there though the numbers would slowly start to dwindle as the Parsi families moved to Bombay or Pune. The upper strata of Muslim society had already thinned out and would reduce further as even more of them moved to Pakistan. But there were still the old class lines, nowhere more evident than at the Cawnpore Club, meant for the upper class, and the Ganges Club whose profile was more middle class.

Not that we would visit either club anytime soon.

After Nainital, Kanpur was a shock. Mills belched out smoke; the stench of the tanneries seemed to lace the air, and people were everywhere. The spacious environs of 3, Temperton Hall were replaced by small one-room houses, first in Arya Nagar and then in Swarup Nagar, while we waited for the house in Friends Colony. We lived in Arya Nagar for about four months and then in Swarup Nagar for about six.

Some links to what was and what is are broken with such force that the past seems like something from your imagination. Looking at the six of us living in one room, Peshawar seemed an impossibility. Had I dreamt it? Was it a fairy tale that I had told myself? Could I be certain of anything that had passed?

Reality was too sharp and in its teeth, it carried hunger and poverty.

We dreamt of days when we used to sit at a fully set dining table and eat a rich meal with fork and knife. Now we ate seated on the floor; we had neither space for a dining room, nor chairs, nor silverware. We studied on the floor, we ate on the floor, we slept on the floor.

Papa slept at one end of the room, then Badi Mummy, then Mummy, then the three of us. Often, I would crawl over to snuggle up to Badi Mummy and sleep, but it was not always easy since Didi and Roopy had the same idea too. Barbara Cage had it right when she said, 'A grandma is warm hugs and sweet memories.'

Badi Mummy, who had never had to cook in her life, took on the cooking responsibilities, making whatever little she knew. Dal-chawal, dal-roti, khichdi, the smoke from the firewood stinging her eyes. There were times we ate khichdi every day, day after day, meal after meal.

My grandfather would coax us into eating it well even as we were sick of it. Trying to feed us, he would rhyme: '*Tatti tatti khichdi te tatta tatta quo, khao mere bachreyo main thwada pyo* (Hot khichdi with hot ghee, eat my children I am your father).' Of course, there was never any ghee. We hadn't seen butter or cheese since we left Nainital. Eggs were a dream.

We developed a private language of our own to convey our misery to each other. If there was no money, we would say 'saipey hin', 'paise nahin' in Punjabi or Pishori reversed. 'Pachhu' meant 'chup', 'tiro' was 'roti' and 'chitta' meant milk.

Even then there were some rays of light. School was one. We had started our schooling at St. Mary's and quickly became known as the Singh Sisters.

Urmiljit Rani Singh. Didi. She was called Uma all her life.

Indira Rani Singh. Me. Ina to all my loved ones.

Roopinder Rani Singh. Roopy.

The library was once again accessible to me. Sports became a focus. Papa had a bicycle, and I could whiz about on it.

Arya Nagar was also where we met Hiroo Advani and started a friendship that would last a lifetime. Hiroo was around six. I don't remember where we met, but we played together in the Brijendra Swaroop Park, went to school in the same bus, and she spent much of her time with us, especially in the evenings when her parents were out. Her parents, Dhamu Uncle (Dharamdas Advani) and the very beautiful Leela Aunty, were socially inclined and they would get home in the early hours of the morning. Papa would wrap Hiroo in his warm choga and lay her on the backseat of her parents' car when they came to pick her up.

Years later, after wear and tear, that choga was thrown away, the guns he had carried from Peshawar were sold for Roopy's education and nothing remained of my grandfather but his binoculars and the books with instructions for pigeon care.

We moved from Arya Nagar to Swaroop Nagar. The Swaroop Nagar house belonged to Ram Asray, a kind man who sympathised with our situation. Once, when we did not have enough money, Asray accepted our radio in place of the rent.

Our worldly possessions were nil. No money, hardly any clothes, no radio, no fan, in fact no electricity. We did not have the money to buy the connection that was being doled at very economical rates.

Papa was angry and resentful at the politics and politicians who had let the country be partitioned and the fact that the politicians, unlike us, had not suffered its aftermath.

He lamented the loss of the life he lived before Partition and how he had lost his holdings and become a pauper overnight.

Badi Mummy would reminisce about the glorious days, how they would get dressed up to be taken to the Governor General every few months to show that they were alive and well, and how she, who had not had a formal education, had been taught to pen her signature to draw money.

Mummy complained.

But I—I was angry. Why? I wanted to yell at the world. Why did this happen? Why did we go from being aristocrats to nonentities? Why were we so poor that we required the charity of others? Why did we have to leave behind our house, our horses, our cars, our lives?

Where was our father who gave us birth and brought us into this cruel world? Why had we lost the support and safety of his presence? In Peshawar, we would meet him every week; in India, he lived in Delhi with his new family. Why were we not able to see him?

There were no answers.

And then, with time, the anger too passed.

~

We had barely settled into the new house when we had an unwelcome visitor.

It was lunchtime. We were all sitting on the floor eating. The meal was more luxurious than usual—dal and roti. The door was open; the door was always open, except at night, and it looked out on to the service lane at the back of the house.

From this direction, in swung a monkey. A huge monkey. Before we could react, it had snatched the roti from the person who was nearest to the door, which happened to be Mummy. We shrieked and scattered. Mummy threw herself in front of us, trying to shoo the monkey away. The next thing we knew it had bitten her calf and ripped out a chunk of flesh and taken a piece of her salwar as well.

Blood was streaming down her leg. It seemed to form a little pool before our eyes.

Mummy was screaming.

Didi was screaming.

The monkey ran away.

Badi Mummy rushed to Mummy.

After the first frozen moment, Papa and I ran out frantically trying to find a rickshaw. We were not on a thoroughfare; it seemed to take an eon to hail one. Finally, we found one and took it home.

Badi Mummy had tied a makeshift bandage with a piece of cloth. It was already stained red. Mummy was helped on to the rickshaw. Papa and a pale but composed Didi went with her.

Rabies was not the dreaded disease it had been just two decades earlier, but even at ten, I knew it was still a major worry. The vaccine was available, but not all hospitals kept it.

This was what Papa and Didi found as they went from hospital to hospital, not knowing the roads or the area of the new locality, as they tried to find one that had the vaccine. It was only at the third hospital that they found the injections and Mummy was given her first dose of vaccination, and had her wound attended to.

My poor mother. The rabies vaccination was a course of fourteen painful injections in the stomach over the period of a month. Then there was the wound. For many a month she just lay moaning in pain and could barely limp.

Poor Papa too. The injections were not cheap. Then there was the daily rickshaw cost. Where did Papa manage that from? Yet, somehow, he did.

Then there was some good news. Hiroo and her family also shifted to Swaroop Nagar. They now lived across the lane from us. She in a posh flat in a beautiful building, we in our one-room small standalone house. Their cook Bhagat would feed us exceptional puddings.

I have never counted Hiroo Johar (née Advani) as a friend. Over the years, we would become like sisters, constantly sharing joy and grief, laughing like mad schoolgirls at our childhood. Like the summer I, along with our neighbour Sherry, spent teaching Hiroo how to ride a cycle.

Sherry was added to our friend circle in Swaroop Nagar. He wore knickerbockers to Church, and his mother made the most delicious gujias for us. He and I spent many afternoons riding his cycle. We would take turns to speed around. Hiroo and Roopy insisted they too wanted to learn cycling, and I broke my back teaching them, but to no avail. My first stint as a teacher was an utter failure.

Papa was also stuttering with learning something new. A friend of Papa's got him a licence to sell stamp paper in court so he could earn a few rupees daily. Papa would leave every morning with a funny-looking steel trunk, locked and sealed, which was opened by the officers of the court only. The stamp paper was like money or traveller's cheques.

As is the case today, all transactions had to be recorded on stamp paper. Purchase and sale or transfer of property was rampant those days.

One day Papa could not sell any stamp paper at court. He came home hungry and tired without any money. My grandmother just sat in a corner with her hands on a forehead looking at my sisters and I. No one spoke.

There was no food in the house, nor any money to buy flour or firewood to make rotis, if nothing else.

That night we went hungry.

I was ten probably.

Many years later, when my son Vineet and daughter-in-law Tinu became property owners, I had their Power of Attorney and would go to court for new tenants every time.

And stamp paper had to be bought.

I made it a point to sit on the wooden bench in the khoka of the stamp vendor and talk to him kindly, call him beta.

I knew he also had to feed a family back home and I prayed that they would never go hungry.

Word got around in Kanpur that a family from Peshawar with three daughters, the family of Sardar Manmohan Singh married to Balmakand's daughter, were in dire straits and going hungry.

Strange people came and met Papa, suggesting small daily wage opportunities, like pasting labels on medicine bottles and making candles, where the family could also help.

We made candles for a dealer. After school we would all sit together, and pour burning hot wax into a large box, and put the wick in the middle and a candle would emerge. These were then packed in the factory and sold to the public.

We also pasted medicine labels on bottles. Empty bottles were given to us and we had to cut out paper, label the size of the doses, and paste them on the bottles. All of us helped in earning a bit of money, but Didi was the most adroit of us.

Then one day Mian-ji came.

He was a man who sat in the nearby masjid and prayed all day. It is difficult to describe him but he comes nearest to a godly image. A frail Muslim peer dressed in a white shirt and an Aligarhi pyjama with a skullcap, he never looked above your feet.

Was it a coincidence that the only similarity between our house in Peshawar and this one in Kanpur was that both were next to mosques? That we had taken care of our neighbours in Peshawar and that we were being taken care of now? I would rather believe in miracles and love, and that when there is love and respect in your heart for everybody, it comes back to you.

Head bent, Mian-ji talked to Papa about the wellbeing of the family. Only Roopy and I were allowed to sit in the room when he came, the rest of the women—Didi, my mother and grandmother—were in purdah.

Mian-ji had thousands of followers in Kanpur and he must have told them that Sardar Sahib's family was not to sleep hungry.

So, every morning when we opened our door, we would find small packets left at our doorstep.

Aata, rice, dal, sometimes fruit, milk or tea leaves, some sugar, firewood.

We were a Sikh Hindu family and maybe ten or more Muslim families were cutting into their children's food of the day to feed us.

The ironies of life.

All this at a time when religion mattered more to people than humanity. Where the friends I had played with, the people who had taken care of me, the people who had saved my Papa were somehow to be hated. Where a language that everybody spoke was no longer to be ours. Where the ugliness of humans was on full display, and nobody could differentiate whether the ugliness of one religion was any different from that of another.

And what were these differences? Didn't we all have the same number of arms, legs, eyes?

I thought of how we made houses, how you could build them any way you wanted, but in the end, you would only have a house. What was so important about the way people reached God, when finally it was only about reaching God?

And yet, here we were, our very meals a testament to the best of humanity.

There was never another day of hunger in our lives.

This went on for months, till Didi began giving tuitions. Didi was a very good student, the nuns would recommend Didi to the students in school who needed help with their craft lessons. And so Didi, at thirteen, took on the role of our family's breadwinner.

She would get thirty rupees at the end of the month. Her hands were sore by the evening using scissors to teach three children paper craft essentials in school. After completing Senior Cambridge she also got a job at the school.

Prithvi Uncle sent us fifty rupees a month. Nanak Uncle (Nanak Mehra, DIG) too.

We somehow survived. But we were poor, very poor.

Once, we didn't have money to pay the school fees. It was very humiliating to be called to the office of the Reverend Mother to be asked why the fees hadn't been paid and to answer that we didn't have the money. But we lived with it till the odd jobs got us enough money to pay the fees.

Mian-ji kept coming, which gave solace to Papa.

Then life changed as seasons change. We finally got possession of the house in Friends Colony.

By the Diwali of 1950 we shifted to our own little house 41, Friends Colony, Kanpur, a block of four homes, two below and two on the first floor. We received an apartment on the ground floor and another on the first floor, which was rented out to Mr Mitra. Later, Shamim and Patto would rent the other block upstairs and enter our lives.

The ground floor was a small house with two rooms, a verandah, a patch of green in front and a garden at the back. There were no boundary walls then; they would come up later, as would two rooms, when the three of us asked Papa for our own rooms, and a mason was hired to slap together some bricks and concrete for the most basic of rooms. We had no rent to pay, and from Mr Mitra we received a princely sum of thirty rupees a month, which allowed us to live in some comfort.

Mr Mitra was our first and last tenant. He lived there for forty years and we sold him the house in thc early 1970s, when we left Kanpur for good.

Papa grew flowers and vines, a guava tree, a papaya tree, pomegranate trees. Every day we watched them grow, finally able to earn some measure of the peace of mind we had lost since we came to India.

Talkhiyoo-n me-n hansi key barey mei-n
Ghum likhey hai-n khushi key barey mei-n

Ja rahi hoon mein aansuon ki tarah
Kya kahun waapsi key barey mein

About laughter hidden in bitterness
Sorrows have been written in place of happiness

I am going like the tears
What can I say about my return

5

The Singh Sisters in School

SCHOOL OCCUPIED MY DAYS. DIDI, ROOPY AND I SET OUT AT 8 a.m. and only returned at 5 p.m.; the long hours included time for sports. Didi then went to give tuitions too.

The three of us were the only children from Peshawar in school. There was only a smattering of Indians enrolled and they were all from affluent, socially prominent families in Kanpur. Studying in a convent school was an opportunity that could be afforded by very few. My friends Cynthia, Audrey and Olga, Gillian Hillman and the teachers were mostly Anglo-Indian or British. The nuns were Irish or German. They were children of Europeans who headed the big mills.

We all did very well in school, especially Didi, who was recommended by the nuns to give tuitions to other students. She taught English, Hindi and craft. My grandfather would accompany Didi to the houses where she gave tuitions and sit outside to escort her back home. When it wasn't possible, Didi would sometimes ride there on the one cycle we had at home.

Didi, Roopy and I each had a set of uniform, white socks and white keds, or PT shoes as we called them then. Our uniforms were washed and cleaned, ironed with a lota with hot coal in it. Papa polished our shoes. When it rained an umbrella was put on the low angeethi and our uniforms were dried on the umbrella. We studied by the light of hurricane lamps.

We looked like ranis, neat, clean, with our shining white uniforms of a blouse, a divided skirt called skorts, white socks, white shoes and white ribbons in our plaited braids. All three of us had long hair.

After school Didi, Roopy and I would play monopoly, marbles and badminton. We would fly kites in the backyard. Papa helped and taught us. He was a good sportsperson.

Didi was the fastest runner in school, it was the only sport she beat me at.

I excelled at all sports and played cricket, volleyball and kabaddi.

I was not too bad at school either. I tried, but never came first. Deepti Mehra (née Bhagat), Sehba Hussain and Dolly Rawson (now Thakore) always beat me.

This group of ours was together from the third standard to Senior Cambridge, or what is now eleventh class or the first year of junior college.

I read voraciously.

In Nainital, I had finished every book in the library meant for little children and was then given access to the senior library.

In Kanpur, I finished reading everything in the senior library and then I was allowed to read from the teacher's library. Mother Cecilia used to say, 'Singh, do you read books or do you eat books?'

I was growing taller too. Pushpa Khanna, or Pushy Aunty as we called her, was my idol. She used to call me Monkey Face earlier, but then renamed me Arms-and-Legs.

The Khannas, like the Kapoors and Mehras, were a prominent family, and the elite of Peshawar. They were extremely wealthy, and besides various businesses and land holdings they owned the Quetta Electrical Supply Company. Pushy Aunty was married to Kewal Krishan Khanna, who was from Peshawar; they had married in Lahore in 1946.

Decades later, their daughter Preeti told me the story of Pushy Aunty's wedding gifts. Pushy Aunty and Kewal Uncle went to Malaya (now Malaysia) soon after marriage as he was a cavalry officer with the 2nd Royal Lancers, and his regiment was stationed there. He was given special permission for his bride to accompany him. They travelled by train from Peshawar to Madras and boarded a troop ship for Malaya. Pushy Aunty lived in temporary barracks. Her father made a detailed list of all the wedding gifts—name and address of the gift-giver, description of the gift and how she should address the person in her thank-you note. The gifts were crated and sent to Peshawar to her husband's home to await their return. Sitting in the barracks in the tropical forests of Malaya she diligently wrote thank-you notes for every gift-giver. But then Partition happened, and she never got to see the gifts as they never went home again.

We were related from my Badi Mummy's side. Pushy Aunty's mother-in-law and my Naani called each other sisters. We called her Maasi Kaushalya. After the war, Kewal Uncle was posted in Kanpur. They lived in a sprawling bungalow opposite our school gate. Their daughters, Pixi, Preeti and Geeti, were with us in school too.

Pushy Aunty would send lunch for all three of us to school. Sometimes we would run across and eat with them, for which she had sought special permission from the Reverend Mother. Those were the happiest, fullest lunches any child could get.

Pushy Aunty died in 2020. She worked with lepers all her life and helped create a colony for them in Kanpur. She continued her social work till she was in her late eighties and stopped only because her body could not keep up.

She came from the distinguished Maira family. Her father was Prem Nath Maira; they originally came from a small village north of Peshawar. Prem Nath was an adventurous pioneer—as a young man he started his career transporting pilgrims in hub mobiles (a station wagon with a wooden body) overland to Mecca and Medina. He then set up a vulcanising shop—none existed on that route. Once he married and had children he moved to Lahore to lead a less adventurous life. Here he amassed a huge fortune both representing car manufacturers and setting up a factory to build trucks for the army.

When he had to leave Lahore due to riots prior to the Partition, homes and establishments belonging to Hindus were being burnt, he had the name of his showroom changed from Maira Brothers to Muhammad and Brothers and handed the keys of his businesses to his trusted Muslim employee.

Like Papa, Prem Nath Maira's government compensation for his assets lost during the partition did not match what had been left behind. He was given agricultural land in Panipat; he knew nothing about farming and did not know what to do with the land. And yet, over time, he managed to make it a success by trying new crops and using progressive methods.

Pushy Aunty had three siblings: Som, Shama and Ravi. Shama, her younger sister, married Sardar Gurbachan Singh who was in the IFS, and their son was the popular Doordarshan newsreader Tejeshwar Singh. We called him Bunny as children.

Pushy Aunty did everything possible to help the three of us, and I was her favourite.

After every summer break, my place in the assembly line or on the playing field moved many places back. But the tallest girls were Geeta Singh and Kamal Kapoor. I came third and stayed there.

I learnt to do many tricks with my bicycle. I could raise the front wheel, I could sit on the carrier and steer the handles with my skipping rope, I could go round and round in a small space like the fire well in the movies. I could take both Didi and Roopy on the cycle for fun rides, Roopy on the bar in front and Didi on the carrier at the back.

There were concerts in school, and one year, the Japanese drama *Mikado* was staged. And when we staged *The Pied Piper*, Hiroo and I dressed as husband and wife. There were dance competitions and debates too.

There were singing classes twice a week with Sister Cecelia. She always had an aspirin on her tongue for her throat and we watched with fascination for when she would open her mouth wide and we could catch a glimpse of it. She did it often.

Frère Jacques, frère Jacques,
Dormez-vous? Dormez-vous?
Sonnez les matines! Sonnez les matines!
Din, dan, don. Din, dan, don.

Brother James, Brother James,
Are you sleeping? Are you sleeping?
Morning bells are ringing! Morning bells are ringing!
Ding, dang, dong. Ding, dang, dong.

The last line was changed under our breath to 'I love you, I love you' with many giggles and snickers.

All giggles and snickers died out at even the shadow of Mother Christine, whose clap was a death knoll. Her eagle eyes would spot an undone shoelace from a mile. Unpolished shoes could not be hidden from her, neither could an untucked shirt nor a hair ribbon that had opened. She wouldn't call anyone by name, she didn't even have a whistle to her lips—usually the nuns carried a whistle in their pocket and blew it to call the girls. Mother Christine would just clap three times and you knew that someone was going to be hanged today. She was a very strict woman, and the first non-white nun I had seen.

At the opposite side of the spectrum was Ms Abel, my class teacher who taught me in three classes. There was something really gentle about her. She taught us biology and undertook the task of teaching us about human reproduction. She neither laughed, nor was shy, just taught it to us in a matter-of-fact manner.

Of course, when I got married, I realised that those lessons had taught me nothing, but I still loved her.

There was also Mrs Saxena, my Hindi teacher, who we called Mrs Sexy, and Mrs Kelly, the history teacher who knew historically significant dates by heart. Bardi, whose name might have been Sister Bernadine, used to garden—I have no memory of what she taught us, but I've never seen roses like the ones that bloomed for her.

We read Shakespeare, Milton, Keats, Byron and knew only

British History. Hindi, that too elementary level, was introduced in the eighth standard. Our generation read about the vastness and the rich culture of our own country much later in life and are still hardly aware of it.

Holidays came around, and we played, we slept, and we also helped in the house and garden.

One day, Badi Mummy was breaking the leaves off a cauliflower to cook. Roopy was five or six. The next thing Badi Mummy knew was Roopy was gasping. My grandmother thumped her back and told her to look up. That's when she saw that Roopy had carefully stuffed the leaves up her nostrils. Badi Mummy was aghast.

Badaltey waqt mein yeh faasla to hona tha
Naye muqaam pay manzar naya to hona tha

Ye aur baat ke manzil pe sab nahi jaatey
Safar pe jaaney ka kuch hausla to hona tha

In these changing times his distance was inevitable
A new vista opening up on a new stage was inevitable

It is another matter that everyone doesn't reach the destination
To have the courage to embark upon the journey is inevitable

6

A Small New World

MY FIRST FORMAL EXPOSURE TO MUSIC CAME EVERY WEDNESDAY night through the *Binaca Geetmala* hosted by Ameen Sayani on Radio Ceylon.

Didi, Roopy and I would sit in the verandah of our home in Friends Colony, Kanpur, and listen to the hit parade in the dark with a hurricane lamp, thanks to our neighbours who were kind and who kept the volume always high.

There was no electricity, we did not have the money to install a meter in this new house that we had been allotted. We had already given our radio to Ram Asray as rent a year ago.

My childhood had a different lilt. There was the homely cadence of geet I had heard at marriages in Peshawar. There was the lullaby of shabads that Badi Mummy sang as she patted our heads and rustled her hair, trying to put us to sleep. *Thir ghar beso har jan pyaare Satgur tumre kaaj savaare,* she sang. Remain steady in the home of your own self, O beloved servant of the Lord. The True Guru shall resolve all your affairs.

She would alternate between that and *Uthat sukhiya, baithat sukhiya …/ Bhau nhi laage jaa aise bujhiya …/ Raakha ek hamara swami …/ Sagal ghtaa ka antar jammi …* (Standing up, I am at peace; sitting down, I am at peace./ I feel no fear, because this is what I understand./ The one lord, my lord and master, is my protector./ He is the inner-knower, the searcher of hearts.)

I grew to love Gurbani, a love that has only grown stronger over the years.

From Pari, my friend, playmate and helper, I learnt the songs of the North-West Frontier Province. Pari loved to sing. Old folk songs would trip off her lips at every occasion. When we were playing on the terrace in Peshawar, when she was making wadi on beautiful white sheets, when she was bathing us.

Suchi wascut waliya sone they button lawaa/ Shaala tu jeevein murada vaikhey Maa (Oh you wearing the beautiful pure damask waistcoat, you should have gold buttons on it/ My son may you live long and may your mother see all her desires fulfilled.)

I remember only fragments, though some have recently been re-sung by the artists of our times, like *Daachi Waaliya* (O camel rider) by Hadiqa Kiani for Coke Studio.

Ve dachi waliya mor muhaar ve,
Soni waliya lai chal naal ve,
Ho teri daachi de chumni aan pair ve,
Tere sir di mangni aan khair ve,
Ho teri daachi te gal wich talliyan,
Ni main peer manaaban challi aan.

O camel-rider, turn your camel around and come back.
O my lover, take me along with you.
I kiss the hooves of your camel with reverence,
I pray to God to keep you safe.
Your camel has small, tinkling bells round her neck.
Oh, I'm on my way to cajole my spiritual master.
Oh, I'm on my way to cajole my spiritual master.

To me music came from within, with its own heartbeats. I read somewhere that with the right music you either forget everything or you remember everything. It has the power to transport us back to any period of life we want to revisit. Music has been my healer and companion all these years.

The beauty of words became amplified with music. Very soon

the sound of words, the harmony of them together started to appeal to me. Poetry seemed the most obvious place I would end up.

Urdu was the spoken language of my childhood. My grandfather recited Iqbal, Ghalib, Zauq often. Later, these turned to phrases of lament that echoed the havoc that had been brought upon us. My grandfather's favourite shair was: *Khudi ko kar buland itna ke har taqdeer se pehle/ Khuda bande se khud pooche bata teri raza kya hai.*

Sometimes our neighbours in Kanpur would also tune in to the geet and ghazals. The first-ever ghazal that stirred my heart or even evoked some romantic feelings was Shanti Hiranandan-ji's:

Nazar nawaz nazaron mein ji nahi lagta
Vo kya gaye ki baharon mein ji nahi lagta

The first seeds of love were sown in me. The literal meaning of ghazal is to make love to a woman. So, Begum Akhtar would look at you and you would melt. Her eyes and her smile were so mesmerising, it could convey ecstasy and take you into a deeper meaning of ghazal.

Then there was Talat Mahmood's *Mera pyar mujhey lauta de, main jeevan mein ulajh gaya hoon, tum jeena sikha do …* So much love and heartbreak in his voice. I memorised it. But what did it mean to me then? I don't know. Who was I pining for? Nobody that I could think of.

Mohammad Rafi's *Pooch na mujh se gham ke fasaney, ishq ki baatein ishq hi jaaney* was another ghazal that resonated with me. Sadness and love, fictions at thirteen? I hadn't experienced romance or a heartbreak, I don't know why these couplets made their home in my heart.

Didi and I had made friends in the neighbourhood—Ibrahim Khan, Mahesh Saneja, Dennis and more. Ibrahim Bhai came from one of the wealthiest families of Kanpur who owned tanneries and buildings and the most famous Nehru Bagh, which even had a planetarium. When politicians came visiting Kanpur they were always taken there for a visit and Ibrahim Bhai's father knew most of them.

I remember seeing Jawaharlal Nehru being taken in an open jeep to Nehru Bagh, as we children lined the streets and showered him with rose petals. As always, he had a rose in his immaculate white sherwani.

As time passed, Ibrahim Bhai became Didi's Rakhi brother. Mahesh was mine.

On my thirteenth birthday, Ibrahim Bhai, who used to write and recite poetry, presented me with a set of poetry books by Rajpal and Sons. These ghazal collections were very popular then and were available only at railway stations. Ibrahim Bhai gave me four volumes of Ghalib, Daagh, Meer and Zauq.

Life has its inflection points and this was mine. There was time before and there was time after. These books became my portal to poetry. I lived with them, dreamt with them, slept with them and could recite a lot of the ghazals with great ease.

I had started writing and listening to poetry when I was eleven, but after I received the four volumes my homework copy would be crammed with my scribblings in verse. I dreamt in class, fantasised with words and devoured Urdu–English dictionaries available in the small Urdu Bazaar to find the exact meaning of the words that so entranced me.

My romance with sound had begun. A beautiful sounding word could make me ecstatic and my restlessness to use it in meaningful, melodic sentences was my very incentive to write more and more poetry.

I realised that I had, buried deep within me, a special bond with words. Urdu was special but English and Gurbani words also attracted me. Later in life the havan mantras enchanted me and I had a Vedic scholar come every Tuesday to teach my children the meaning of the Sanskrit words of this oft-repeated ritual in our domestic life.

There were other influences too, such as Shakespeare, Milton, Keats, Shelly, Tagore and Premchand whom I read at school.

~

'We are getting new neighbours!' Roopy skipped around the backyard as she sing-songed the news. It was Sunday and we had just oiled our hair. Didi and I were sitting in the sun; Roopy never seemed to be able to sit still. We looked up instinctively, the adjoining flat upstairs was vacant.

'Do they have children?'

Nobody was sure, but the general feeling in the air was that there were no children in this new deal and I lost interest. To be fair, as a fourteen-year-old my interest in the world of adults was limited to whether they cooked or fed me well.

The crates appeared soon after. We watched with interest. Then came our new neighbours. They were very young. They must have got married soon after graduating from college. Maybe I had been too quick to write them off.

They came over and introduced themselves to us—Shamim Raza and Pashupati Nath Mittal.

'Call me Patto. Everybody does,' he said. All of us nodded. There was little possibility of Pashupati Nath rolling off our tongues easily.

I don't know if I ever heard the story myself, but as if by osmosis, we all knew it. It was a story that could have been made into a movie. She was a beautiful Muslim girl and he was a handsome young Hindu Kayastha lad. They had met in Lucknow University.

Shamim belonged to the Raza family and her father used to be a Commissioner in Patna. Shamim's chacha was Mustafa Zaidi, the well-known poet. Shamim had been either engaged or had been pledged to be engaged to the famous poet Majaz Lucknawi.

But Shamim and Patto fell in love, the engagement was broken, and they married, against their families' wishes. It was a great love affair that created a furore in Lucknow.

They were young and fun and welcomed us into their home. Their house was full of books and young people, all of whom wrote, recited or listened to ghazals. Their friends came from the intellectual and cultural hubs of the day—Aligarh Muslim University, Banaras Hindu College and Lucknow University, which was the hub of Urdu adab in those days. Couplets were recited, created and exchanged as easily as breathing. I sat fascinated and took in as much as I could.

I listened to ghazals with them. It was then that my love affair with music, especially with the ghazal, began, and I became interested in the likes of Begum Akhtar, Kundan Lal Saigal, Kanan Bala and Iqbal Bano, among others.

I started reciting Majaz, Mustafa Zaidi, Sahir, Jigar and a host of contemporary poets. Sixty years have passed but I can still recite Majaz's *Noora* and Mustafa Zaid's *Aakhri Baar Milo* flawlessly.

Shamim encouraged me to read, and when I would recite she would correct my talaffuz. She taught me the importance of pronunciation. 'If you cannot pronounce the word correctly, the meter of your ghazal, the rhyme of your couplet will be incorrect. The rhythm of the ghazal would be awry,' she said.

I practised the q's from the back of my throat, worked on getting the nukhtas right—where should it be a 'za' and where should it be 'ja', and where should it be a 'kh' or a 'ka'.

The words started to mean something. Short rhyming words came to my mind too and I tried to put them together. Sometimes it made sense, at times it was rubbish. My schoolbooks were crammed full of little sentences and poems.

Some were in books they shouldn't have been in. Mrs Sexy caught me once.

'Are these written by you?' Mrs Saxena asked. 'If it's written by you this is really good.'

She let me off with a warning not to doodle in my submission books.

I did not know then that my father was a respected poet. That well-educated people compared him with Bulleh Shah and Shah Farid. I did not inherit property from my father, neither did I receive his love and care, but poetry was perhaps an inheritance from him, and it was manifesting in my blood.

Poetry became a friend and we talked to each other and wrote to each other. I became quieter, more immersed in my thoughts. I surrounded myself with books, I knew a splattering of Urdu, so I read Urdu poetry, a bit of Hindi (introduced only in the eighth class) and, of course, English.

I still have my first kaida of Urdu from Peshawar. The first poem was *Tik tik karti gharhi raat din.* We were taught how to write on the takhti but I relearnt it later in life.

Meanwhile, Shamim and Patto had become our family. Shamim would share with us the rhymes that were famous in Lucknow and Kanpur. *Khuda bhala kare Punjab ke fasadon ka/ Hamare ujde hue chaman mein bahaar aayi.*

Patto worked part-time at British India Cotton Mills, but Shamim was home and we were together all the time; my grandmother regarded her as her fourth daughter. They became guardians to my sisters and I. We went out with them to the movies, for chaat, to dinners and for walks. We spent so much time together that we could not say who lived in whose house. We were family.

7

Interesting Proposals

THERE SEEMED TO BE TWO OF ME. THERE WAS THE ME WHO HAD found poetry and was almost like Mirabai in its worship, and there was the me who was fourteen and liked to giggle with schoolfriends and was an avid sportsperson.

That year there was a lot of giggling. We had discovered boys. What fun! The school bus was where we giggled over them, watched them, and sometimes even met them at stops. We also sang. Some girls had boyfriends, and they would come and see them off in the mornings or stand outside the school gate.

Once, on our way to school, we were singing away at the top of our lungs, when the bus came to a stop in front of the Bashir family house. (India's green beauty doyenne Shahnaz Husain married into that family.) From the corner of my eye, I saw a game of cricket being played. The next thing I knew there was a hard whop to my head.

When I opened my eyes, I was in the school Infirmary. Didi and Roopy were watching over me anxiously.

'The lump on your head is huge,' Roopy said admiringly. 'It's almost the size of the cricket ball that hit you.'

'How do you feel?' Didi asked. I looked at her gratefully. I could always rely on Didi's concern. 'Is your brain what it used to be or is it scrambled?'

'And which is better?' Roopy laughed.

They both laughed like it was the witticism of the century.

'Very funny,' I said, coldly.

The nurse discharged me after I had missed only one period and told me to return to class. I frowned at this lack of concern for me. Surely I could have been sent home.

I was the talk of the class and bus that morning, and all my classmates watched me eagle-eyed for the rest of the day. Soon though a sense of disappointment seemed to permeate the air. Besides the lump on my head I had no other injuries; I wasn't trembling, I didn't faint again, I ate a hearty lunch; all in all I showed every sign of being disgustingly healthy. I even chased Roopy down the hallway when she made jokes about my scrambled brain.

I had to do that a lot over the next few days as Didi and Roopy managed at least two references to my scrambled brain every day. They only stopped when I learnt to resolutely ignore them.

Sometimes I would take the cycle to school. I could only do that if I had missed the bus. You had to plan in advance to miss the bus. Papa was very forbearing; my reasons for missing the bus never stood much scrutiny.

Especially when a hundred metres down the road I was joined by two other friends who had also 'missed' the bus. I was a speed freak and my goal was always to race the bus and see whether we could reach earlier. I would fly on the cycle. Even later, when I learnt to drive, I loved to drive fast.

I was fifteen when Didi gave her Senior Cambridge exams. The equivalent of what is eleventh class today, it was the final year of school then. We had missed more than a year during Partition and the delay in transfer certificates had made us older than our friends. Didi was seventeen.

Didi got 100 per cent in history in Cambridge and was offered a scholarship, but the need of the hour was to feed us. She got a job in our school and taught the kindergarten kids in a new wing that had been built recently.

The best thing about the new building was the cake man who

ran the school canteen opposite it. Mummy used give us 4 annas as pocket money, a princely sum in those times, which would get us multiple eclairs, nankhatai biscuits and patties; they were only half an anna each. Till date I've never had better eclairs or patties.

We had all turned into pretty girls. I did not look like Didi and Roopy, with my green eyes and light brown hair. I looked just like Papa, while they looked like Mummy and my father. I was considered classically beautiful, Didi was said to have had an old-world elegance, and Roopy would grow up to be a bombshell. Each one of us was attractive in our own way.

My role in the three of us was clear. I was their protector, since I was the toughest of the three, the tallest and the strongest.

I attracted interest early and even started to get proposals.

The first proposal I received was dramatic, a letter written in blood by a family friend's son who was studying in Colvin Taluqdars' College in Lucknow. He had drawn his blood with an injection to write to me, and I have always wondered how he filled his ink pen with it!

In the end, I handed over the letter to Papa, who met the boy's father and told him to get the boy a penicillin shot to stop any infection.

Another proposal came in the form of a record from a boy called Pradeep. It was the famous song from the movie *Sone ki Chidiya: Pyar par buss to nahi hai mera lekin phir bhi tu bataa de k tujhey pyar karun ya na karun.*

Others were more sedate, like the one from Dr Bhatia, who would call on my mother once in a while to check on her. I took them all in my stride and we had many a laugh at home.

Didi too had her share of romances. Once, to meet a doctor from Lucknow, she took me along and told Mummy, Badi Mummy and Papa that we were spending the day with some school friends. I knew I was part of her romantic rendezvous but even I was surprised when she dragged me to the railway station. I was going to travel, how exciting!

Didi whisked out a platform ticket and gave it to me. I was to sit on the bench till she returned. She caught a train and went to Lucknow. Hours passed. I was anxious and hungry. When she returned I was almost in tears.

Roopy was much younger than us, but one family saw her at a wedding and was smitten. They wanted one of their twin sons to marry her. Anyway, she had her share of affairs later in life and got married to the best of the lot.

What did I care for romance? It moved me in ghazals, in nazms, in poems, but in life I wanted to be a doctor—there was a medical college close by and when I thought of the future that was the image in my mind.

Love was for adults, and we were not there yet. Anyway, all three of us knew we had to be extra careful in this regard. Three young girls, refugees, whose mother had separated from their father, and with only an elderly grandfather as the sole male in the family to protect or support—we knew we could not do things that girls from normal families might. The shorthand from our relatives and well-wishers seemed to be 'get them settled quickly'. People would say: 'Iski shaadi kardo jaldi warna koi utha le jaayega'.

But all of this was a long way off. I was content with my position as the middle child, whatever happened would happen to Didi before me.

Be simt be chirag safar hum ne kiya hai
Mushkil bahut tha dost magar hum ne kiya hai
Thi Indira udas bahut zindagi magar
Jaisey bhi ho saka hai basar hum ne kiya hai

Directionless, lampless, I have journeyed
It was difficult, my friend, but I have travelled
Life was sad, Indira, and yet
However I could I have lived it

8

A Trip to Shimla and an Unexpected Encounter

'HAVE YOU PACKED EVERYTHING?' MUMMY ASKED.

'Yes, Mummy.' I forestalled her questions. 'I have kept the powder, the ittar, the earrings and the jumper.' The last item she had knitted for Didi and I to wear in Shimla. Mummy was a whiz at knitting and would knit us jumpers overnight.

Badi Mummy entered the room. 'Yes, Badi Mummy, the scarf, the flannel pyjamas, the torch are still in the suitcase.' The suitcase which she had helped me pack two nights ago.

She was trailed by a sulky Roopy. Now that the time of our departure was drawing near, Roopy had finally realised that she was going to be left alone in Kanpur for the holidays, while Didi and I would be going to Shimla. She was wasting no opportunity of making her displeasure known.

Didi and I were going to Shimla! I still couldn't believe it. This was going to be our first holiday since we came to new India.

Papa's friend from Peshawar, Sardar Pratap Singh Dhingra, had paid us a visit in February. He was the Conservator of Forests in what is now Himachal Pradesh. He had insisted that we all come for a visit. That was not possible given our finances; so it was finally settled that Didi and I would go. Didi was eighteen, I was sixteen, and we were old enough to travel unaccompanied. Moreover, his daughters would be our company.

I held the warm glow of this promised holiday close, adding to the details of the plan as it was made. The summer of 1956 was going to be very special. I must have had what we called chhati hiss, a sixth sense about it, a gut feeling that something was going to happen.

We would take the train to Delhi first, where we would break our journey for a day. We would spend this day with our relatives, the Horas. They lived in Windsor Mansions behind the then Cottage Emporium, I had been told. I knew that Pearl Didi, Ruby and their younger brother Tejpal would be there, and I looked forward to meeting up and renewing our relationship that had been lost in the turmoil of Peshawar.

From there, Didi and I would catch a train and go up to Shimla, where we would stay at Pratap Uncle's bungalow, Charlie Villa.

It was to be a summer holiday in the hills, like the ones we used to take from Peshawar. It would be golden.

We arrived in Delhi. Swarup Uncle picked us up. Delhi was a medley of noise and people. Such wide streets! Connaught Place! And we hadn't even arrived at our uncle's house yet. We were welcomed warmly. Swarup uncle's mother, Mano Bua-ji, was Papa's first cousin and was considered the head of our family. A grand meal was laid out and we were given huge servings. Poor Didi struggled to finish the food and I had to distract our hosts with stories about school so she could refuse second helpings without too much fuss.

That would have been enough to make this holiday memorable but after lunch Mano Bua-ji dropped a bombshell.

'Your father wants to meet the two of you,' she said. We knew she had been in touch with him over the years because her sons and my father were friends and of the same age.

But still, what?! Who?!

Didi started to cry. I stared at Mano Bua-ji in disbelief.

Our father wanted to meet us! The man I had only seen in faded pictures. I couldn't take it in. You never know you have missed something till it is given to you.

Until that moment, I had never realised that there was a father-sized hole in my heart. We had been brought up with so much love by my grandparents and were so protected that I had never missed him in day-to-day life.

The only time his absence cropped up was when I was filling out forms in school where I put in my grandfather's name in the section that said father, but my mother's name, Satwant Kaur, where it said mother.

But I must admit he was always on my mind. Imagination has been my defence mechanism. I imagined that one day he would come, one day he would call us his daughters, one day he would say that he missed us.

I did not actually think that imagination would turn to reality.

My father had always been an enigma in my life.

I don't remember living with him at all but I am told that Didi and I were sent weekly to his house for mulaqat and that he would give us silver coins.

I was around three or four years old when my parents separated in 1944 or 1945. No one remembers why now and no one really cared for there were no formal divorces then. My father remarried in 1946 and we hardly ever saw him after that.

Later I discovered that he was a brilliant lawyer. He wrote the patency law of India and was a specialist in UN Affairs. His portrait stands in the Supreme Court; some dear friends sent me that picture.

Sometimes I yearned for him. When we were living anna to anna, and my grandfather was not able to work, I dreamt that he would swoop in and be our saviour, give us back the safety and comfort of our childhood. But they had only been dreams.

I had met him a million times in my head.

As it turned out, I was destined to meet him only twice.

It was all decided quickly, we were to meet him in an hour, at 4 p.m., for tea at Gaylord. It was not far from the house we were staying at and we would be able to walk to it.

I will never ever be able to explain that one hour of waiting, and what Didi and I went through. The hope, the joy, the anxiety … my heart sounded like a drum beating and my palms were sweating.

Details from that day are frozen in my mind. The white blouse and blue pleated skirt I wore, Didi's salwar kameez, the intimidating expanse of Gaylord where we reached half an hour earlier than the given time. The tables set for four, the smell of freshly baked bread.

We waited by the door where there was a crowd. It was less frightening, less lonely there.

We stood there waiting for our father who we had never known or remembered. We stared at every Sardar that walked our way, once or twice Didi and I looked at each other questioningly before deciding that no, that was not him.

And when he did appear we knew from far. He was wearing a greyish blue suit, with a light blue shirt and a striped tie. His pagri was white. I am not sure if that was a court diktat, but unlike the colourful ones worn by my cousins and uncles, my father's pagri, even in the few photos I was able to cobble together later, was nearly always white, or very infrequently with black polka dots.

How can you be drawn to a person you do not know and haven't seen for years? Can your blood flow towards another person, like there is the pull of gravity? We went to him and he just hugged us tight and held us both to his chest. I think all three of us were crying silently, broken from the inside, trying to keep calm on the outside.

We did not even realise when we entered or when we were seated.

There was awkward silence. Not really a silence though, since Didi had tears in her eyes and was sort of choking. I was trying hard not to cry, to seem normal. But there was an absence of words.

Finally, our father spoke. He asked us our names. He did not know who was who. The lump in my throat seemed to expand. This was my father, a stranger. What a bitter truth to be thrown in our faces. What were we supposed to do?

Did you never care about us? How could you not see us all these years? Did you ever think how we have lived without a father? Do you know that Didi had to start working at thirteen to help run our house? Didn't you want to know your daughters? I missed you so much. I hope you will be in my life always. Recrimination, heartache, loss, hope, prayer. There was a jumble of emotions within me, and I could not force a single word out.

Didi drew herself together, and behaved like the elder she was.

'How is Dadi?' she asked.

Haltingly, he replied. Her health, her days, her keenness to meet us. Slowly our conversation became less stilted; the tension eased, and we spoke more comfortably.

I tried to memorise his face. It was both familiar and unfamiliar. It was the face I saw on my younger sister Roopy, but it was also his own, one of a good-looking Sardar, with a broad forehead and aquiline nose. Later when I met my stepsister Manju, I would find another person who looked like him. In fact, if you were to put Roopy and Manju together they would look like twins. The face structure has passed down to another generation—one can see it in my son Suneet, Didi's son Tanuj and Roopy's son Siddharth.

He must have been only forty-six and there were lines of age and care, but what we saw was the twinkle in his eyes. He smiled and looked at us both. He asked me whether I still wanted to become a doctor. I could only nod. Why would a simple question make my eyes overflow? I found myself wiping away tears.

'You gave me millions of injections as a baby,' he said.

He ordered the famous Gaylord chicken sandwiches and chocolate pastries. Didi and he had tea, I had hot chocolate.

We talked. About school, marks and some known family members. He asked me what I liked to study, so I told him I liked poetry and history.

I don't think he heard my answer, or what I said was lost in the din. Neither of us spoke about poetry. Neither did he mention that he wrote nor did I.

'Agar tumhari Maa ne saath diya hota to mein taarey torh laata (Had your mother supported me I would have plucked the stars for her),' he said. Something about his words lodged themselves deep inside me.

He had been very humiliated by my grandfather, who was a lion in those days, the king of all he surveyed, hundreds of people working for him and who had saved vast amounts of money for each of us.

My parents did not get along and my father was thrown out of the house many times. While my grandfather was a rich, strong zamindar who behaved like one, my father was still studying law and reliant perhaps on my grandfather for money.

No one realised how soon things would change.

The question could not be denied any longer. Didi asked it. 'Why have you never met us?'

'Main do kashtiyon pe sawar nahi ho sakta, toot jaunga (I cannot straddle two boats, I will be torn apart),' he said.

We nodded as though we understood. But could any child really understand?

He asked about Roopy whom he had never seen. She was born three months after my parents separated.

He gave us money, a hundred rupees each from him and another hundred each from my Dadi. And then we parted. No promises were made to meet again from either side. I knew the words would not come, yet I had hoped to hear them. The lump in my throat returned.

We hugged. Tears coursed down all our cheeks. He wiped them with his handkerchief. Then he turned and walked away. One moment he was there, the father we had longed to see, and the next he had become a part of the milieu that moved around in front of Regal Cinema.

Didi and I stood watching long after he had disappeared, unable to gather ourselves. Didi cried unabashedly and I cried silently; I always cried silently. Even my anger and hurt were muted.

We had never lived with him and he was alien to us, yet all of us felt the painful pangs of someone special being separated from us. Something had happened in those moments.

It took a while for movement to return to our limbs and we started the walk back to Windsor Mansion. What could we say about what had just passed—Didi and I never discussed it. Instead, we focused on the excitement at the large sum of money we had received; neither saying that we would exchange all that money for another meeting.

The next afternoon we left for Shimla.

With so much money we boarded the train and both of us had a Coca-Cola that cost 4 annas each. It was a luxury we could never afford.

Our host, and fellow Pishori, Sardar Pratap Singh Dhingra had two grown daughters who were married. Amarjit Aunty was married to Agya Uncle and had two sons Sherry and Duma. His other daughter had two sons as well. Their younger brother, Amarmohan, was a little older than us and extremely nice. We kept in touch till well after marriage, exchanging regular picture postcards. We used to call him Amy.

Our holiday felt like a time from a past life. Mornings began with full English breakfasts—scrambled eggs, sausages, toast, baked beans—presided over by Pratap Uncle and his wife. Days were idyllic, spent roaming around Mall Road, skating, riding horses, cycling, eating channa jor garam, and playing board games and cards with Pratap Uncle and his family.

Didi was a superb skater and came first in a local competition. She used to skate in Nainital too. Her partner was Ravi, the son of the J.B. Mangaram family who owned the most popular shop on Mall Road. Ravi was good-looking and wore beautiful cardigans. I liked him best in his yellow turtleneck cardigan.

I embraced the outdoors, going horse-riding and cycling at every opportunity, while our hosts and Didi huddled at home and played card games like Court Piece and Flash for money.

One day I hired a cycle and went down the ridge to the Mall. I pedalled away, noting appreciatively the lack of other cyclists on the path. A police whistle blasted through my pleasant reverie. The whistle was attached to a policeman who was running towards me, waving his hands and shouting.

'Stop … No … Cycles …'

I understood why I had not encountered any other cyclists on this road. But what could I do? I was on a steep slope, the bike gathering speed as I hurtled downhill, and I could not follow the policeman's instructions.

Both the policeman and I sped downhill, his burst of whistles getting shorter as he huffed behind me, both of us unable to stop because of the steep decline.

I rolled to a stop at the bottom of the hill well before the officer; in fact, the policeman, proving the law of inertia, overshot me and had to walk back.

I apologised prettily and profusely; I was a tourist; I didn't know the roads; it wouldn't happen again.

Mollified, he let me off, with a 'Don't let it happen again.'

That summer, I won the Miss 16 crown in Shimla at Devicos.

Devicos had a live band and a popular tea service, which made it the most stylish and trendy restaurant in Shimla.

It was the first time that I had ever gone out dancing. I was quite shy but everyone in Uncle Pratap's family insisted we go. A gharara–kameez was found. Blue and golden printed satin even though I never wore blue because it clashed with the green of my eyes. There they announced the Miss 16 dance. It was like the films. I had danced in school and school birthday parties and concerts, but never quite like this and that too with a man. The partners were chosen by lucky draws. I don't remember the name of my partner, but he was the younger brother of Veera Sunder Singh, later known as the actress Priya Rajvansh, and was a Second Lieutenant in the Army. We competed against his sister but eventually won and I became Miss 16, much to the pleasure of my Shimla family.

And the displeasure of my father.

I heard from my cousins in Delhi, on our way back to Kanpur, that he did not like this escapade of mine.

The next and the last time I met my father was at Swarup Uncle's chautha in September 1986. This was the same Swarup Uncle with whom we had stayed on our way to Shimla.

Didi and I were standing after the prayer meeting with our husbands, Sushil Bhai and Baldev. Didi was a mother of two, and I a mother of three. We were in our late forties.

Someone came and hugged me from the back.

Shocked, I turned around.

It was my father. Older, his beard grey, still good-looking.

He wore a white polka-dot pagri, as he seems to have much of his life. I wish I could have asked him why.

We were all surprised.

Politeness reigned. Pleasantries were exchanged. We introduced Baldev and my brother-in-law Sushil Bhai. He introduced his son. There was family all around watching. We were too surprised and too conscious to say anything or ask anything.

I wanted to tell my father that I loved his poetry and had all his books, that I read them daily, that I knew him as much as I knew myself. But nothing was said.

We met as strangers and then he went to his car, and we to ours, and we drove away in different directions.

Hawa se phool saare chil chuke they
Hum aksar iss tarha bhi mil chuke they

Koi harf e gila kaise nikalta
Kisi ki hum, zaba'n mein sill chuke they

The flowers were stripped from the winds
And that is how we had often met

How could a word of reproach escape
We were stitched up in someone's tongue

9

A Surprise Engagement

I HAD BECOME A SENIOR IN SCHOOL. I WAS IN MY FINAL YEAR, WITH the Senior Cambridge exams awaiting me at the end of the year.

The days seemed long, full of things, yet they were speeding by so quickly. I was the captain of the cricket, volleyball and kabaddi teams. I became the captain of the Gold House, a prestigious position in school. The principal's office had photographs of all the houses and captains displayed on the wall and so was mine.

I was busy with schoolwork and my sports schedule. I had the honour of playing an exhibition match for charity with Frank Worrell who would go on to become a legendary captain of the West Indies cricket team, at Green Park Stadium in Kanpur, which was an important venue for all test matches.

It was the year I read *Jane Eyre, Wuthering Heights, Thelma, The Valley of Decision* and *The Old Man and the Sea.*

I was always awarded for the neatness of my desk. There was a place for everything, and everything was in its place. Everybody would write their names on the desks at school or scratch out a design with a compass. I couldn't bear it.

Mine remained the one untouched desk in every class. Even today, if you come home and ask me for anything, I can say which drawer, and where in the drawer you will find it. Every shelf in my house has little compartments, and everything is neatly arranged in them.

'Singh, this is your last year. Can you finish your needlework on time?' Mrs Chatterjee asked.

Implored might be the better word. The one thing that neither school nor home had been able to teach me was needlework. Crocheting, knitting and sewing were beyond my capabilities. Mummy had passed on her genes to Didi. I did not even envy her. I still wished that I could understand math, the only other subject I struggled with, but I was indifferent to needlework.

I had never improved through my school years. My needlework still sat in the Lazy Corner. At the end of the year, everybody in school would go and look at the corner, and my name would always be displayed, but even this public shaming didn't help. I just could not sew or knit. It always took me a year to crochet, knit and sew.

I could not look her in the eye and mumbled something that could be taken for assent.

As the year progressed, a certain anxiety seemed to grip our class, even the best students were rendered nervous. Study timetables were created and circulated. I optimistically tried one that required me to wake up at 4.30 a.m., but when it was time to set the alarm, it occurred to me that the exams were three months away and Didi would be disturbed. Best to study later in the day, I figured.

One month later, I needed no alarm to wake me up in the morning. My anxiety about the exams in December was enough of an alarm clock. Like the razor-sharp pendulum in Edgar Allan Poe's *The Pit and the Pendulum*, the Senior Cambridge exams were descending.

Life after the Senior Cambridge exams played out in my daydreams. I would be a doctor; I had spent a lot of my childhood playing with doctor sets; I had an avid interest in watching people get injections; and the college years would be easy because the medical college was opposite our house.

'Papa, Ina is daydreaming again,' Roopy the traitor would rat me out.

12 September 1958. Two months to go for the Senior Cambridge exams. A little less than a month before I turned eighteen.

It was the day of Sangrand.

In Sikhism, Sangrand is the start of a new month.

It is said that on this particular day one must hear the name of the new month either from a Granthi or someone very good, and luck will follow all month.

Even though Guru Granth Sahib-ji says, '*shogun apshagun tis ko lage jis chit na aawey*', meaning good omens and bad omens affect those who do not keep the Lord in mind, and effectively there is no concept of auspicious or inauspicious in Gurbani and Guru Granth Sahib, my grandmother always announced the Sangrand and blessed us children.

It was Friday evening, around 4 p.m. and Didi, Roopy and I were celebrating the beginning of our weekend. Badi Mummy had gone to the Gurudwara for Sangrand, Mummy was sleeping and Papa was tending to his garden.

The bell rang. It was Kumsie. He had brought along with him a friend carrying two records and two telegrams.

Kumsie's name was Arun Kumar Arora, but nobody called him Arun.

I had first met Kumsie in Nainital shortly after Papa arrived from Peshawar in 1947. I was six. Mummy had been admitted to Crawford Hospital for some check-up. Adjoining the hospital was a large playground and I would play there most day—cricket, marbles, football. Kumsie joined in and though he was almost four years older, I beat him at marbles every day. At the end of the game, he owed me a lot of marbles, but did not have as many.

Instead, he went to my grandfather and gave him the pen he was carrying and told him to please keep the pen as collateral till he brought more marbles the next day. Papa smiled involuntarily, before solemnly agreeing to the deal.

We were friends ever since. His sisters too were in the same school as us. I soon became friends with his sister Papsy (Prabha); she and I would hold hands and walk to school. Didi became friends with his older sister Kitty. Both families became close. His parents ran the famous restaurant Shady Grove in Nainital; they later opened a branch in Kanpur, which Kumsie was sent to manage.

Papsy became a librarian and moved to America, married a priest Gene Lockwood, who was the principal of St. Xavier's in Delhi. She created quite a furore in the Christian world; he was excommunicated. But love has no boundaries. Kitty married J.C. Mendiratta, an Income Tax officer, who was very popular with the ladies because he did palmistry and made predictions about the future.

Kumsie married, too, but rather late in life. He married a soft-spoken, adorable lady named Arvind. A doctor, she took to us immediately and came and stayed with Baldev and me in Delhi after her marriage to Kumsie. It is she who taught me the Friday fast. Kumsie and Arvind have a son, Sharad.

Life, they say, can only be understood backwards, but it must be lived forward. So here was destiny knocking at my door, holding my hand and leading me forward while my mind, body and soul were still living in the past—in Peshawar, Nainital, Rampur, Lucknow, Dehradun and Arya Nagar.

Once he moved to Kanpur to run Shady Grove, Kumsie came home often. It wasn't unusual for him to bring friends along; though this one, a fair, slightly plump young man, with salt and pepper hair, seemed older. Friends with records were also normal enough. But the two telegrams were definitely odd. Apparently, two children had been born in his family, Raju and Anju.

Kumsie's friend was introduced as Baldev Varma, who was shifting from Amritsar to Kanpur to set up a hundred-loom spinning factory.

Just then Badi Mummy walked in from the Gurudwara with prashad in her hand. Baldev got up and bent forward to touch her feet.

Roopy and I exchanged glances. Didi and I exchanged glances. I gave him the benefit of the doubt—maybe it was an older person thing.

'Can we play the records?' Kumsie asked.

The reason for his visit with Baldev became clear. Since nothing had yet been unpacked in Baldev's house, Kumsie had brought him to our house to listen to the records.

Kumsie moved to the gramophone. Baldev walked with him, holding on to his precious vinyls, two 75 rpms.

Our gramophone player was large and bulky and looked like a wooden box. You had to raise the lid to access the turntable and the controls. It had been given to us by a friend of Papa's who was migrating to Pakistan. It was a reminder of the irony of life: years earlier, we had parted with our radio, and now we had been given a gramophone as a gift.

We kept it in a corner of the front room. Opposite it was a settee made from trunks joined together, trunks that had come with us from Peshawar. Didi and I were sitting on these, Roopy was too restless to stay in one place.

Kumsie and I listened to music the most. We didn't have too many records, but the ones that we played again and again were the lively *The Breeze and I* and *Zambezi*.

'Well if I have a whim,' Kumsie would begin.

'I either sink or swim,' I would take up. And then both of us would dance a little. *Moon River* was another favourite.

Baldev slid a vinyl carefully out from its cover, held it gingerly with his fingertips and put the stylus on. On some of our most played records, the needle would skip or not find the groove to start, but that evening it behaved perfectly. Out of the speakers came the rich baritone of Bing Crosby singing *'I'm dreaming of a white Christmas'.*

Tea was served.

We listened to the records repeatedly. Then we played *Zambezi, The Breeze and I* and *Moon River,* and so the evening meandered forward, while we should have been preparing for exams.

From that evening on, Kumsie and Baldev would often drop by. Baldev offered to help me prepare for history and literature, especially Shakespeare.

He was a double MA in English literature and had been a professor in Amritsar till the family insisted he carry forward the flourishing textile business.

His uncles and grandfather owned the oldest weaving mills in Amritsar. They had been set up in the late 1800s and they exported taffeta and linen to Europe and Africa.

December came by, and soon the exams were over.

I lived in free time. There were talks of college—the medical college opposite was still my goal—but we had to wait for the Senior Cambridge results to come out first.

I spent all day playing cricket and tennis in the neighbouring parks and empty lands—Kanpur was not the concrete jungle it is now—without an iota of fear that accompanies children and public spaces now.

We even managed to make a mini badminton court in our backyard. Sometimes Papa would play with Didi, Roopy and I, and sometimes Shamim and Patto would join us too. Shamim and Patto always won as they were champions from Lucknow University.

One day, in early January 1959, I cycled home after cricket practice and, as was my habit, I lifted the front wheel of the bicycle to land it on our verandah.

To my dismay, my cycle landed in the midst of four unknown ladies who had watched my stunt with amazement.

I quickly got off, said a respectful namaste, and went inside.

Very rattled and red-faced by embarrassment I asked my mother who those ladies were. She said she would tell me later.

That later came sooner than expected.

The ladies were Baldev' s family and they had come to get him married.

At first, I thought it was Didi they were interested in and I said that it seemed too soon, but I was even more shocked when I realised I was the target. Baldev had asked for my hand in marriage.

I was engaged to Baldev on 10 January 1959. My soon-to-be mother-in-law took off a ring from her hand and put it on my finger. *Roka ho gaya, shaadi teh ho gayee.*

After our engagement, Baldev confessed, 'The moment I saw you, I knew I wanted to marry you'.

Proposal and acceptance letters were exchanged between my soon-to-be father-in-law and Papa. I have both the letters still.

There was no question in my mind, I couldn't say no.

They strictly wanted an Arya Samaj wedding.

Papa agreed, though he expressed that they would have preferred an Anand Karaj.

We were married on 8 February 1959. Twenty-eight days after the engagement.

The Senior Cambridge results were yet to come out.

You'n wafa ke sare nibhao gham ke fareb mei'n bhi yaqeen ho
Koi baat aisi kaho sanam ke fareb mei'n bhi yaqeen ho

Mere intizar ko kya khabar tumhei'n ikhtiyar hai is qadar
Mujhe do saliqa ye kam se kam ke fareb mei'n bhi yaqeen ho

Be faithful to all the sorrows of loyalty so we may believe in deception too
Say something to me, my dearest one, so we may believe in deceit too

Little does my patience know that you have such boundless rights
Grant me at least enough grace so we may believe in deceit too

10

A Wedding and a New Family

HOW I GOT MARRIED IS A MIRACLE.

Firstly, Mano Bua-ji, Papa's cousin, was conferred with. She was the head of the family and Papa never did anything without her consent.

Baldev's family were Hindus and we were Sikhs.

Mano Bua-ji discussed the feasibility and, seeing the circumstances of our family, gave her consent.

Then relatives came forward to help.

Pushy Aunty got her friends together, Raj Thapar (then Srivastava), and Laxmi Sehgal of the Azad Hind Force. They were the elite of Kanpur and did a lot of relief work during partition. A lot of displaced refugees were resettled in Kanpur.

These ladies put some sarees together by way of a trousseau, they got someone to donate money for the tents, somebody else to donate for the chairs and tables. More friends of theirs came to help the refugee girl's marriage, taking care of the food and lights.

I broke the news to my friends, who refused to believe it, till I gave them the wedding invitations. To say that they were shocked would be an understatement. I invited all my teachers and nuns for the wedding.

Mahesh, Ibrahim Bhai and Dennis put up a small mandap in our backyard and that's where we took our seven pheras. I did not understand a word of what the Pundit-ji said. He was a learned person and came with Pita-ji, my father-in-law, in the baraat from Jalandhar. I did not know Punjabi too well, let alone Sanskrit. At home we spoke a mix of Pishori, English and Urdu.

Baldev took one rupee at the wedding at Kanyadaan. This then became a tradition in the family.

I concentrated on not tripping over my saree. It was a red silk saree with golden polka dots. I had never worn a saree in my life. Didi had put about a hundred pins in it to secure it from any accidental slippage and to ensure that even if I stepped on it, it would not unravel.

Baldev never forgave her for this.

The baraat was huge, almost a hundred people. Baldev's young cousins danced on the tables, sprinkled Evening of Paris on my school friends and teachers who had also come in huge numbers. It was the first time the nuns and the teachers had come to a private function; I had been a popular student.

Some of the cousins from the baraat trampled on Papa's green roses, who was so upset by the untimely demise of his prized flowers that he refused to meet them again.

I believe my father came to see my baraat from afar but did not make his presence known.

I wish he had.

8 February 1959. I was eighteen years old.

Not even twelve years since the Partition.

Just like that I was married, a wife, a daughter-in-law, a sister-in-law. I went to live in Kunj Vihar Palace—which had twenty flats—in Gumti No. 5. It was an imposing white building. Gulzar's family were our neighbours. Many moons later he came to my house when Zehra Nigah was visiting, and I reminded him of Kunj Vihar Palace.

Life has had a change waiting for me at every corner. When I look back, I see that I have lived many different lives.

My Senior Cambridge results came out in March, a month after the wedding. I did not do too badly. Barely passed maths but did well in literature, history and geography. What to do with those results though?

Mata-ji, my mother-in-law, gave me a guinea.

A new life, a new displacement, a new family, adjustments, compromises.

The difference between our dreams and our reality comes down to one thing—our expectations. If we don't think that our dreams stand a chance of coming true, we allow them to become far-fetched. And, if we think reality is full of frustrations, we tend to set our sights low.

Yet realism should never be an excuse for hopelessness.

Some dreams are truly attainable.

I left two sisters behind and acquired a large family. My name was also changed to Indu, as one of Baldev's chacha-ji was called Indra Nath.

Kunj Vihar was not far from Friends Colony, a rickshaw took 4 annas to get me home. My mother-in-law at times said this 4 annas that I spent on a rickshaw could buy vegetables for all the meals in the day.

Pita-ji, my father-in-law, came from a large family. They were five brothers and one sister.

Pita-ji, Shri Harbans Lal Varma, was an executive engineer in the Railways. He was married to Shakuntla Devi from Gwalior, who was originally from Lahore.

All of Baldev's siblings, his sisters Vimla Behen-ji, Urmill Behen-ji and Sunita, and his brother Bunty Suresh Varma were born in Lahore.

Baldev, however, was born in Delhi, as my father-in-law had been posted there because of his job in the Railways.

We never got enough of hearing about the Sareena da Mohalla in Lahore. It was an elite area where my mother-in-law used to live.

Her grandfather was the Privy Council to the Maharaja of Gwalior and a large part of her family still lives there.

Once, I visited the Gwalior Palace and found a large portrait of him hanging in one room with those of other dignitaries.

It's a painting that I think about often, like the portrait of my father that hangs in the Supreme Court, as well as the Ghantaghar built by my great grandfather in Peshawar. They have become paintings and landmarks whose original subjects and benefactors are now unknown, just part of the unremarked landscape of everyday life and days past. Even the family does not know them any longer; after all, who has the time to look up the generations past? And yet they were real, they lived, and they were loved, they created families ... is it just the course of nature that we gradually lose everything that matters at some point, right down to the last physical mementos?

Baldev was the middle child of five siblings. It was known as thrikhaa in Punjabi because he was the boy after three daughters, one of whom did not survive. His two elder sisters, Vimla Behen-ji and Urmill Behen-ji, were twelve and eleven years older than me. Baldev himself was eight years older.

Sunita was Baldev's younger sister. She was almost my age; I was older by six months. She got married only five days before me. We had a joint wedding card. The youngest was Bunty, who was the only one amongst the five living with his parents. All the others were married; both Vimla Behen-ji and Urmill Behen-ji moved around often because of their husbands' jobs.

It was overwhelming to suddenly become a part of this huge family unit. Vimla Behen-ji had two sons, Urmill Behen-ji had two sons and a daughter. And Baldev and I lived were to live with his Chacha-ji and Chachi-ji with whom he had set up the mill.

I was always a bit in awe of Vimla Behen-ji and a little nervous around her. We became very close much later, near the end of her life. She lived a minute away from where I live now in Friends Colony, New Delhi, and I would see her every day on my way back from work. She was on crutches since she was thirty, when a procedure on her knees had gone wrong.

She was married to Shri Baijnath Bhalla, who was also in the Railways. Baijnath Bhaisahib was posted in Jagadhri Punjab and later in Lucknow and eventually in Delhi where they built a house in New Friends Colony just before his retirement. Bhaisahib was a brilliant engineer and had studied in England before his marriage.

They had two boys, Karan and Arun, who are now settled in two extreme ends of the world. Karan lives in Toronto and Arun in Sydney.

Urmill Behen-ji was a woman with a heart of gold. She was married to Prakash Nayar, the don of our family. He was in the IFS and had a great swag to him. He lived life king size. Bhaisahib's postings saw them live in places like Sri Lanka, Tanzania and Belgium. Urmill Behen-ji made the trousseau for every girl in the family. I still have the beautiful crockery she gave Baldev and me. So does Sunita.

She was a cook par excellence, and though a strict vegetarian herself, she could serve the most delicious non-vegetarian food. All three sisters, Vimla Behen-ji, Urmill Behen-ji and Sunita, were vegetarians and so was Mata-ji.

There was a large age gap between Baldev and his younger sister, Sunita. She was married to Virender Kumar Verma, a geophysicist who was with the group general manager at ONGC and did extremely well.

I have been the closest to Sunita, we are soul sisters. We stayed a lot together in Aligarh, in Dehradun, had our children together and she has supported me under all circumstances in my life. Till date we share our innermost feelings with each other. In many ways she comes the closest to an ideal woman. There is an obvious peace that reflects on her face. She has always lived within her means. Giving something to Sunita is like going to war, she just will not take. She and VK Bhaisahib were posted in Iraq for five years. They have two children, Vivek and Ritu.

Vivek was born in Aligarh, a year after my son Vineet. Ritu was born in Dehradun.

The youngest of the brothers and sisters is Bunty, S.K. Varma, a chartered accountant and my great support.

He has stood by me in sorrow and joy.

He has been a father figure to my children and guided them in their careers and life. We have grown up together. When I lived with my in-laws, he became my confidante. I was eighteen, he was fifteen.

We played together and had a very close respectful relationship. I hid his cigarettes in my room and many a secret from his bachelor days.

He is married to Poonam Kapoor, a doctor and the daughter of a family friend from Aligarh. It is my fervent prayer to God that every family on earth should have a Poonam. This God-sent messiah has helped four generations in our family. They live close by and are my moral support in this age. They have two daughters, Meghna, now a mother of two herself, and Shibani, who is married to Gaurav Gambhir, her school sweetheart. They have two sons. One is aspiring to be a cricketer for India.

Khuwaab ban kar guzarti rahi zindagi
Kis qadar tujh se kam mein mili zindagi

Khauf lafzon ka mein oorh kar so gaee
Aur rishton main bat ti rahi zindagi

Turning into a dream, life kept passing by
How little I met you, O life

Cloaked in the fear of words, I slept
And life kept getting divided into relationships

11

A Birth and a Death

My marriage to Baldev was a marriage of two different cultures. I may have been born in a rich land-owning family of zamindars where everybody's card read 'Banker and Landlord' but in the present circumstances, when the marriage happened, I was a daughter of a refugee family, displaced during the Partition like many others.

I was sheltered and protected by old grandparents. I was fatherless and brotherless. Just eighteen.

I did not know much Punjabi, had never worn sarees, had never covered my head in front of elders, and had never eaten food, especially rice, with my hands. I was soon nicknamed Mem Bhabhi as I would roll up roti and put sabzi in it and eat with a fork and knife.

He came from a large and rich business family, well-known and respected in Amritsar.

He was eight years older than I. He had seen life, lived in college hostels, and had his string of love affairs. He was brilliant and well-read, but also spoilt and the much-indulged son of his mother since he was born after three daughters.

I discovered some wonderful and outstanding qualities in him when we became a couple.

He was kind, very respectful with elders and he loved children. He was so well-read, so knowledgeable about history, that it was difficult to comprehend. He loved and had read all the great Russian writers: Tolstoy, Dostoevsky, Pushkin, Turgenev, Gogol, Nabokov, Bulgakov, Pasternak, Lermontov, Chekhov.

Chekhov once said, 'Medicine is my lawful wife and literature my mistress; when I get tired of one, I spend the night with the other.' In Baldev's case, literature was his lawful wife and art his mistress.

I too started to read the Russians; *War and Peace, Anna Karenina, And Quietly Flows the Don, Don Flows Home to the Sea, Brothers Karamazov,* becoming absorbed in stories that were both large and yet felt personal, both foreign and relatable, and was once again given a new insight into human nature and love. His collection of books is a vast treasure which he has left for his children.

He bought the *Time* magazine like it was an addiction and we were regular customers at the Universal Book Store in Kanpur.

He pored over books about art, buying coffee table books about every famous painter in the world. Later, when he started to travel, he would visit as many museums as he could, and all his travel recommendations included art works to be seen.

Baldev loved music too. His collection of records, and later cassettes and CDs, was vast, ranging from pop and Bollywood to Indian and Western classical music. His appreciation of K.L. Saigal was no less than that of Kamla Jharia, Kanan Bala, C.H. Atma, Lata Mangeshkar, Asha Bhosle and Mohammad Rafi. He had LPs of Bach, Beethoven, Mozart, Brahms and Tchaikovsky; *Swan Lake* was a favourite.

Baldev knew so much poetry. He would quote Sahir, Majaz, Shakeel as easily as he quoted Keats or Byron. I have never met a more well-read person. It was a glorious period of our lives. The soirées held in our houses are still remembered and their recordings are a family treasure. We soon became a sought-after couple in Kanpur, he for his jokes and me for my ghazal recitations, and people vied to be invited by us.

The cricket craze in Kanpur is well-known, the Green Park there is a very important venue for Test matches.

Baldev knew Farokh Engineer and once invited the entire cricket team for dinner.

We became heroes in Kanpur.

Soon, Baldev's factory began to produce, and our house was often filled with bales of linen. I gave a lot away to many needy people, especially the swamis who came to our house to meet my parents-in-law or for havans.

My house was also always full with relatives—Baldev's uncle Vishwanath Chacha-ji and his wife Pushpa Chachi-ji with whom he had started this business and factory, his gaddidar, Khem Singh, who sat at the wholesale shop, his cousins and my parents-in-law.

It was as if all roads and routes led to Kanpur and, once there, to 13, Kunj Vihar Palace.

And then a bolt from the blue … I was pregnant.

I had told Pushy Aunty that I was feeling unwell as I did not want to worry my family. When I married, I knew nothing about sex, and when I started to feel queasy, I thought I had caught something.

I am still astonished at how women were told to always cover their heads, and then suddenly are married off one day and expected to give their naked bodies to men without being told anything.

Pushy Aunty brought along her friend Dr Laxmi Sehgal for a check-up. Once finished they did a small jig.

'We are going to become grandmothers,' Pushy Aunty said.

I was dumbfounded. What did that mean? I, Indira Rani Singh, was going to be a mother? I was going to have a baby?

There was rejoicing, more family came till the house was bursting at the seams.

More desi ghee was stuffed down my throat, milk three times a day and panjeeri with sund.

I hated sweet things.

Baldev and I, we did not really know what hit us.

All that I wanted to do was cuddle up to my Naani and hold her like I used to in my childhood.

But that was not to be.

Badi Mummy woke up one morning and told us that she had a dream in which Baba Nanak-ji had appeared.

'Let's go,' he said. 'It's time for you to come with me.'

In her dream, she pleaded with Baba-ji. It's my granddaughter's first Diwali after her marriage, please do not ruin it.

He agreed. 'A day after Diwali?' he asked.

She said the day after Diwali is Tika (also called Bhai Duj in some parts of the country), you can come after that day.

She had already become very frail with diabetes, though she was taking regular medicine.

Diwali came on 31 October that year. It was my first as a married woman, and it was a joyous occasion. Tika passed the next day.

Almost to the day promised to Baba-ji, Badi Mummy fell into a coma due to diabetes and was admitted to the hospital. She passed away on 4 November 1959.

Our guardian angel, our cushion of security, our shoulder that we leaned on in sorrow and joy was no more. All three of us would fight to sleep on her lap and would eventually take turns. We would look forward to the navala (mouthful) of food mashed in gravy or dal she fed us; even when it had been khichdi it tasted heavenly.

The three of us felt ripped off our guard. She was only fifty-nine.

Partition had wrought havoc on my grandparents.

Mummy was young. The three of us were very young and could fight to survive. But Badi Mummy and Papa were mere shadows of the handsome aristocratic couple they used to be in Peshawar.

She could not endure the Partition. She could not endure the life changes. She could not endure the hard domestic work that came onto her. She could not endure the frailty of the family.

Ramesro Devi, daughter of Sir Balmakand, the woman who fought all ends after Partition to protect us, left for her heavenly abode. There were no phones and so no means of quick communication. Relatives were advised by telegrams. I was fetched by Papa just before her hospitalisation.

There was an Akhand Path in the house. The continuous recitation of all the verses in the Guru Granth Sahib from the beginning to the end, in thirty-one ragas as specified, in all 1,430 pages, that lasted more than forty-eight hours.

Later in life I followed this tradition regularly. Every year I had an Akhand Path. Baldev and my in-laws were so accepting and supported me throughout. We had regular havans too. Every Tuesday Baldev and I performed the havan in our back verandah and the children joined in if they wanted to.

But after the readers were gone, after the relatives had returned home, we were left in a house devoid of Badi Mummy's presence, without her continuous rounds of tea, without her little kettle and tea cosy, without her sitting in the kitchen.

I wandered around the house, haunted by her absence. The wooden takhtposh in the verandah where she would sit after a full day's work and say '*Ni kudio ik glass pani pila dyo* (listen you girls, please get me a glass of water)', gently mopping her sweaty forehead and brows with her dupatta.

Papa was inconsolable. His Malika Rani was gone.

Mummy wept bitterly. My sisters and I huddled together. We had never experienced death before.

It was a bitter, cold winter.

Jab dil mei'n utar jayega chahat ka nazara
Bay hosh sa ho jayega ye zahan tumhara
Kuch kaam na aayega kisi ka bhi sahara
Tab dhoondne lagoge meri chahato'n ko tum
Phir mai'n nahi'n milu'ngee
Phir mai'n nahi'n milu'ngee

When the panorama of love seeps into the heart
This world of yours shall become insensate
And no one's support shall be of any use to you
Then you shall begin to search for my loves
But I shall not be found again, I shall not be found again

12

The First Break of the Umbilical Cord

SPRING CAME AROUND.

Papa's garden was abloom, but he had become quiet and mostly kept to himself.

The world turned. The baby grew. Things set in motion before Badi Mummy died took their own course.

Didi got a job in Delhi.

Mehr Chand Khanna Uncle, a close family friend, recommended a job for Didi at the Cottage Industries Emporium in New Delhi. He was then the Union Minister for Rehabilitation. He and Prithvi Uncle convinced Papa that working at the newly opened Cottage Emporium would be safe for Didi. The Emporium was mostly led by ladies who were helping the refugees settle down and start earning a living.

They also said that they would get Didi a room in the Working Girls Hostel at Curzon Road, now the Mahatma Gandhi Road, a few minutes away from Janpath.

With marriage, I had already left home a year ago. But I was only a rickshaw ride away. Didi would now be in a different city. Distance, time and death were splintering our family unit.

Didi. A classic beauty with a strong bone structure and fine features. Beautiful hair, beautiful brown eyes, which she fluttered very often. At times in bewilderment and at times in desperation. She laughed with total abandon and yet disliked dirty jokes. It went against her grain, as one would say. She cried very easily too. One had to be careful not to offend her. She was always frail. I had always felt like her protector, though I always called her Didi and revered and looked up to her. She had been as responsible for bringing us up as my mother and grandparents had been, sometimes I felt she had even taken their place.

Didi had been the breadwinner of the family and the warrior that kept hunger at bay. Her adolescent years had been spent earning money to feed us.

She cut and matched old cushions and curtains and made shirts and skirts. She hated geography and loved history. Mrs Kelly, her teacher, often quoted her. She had been giving tuitions since the time she was thirteen.

Even now she was taking on the responsibility of the family. She was only twenty-three.

Her salary was 180 rupees a month. It was not a princely sum but enough for her monthly rent and rations. She promised to send hundred rupees home every month as money order. She also promised to take care of herself in the new city and turned over the responsibility of the house on the young shoulders of Roopy.

Roopy was in Senior Cambridge, and soon she would be going to college.

Papa had retreated into himself. He hardly smiled, his body had bent with age or perhaps the grief of Badi Mummy's passing. His breathing had become heavy. He was on medication. He spent much of his time in the small room lying on the settee looking out at the garden.

Mummy had to be taken care of.

Through the years, I often played a game of what if.

What if we were still the Singhs of Peshawar? If Papa were still landlord and banker, king of all he surveyed. What he had learnt about work from his family was to own and manage the lands, go hunting, and have pets. As children of this zamindar we would have led lives of comfort and luxury.

But we would have been bound by the family outlook—that women should not go out. We would have left home only at marriage. We would all probably have been married and would have become mothers at young ages.

I could never, even after marriage, wear a sleeveless blouse in front of Papa. I could never come before my father-in-law without a pallu. Papa would say, your father-in-law is coming, you should take a pallu. In Peshawar, our tonga and car had purdah; Mummy wore a burqa when she ventured out; and we wore a purdah to school as Papa didn't like that we had to wear skirts.

And Didi, she would not have given tuitions after school, she would not be working, nor would she live alone in Delhi. Would that have been a better life?

I always found myself unsure. But one thing I was sure about, if we had men in the family, life would have been better and safer. If we had a father, we might all have studied further. My father's sons became advocates and his daughter from the other marriage a doctor. We only had an ageing grandfather who had been unable to cope with the change Partition had wrought. We would not have to be married off in a hurry, and would not have considered it a sin to be good-looking.

We saw Didi off at the station a ticket of third class in her hand, a slim, slight figure in a salwar kameez, with a big suitcase.

Didi got a room in the working girl's hostel at Curzon Road, just a five-minute rickshaw ride to Janpath and Cottage Emporium. We had already been reassured by Prithvi Uncle and Mehr Chand Uncle that the Working Girls Hostel was a safe place to stay and Cottage Emporium a very good place to work, reassurances we clutched to ourselves and tried to smile.

Mummy told Didi for the third time that she should finish the food packed for the journey. Papa was quiet, as he went up with her on the train and saw her to her seat. I was only weeks away from Vineet's delivery; Didi promised to return at the time of my child's birth.

And so it came that Urmiljit Rani Singh, whom the world knew as Uma, left Kanpur in 1959.

Shauq-e-junoo mein ishq ki sun li sada alag alag
Qissey tamaam ho gaye apni jagah alag alag

Aansu gira to aankh ne pucha ye sarey jism se
Jan-o-jigar ke sath ko kis ne kiya alag alag

The song of love was heard on its own in a state of mad ecstasy
All the anecdotes came to an end and on their own separately

When the tear dropped, the eye asked the rest of the body
Who has wrenched the life out of my heart and put them separately

13

Learning the Language of Babies

BABIES GROW AND SEASONS CHANGE. WHEN SPRING CAME AROUND, it was time for my delivery.

The delivery was expected around the day of Holi. I wanted to be with my family.

Baldev's aunt, Pushpa Chachi-ji warned me that if I went home, it would be difficult for them to be informed—how would Baldev know if I went into labour? Especially since I was so close to my due date, I could go into labour at any moment.

But I did not want to be anywhere near the celebrations and the revelries of Holi. Badi Mummy's absence was still too raw and then there was Didi, who was home from Delhi for the first time after joining Cottage Emporium. Anyway, men never came to the hospital for deliveries in those days. Baldev just followed his Vishwanath Chacha-ji to work and back.

I went into labour on 13 March around 3 a.m. There was no one to take me to the hospital. Mummy woke up Papa in the next room who rushed to neighbours, the C. Lal Chemists family, who had a car.

Mr Lal offered to drive us to the hospital himself. We hurriedly stuffed ourselves into the Fiat and drove to Dufferin Hospital. Didi, Roopy, Mummy and Papa were all in more agony than I.

I was healthy, I was young.

Pushy Aunty was informed and reached soon after. Then I was wheeled away into the labour room.

Vineet was born in the afternoon on 14 March. It was an easy delivery—scoring a century in cricket is harder. He was a healthy baby, almost nine pounds, with a mop of black hair.

After the delivery, I was very hungry. Pushy Aunty asked me what I wanted to eat and I said two fried eggs and two toasts. I devoured them while still at the delivery table. Thankfully my mother-in-law wasn't present, or she would have fainted; it was the custom in their house for the mother to have only vegetarian food for forty days after childbirth.

Then I insisted that I would walk to my room, and not be carried there on a stretcher. I got up. A chorus of protests arose, and there was a lot of staring at this unusual behaviour in the delivery room. Eventually I agreed to go on a wheelchair.

Outside the delivery room another emotional drama was unfolding. Papa was howling like a baby. I had never seen him cry, that sturdy, handsome Pathan had broken down. He kept saying, *'Tuwadi Mummy nu khabar suna k aana.'*

Roopy, Didi and Mummy came into the room and soon Vineet was brought in too. There were squeals of delight and they just stared at him as if a miracle had happened. Three cry-babies and a crying baby!

I saw a shadow of Baldev from the jaali window.

Later in the evening he came and looked at Vineet in the crib endlessly. Husbands never picked up their babies in those days, I never understood this taboo. Why was that not deemed an appropriate expression of love for your own child? Sometimes Baldev would, but it was an exception.

Then a new hurdle had to be overcome. Feeding the baby. Whenever I fed Vineet, he vomited.

My milk was tested and I was told it was healthier than a cow's. The family did more sadka.

Didi and Roopy giggled with their hands on their mouths.

Finally, a solution was arrived at. Give Vineet a little water before feeding him.

Back home another new life began. Another new routine.

New feelings.

Bewilderment.

How had I produced a human! I loved the beautiful tiny hands, the pink blossom-like toes, I could not take my eyes off the child. There is something so angelic about a newborn. The smell, the little dimples on the knees and elbows.

How important is that burp! His burp after feeding brought a relief not only to Baldev and me but to the entire household.

Gone were the days of cricket and volleyball, instead there were bottles and spoons and nipples to boil. There is no night and day for a newborn. Papa used to dry our uniforms; my biggest worry now was drying Vineet's handstitched napkins. The days of Pampers came decades later.

So, what is motherhood? Ask any new mother and she will have a myriad of answers from ecstatic to anxious and hysterical.

Motherhood exposes raw nerve endings, it makes you more alive, and it's also absolutely exhausting.

Looking at your child is both like looking in the mirror and looking at a stranger.

When I had time to think, I worried how I would shape this new life. One moment I was ready to cry, another day I was hysterical with laughter. It was a continuous personal comedy show twenty-four hours a day.

Our house was large. Baldev and my room had a small room attached to it, which I turned into a nursery. Pushy Aunty gave me a cot and life began to revolve around that little cot.

Our little doggy Brownie (who was given to me during my god-bharai) sat near the cot day and night and woe betide if someone unknown came near. They could consider themselves lucky if he gave them a polite warning about the trespass by pulling their pants off. If they didn't get the hint, his fangs would find the flesh of their calves.

As time passed, Vineet evolved a language of his own to convey to us what he wanted. 'Gumma' was his milk bottle, 'bum' was falling down. Whenever he heard cutlery his eyes would brighten and he would scream 'khana khana khana'.

One day Vineet started to cry, and we heard a new word.

'Umphy.' Baldev and I looked at each other.

We showed him the dog, the milk bottle, fruit, chocolate but that 'umphy' would not go and neither would he stop crying. I asked Baldev to take him out of the house in order to distract him. And suddenly Vineet looked at a thela of peanuts on the street and screamed 'UMPHY'! Someone in the house must have eaten peanuts in front of him. He wanted moongphali.

When I meet God, I will request him to make some sign language for mothers and young children to understand each other; poor, tired mothers have to solve puzzles 24/7.

Vineet kay Naam Ek Nazm

Merey ehsas mein jazbat hazaro'n hai'n magar
Main ney her fikr pay ash-shar likhey hai'n dil say
Jinki tareef huee daad mili hai sab say
Halqa-e-dost ki mehfil mein huye charchey bhi
Aaj main chah rahi hoo'n ki ek maa'n ki tarah
Apney betey kay liye nazm lihku'n palko'n say
Merey shano'n pay mera mazi liye hai darpan
Jis say kuch rang-e-dhanak beetey dino'n kay chamkey
Jab ki, ek aalam-e-masti mein nahaya tha sama'n
shaher-e-ummeed pay chhai thi baharo'n ki phuhar
Dil kay aangan mein barasta tha gulabi sa gulal
Shadmani kay taqazo'n say chamak ut-tha hilal
Jiski her jyot say khushio'n kay ujaley phootey
Jiski aamad nay mujhey Maa ka diya tha rutba
Balapan jiska meri gode ko deta tha ghuroor
Jiski kilkari pay kehti thi mein chashm e badoor
Wo meri zeest ka maqsad bhi tha sarmaya bhi

14

Time Tests Us Again

PROSPERITY. THE DICTIONARY DEFINES IT AS THE STATE OF BEING successful and having a lot of money.

Marriage was giving me a taste of it.

It was bittersweet, tinged with a sense of regret that my family could not be part of it, with the knowledge that once upon a time, I would have taken prosperity for granted.

The year Vineet was born, my in-laws shifted to Aligarh from Jalandhar; Pita-ji was doubling a new railway line from Delhi to Allahabad.

They had fourteen trolley men allocated to them. They were always on the move, bringing us gajar ka halwa, another getting desi ghee, makki ki roti and saag, collecting fresh eggs and home-grown vegetables.

My life now lay between Kanpur and Aligarh.

In Aligarh, the house we lived in belonged to one of the nawabs. It was a palatial bungalow, right opposite the railway station. We had dozens of rooms, tennis courts, a greenhouse, parks. The drawing and the dining halls were so large they could be used for weddings. We even had our own wheat fields. There was a greenhouse where the family sat in the evenings for tea. We slept out on charpais with mosquito nets.

We had a new transistor in the house and it had become our favourite plaything. My brother-in-law Bunty and I would listen to *Forces Request*, a beautiful programme on All India Radio, which played all our favourite Western music. We would send requests for our friends and were thrilled to hear our messages when they were selected. The presenters, Melville De Mellow, Roshan Menon, Lotika Ratnam, Surojit Sen, Pamela Singh and many more over the years, became household names, capturing their listeners' attention with their authoritative and informative patter.

In this sprawling Aligarh house Vineet's naamkaran was a landmark event. A hundred guests attended. Poonam, who was to become my sister-in-law years later, danced to *Mohe panghat pe Nandlala cher gayo re*. She was around nine. In my family a male child had been born after sixty years. There was happiness all around.

Didi was working at Cottage Emporium in Delhi.

Roopy was in college in Kanpur and was staying with Mummy and Papa.

Baldev's work was going well.

I was busy with Vineet. I saw Papa, Mummy and Roopy whenever I could. Mummy knitted dozens of sweaters for Vineet, which he outgrew in a trice the way only babies can. Seeing Vineet was guaranteed to make Papa smile, though he couldn't lift him or play with him.

When Vineet was less than two, Baldev and I took him to Gwalior to meet Mata-ji's family. There we received a telegram; Papa had passed away.

He had been in intense pain in the last year of his existence. Still, the devastation was severe.

My grandfather, my protector, was gone. I was not with him on the last day of his earthly journey. 6 July 1961.

Even though this was his physical death, the Partition had killed both our grandparents much earlier; they were just mere shadows of who they used to be.

A devastated man broken and bashed with no shore in sight. No monetary help, nothing to look forward to, especially after Badi Mummy's death. He had no will to live. He died of pleurisy. Neither Papa nor Badi Mummy had lived to sixty.

Children tie you to the here and now, and yet I felt adrift. I attended to Vineet's needs, but days went by, and I did not know how they had passed. I had lost my anchor; my home, my family was broken; even the protection of having a male figurehead in our family was now gone. My sisters and I had only each other to lean on.

Things seemed to go downhill from there. The next year, India went to war with China. The supply of silk yarn to India stopped. Our factory fell silent. Baldev tried to get yarn from Bhagalpur or Faizabad. But he had no luck.

The factory stayed shut.

Baldev went away to the factory and tried his best, but work was at a standstill. He whiled away his time and stayed there recreating two sculptures for me—Auguste Rodin's *Kiss* and *Thinker*—with Gurbachan a worker who was a moulder. Later, in similar circumstances in Bhagalpur, he would also sit at the loom and weave for me a saree, a beautiful striped grey and off-white saree in silk.

There was no income once again.

Baldev had only one solution: pack the family off to the in-laws, while he went all over the country trying to revive the business.

Once again, I had been rendered homeless. The only difference was that I was now at the mercy of my kind in-laws. I had a roof over my head and two square meals for my children.

In the Ramayana, Ram and Sita's vanwas was for fourteen years. I lived without Baldev for roughly ten years. Somehow, I survived. We had Suneet and Geetika, too.

We were in and out of that house in Aligarh for almost seven years till Pita-ji retired in 1965.

Sometimes I lived in Aligarh, sometimes in Delhi either at the Working Girls Hostel with Didi or my sister-in-law, Urmill. When my father-in-law retired, they moved home to Dehradun and sometimes I lived there as well.

Baldev's parents were burdened with me and three children, children who never went to school. Vineet wore torn shoes.

One night in Delhi, I had nowhere to go. I was out on the streets holding a suitcase, Geetika in my arms and Suneet by my side. Geetika was a few months old and Suneet around three.

This is another night that is etched in my mind for its sheer helplessness and hopelessness, just like the night we went hungry. I had absolutely nowhere to go. I had no money.

We were living with Didi in the Working Girls Hostel, but their rules did not allow guests to stay for over fifteen days.

All too soon we were asked to leave. Then we were smuggled back inside and made some other girl's guests.

It was a precarious life.

There wasn't much to do in Aligarh. I would cover my head and, accompanied by the chowkidar, cross over to the railway station and make a beeline for the AH Wheeler book stalls, which had poetry books. I would sit on the platform and read often. That was the only outing.

In between, in 1965, Baldev and I lived in Amritsar for a few months. The factory in Kanpur had shut down but he tried to revive the one in Amritsar. Then the Indo-Pak war started. Our factory was located next to the border, and it was bombed. It had no insurance against war.

Once again we were left without a source of income.

Back to Dehradun.

On one of my visits, I was chosen May Queen at the Doon Club May Queen Ball. I was twenty-four and a mother of three. Hilarious and tragic.

Our marriage was like many other marriages. Full of trials, full of joys and full of pride. God gave us so many opportunities, so many bounties.

Wonderful families. Wonderful children who have done us proud.

Though Baldev made many wrong decisions his goodness outweighed all the wrongs. I never met a more brilliant, kind, well-read, well-travelled man. Once on his way to Aligarh, after buying his ticket, he had only about one rupee left. He had to make a choice, either he could eat, or he could buy *Time* magazine. He bought the magazine.

Hazaar khuwab liye jee rahi hain sab aankhey
Tere bina hai magar meri be sabab aankhey

Chamakte chand sitaron gawah tum rehna
Lagi rahi hain falak se tamam shab aankhey

Bearing a thousand dreams, these eyes live on
But without you, mine are reasonless eyes

You bright moon and stars, be my witness
Gazing skywards all night have been these eyes

(top, left) My grandfather, Sardar Manmohan Singh; (top, right) My grandmother, Rameswaro Devi; (bottom, left) My mother, Satwant Kaur; (bottom, right) My father, Sardar Anoop Singh

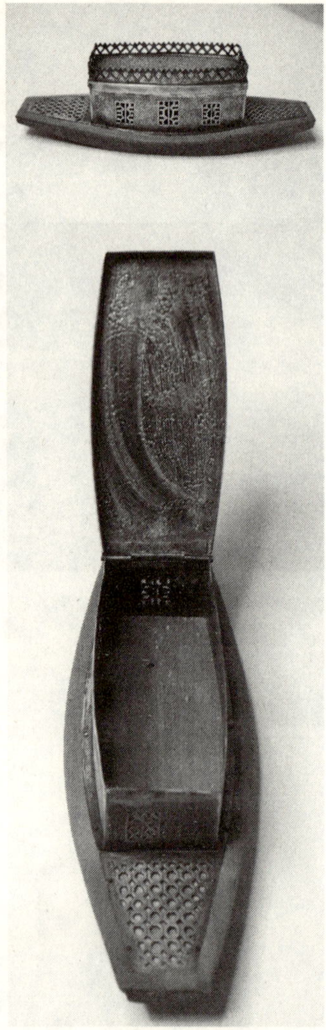

(top, left) A book on what to feed pigeons that Papa carried with him
(bottom, left) Papa's binoculars that saw it all; (right) The silver shikara that held my mother's trinkets

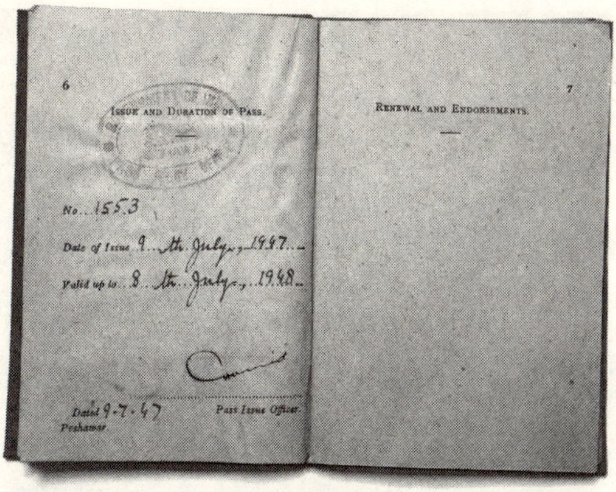

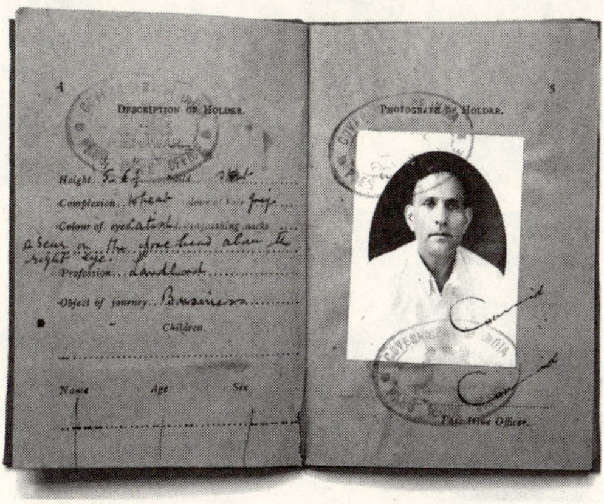

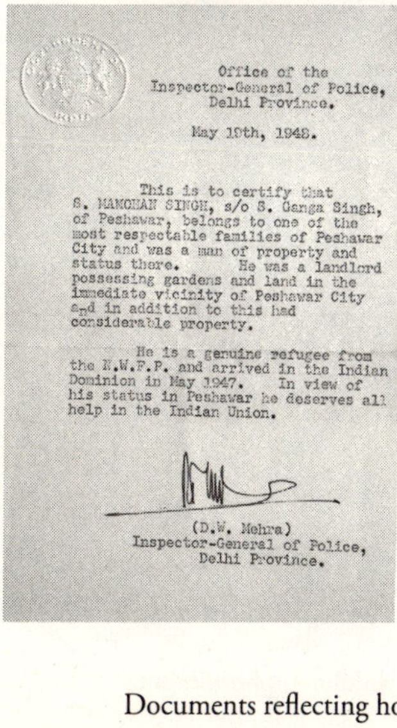
Office of the
Inspector-General of Police,
Delhi Province.

May 19th, 1948.

This is to certify that S. MANOHAN SINGH, s/o S. Ganga Singh, of Peshawar, belongs to one of the most respectable families of Peshawar City and was a man of property and status there. He was a landlord possessing gardens and land in the immediate vicinity of Peshawar City and in addition to this had considerable property.

He is a genuine refugee from the N.W.F.P. and arrived in the Indian Dominion in May 1947. In view of his status in Peshawar he deserves all help in the Indian Union.

(D.W. Mehra)
Inspector-General of Police,
Delhi Province.

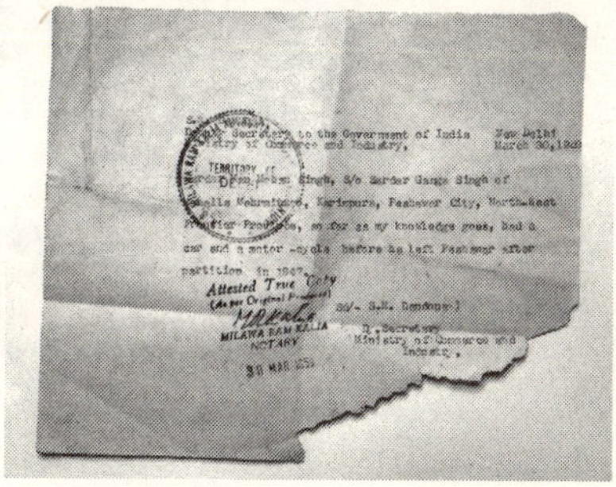
[illegible] Secretary to the Government of India New Delhi
[illegible] of Commerce and Industry, March 30,[illegible]

Sardar [illegible] Singh, S/o Sardar Ganga Singh of [illegible], [illegible], Peshawar City, North-West Frontier Province, so far as my knowledge goes, had a car and a motor-cycle before he left Peshawar after partition in 1947.

Attested True Copy
Sd/- [illegible]
MILAWA RAM KALIA
NOTARY
D. Secretary
Ministry of Commerce and Industry.

Documents reflecting how the Partition impacted our lives

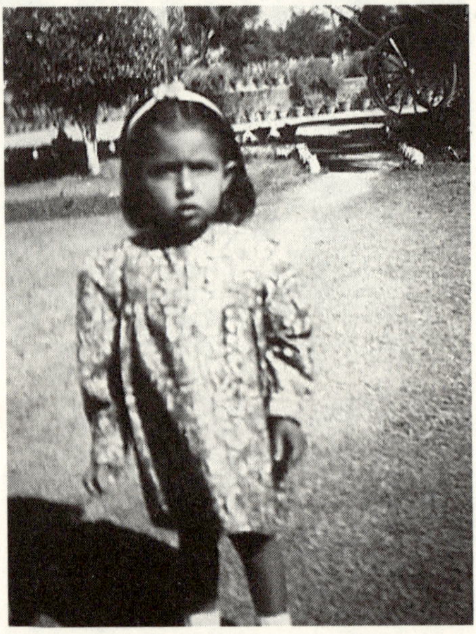

(top, left) Didi and I with Qadra; (top, right) A childhood photo of me; (bottom) Roopy

(top) Hiroo Johar (née Advani) and I, dressed here for the staging of *The Pied Piper* at school; (bottom) A group photo from my school days

(top, left) Baldev and I on our wedding day; (top, right) Didi as a bride; (bottom) A photograph from Roopy's wedding

Regd. No. L-95

Vol. I. No. 42 DEHRA DUN, May 22, 1965, PRICE 15 PAISE

WITNESS

the newsweekly with a difference

Editor : RAJ KANWAR

Sumptuous Fete At Welham

The students and the staff of the Welham Girls School last week organised a sumptuous fete to raise funds for the school building.

Hundreds of citizens and students thronged the Welham lawns to seek amusement and joviality. There was fun and merriment for every taste and pocket, although most visitors came back with nearly empty pockets. There were, however, a few lucky ones too who won attractive prizes in the raffle draw, the luckiest being the young Miss Dhand whose little dog won the prized gift of RAJDHOOT motor cycle donated by Mr. Nanda of Escorts Ltd.

A notable feature of this year's fete was the introduction of "Horror House" and "Gypsy Girls." Dressed like typical gypsies, these girls successfully delineated the role of fortune-tellers. Among their main customers were the gentlemen cadets from the Indian Military Academy. The Horror House could not match the "horror" of Dracula, but it did succeed in earning a fat amount for the

Rename Circuit House AS NEHRU HOUSE

BY RAJ KANWAR

Nehru's first death anniversary falls on May 27; he had a special regard for Dehra Dun and its people. Whenever he felt tired and fatigued, he invariably came to this beautiful valley for rest and relaxation. A few days' stay in the Doon Circuit House always did him a world of good; it gave him a new strength and freshness which in turn enabled him to give his best to the complex problems that awaited him in New Delhi.

"BEAUTY QUEEN"

INDRA VARMA BECOMES 'MAY QUEEN'

BY WITNESS STAFF REPORTER

A pleasant surprise was in store for the tall and graceful Indra Varma and her husband,

(top) Didi ready to leave for Delhi to take up a job at Cottage Emporium; (bottom) A clipping from *Witness* carrying the announcement of my being declared 'May Queen'

(top) Baldev and I, in Kanpur; (bottom) Mata-ji, my mother-in-law, with Vineet and Suneet

(top, left) Mata-ji and Pita-ji, my parents-in-law; (top, right) Baldev with his brother Bunty; (middle) Our immediate family in Aligarh, 1962; (bottom) The larger Varma family

(top) Kumsi and I; (middle) Kumsi and his wife Arvind with Baldev and me; (bottom) Papsy, Kumsi and Kitty

BEAUTIES WITH BRAINS

Vol XI No. 5 December 1964

This charming sextet of girls will soon be serving BOAC passengers with traditional courtesy on flights between London and the Orient. For this is no beauty contest line up. These girls are highly qualified and have just successfully completed an intensive six weeks training course in which they had to pass stiff examinations on all the varied duties of an air stewardess at the BOAC Cabin Services Training School at London Airport.

Pictured from left to right are: Miss Harinder Bhela and Miss Roopy Singh of New Delhi, Miss S. Mirchandani of Nagpur, Chief BOAC Instructor at the Training School, Mr. John Lawrence, Miss Dilnaar Talati, of Calcutta, Miss B. Ali of Karachi and Miss Veena Multani of Bombay.

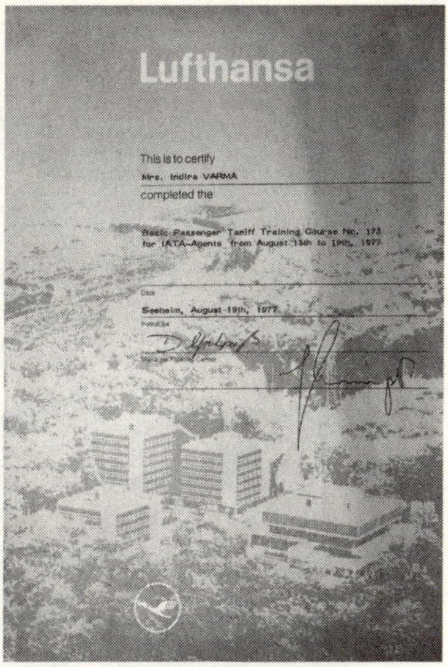

Lufthansa

This is to certify

Mrs. Indira VARMA

completed the

Basic Passenger Tariff Training Course No. 173 for IATA-Agents from August 15th to 19th, 1977

Date

Seeheim, August 19th, 1977

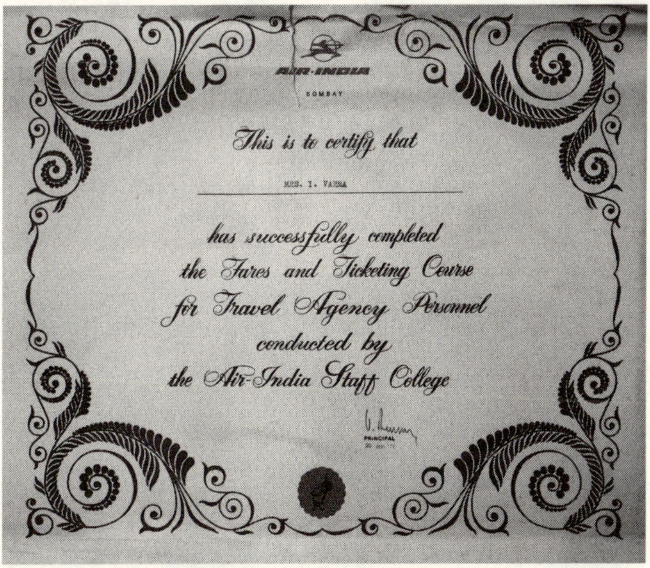

AIR-INDIA

BOMBAY

This is to certify that

MRS. I. VARMA

has successfully completed the Fares and Ticketing Course for Travel Agency Personnel conducted by the Air-India Staff College

PRINCIPAL

(top, left) Roopy recognised as a 'Beauty with Brains' during her stint at BOAC; (top, right) The certificate of completion issued to me for the basic training course for travel agents at Seeheim; (bottom) The certificate of completion issued to me for the Fares and Ticketing Course conducted by Air India Staff College

(top, left): As platform officer at Citibank; (top, right) Kasturi Lal-ji giving us Union gyaan at Citibank; (middle) The empty desk where I sat and opened accounts; (bottom) A group photo taken at a Citibank staff meeting

Vineet's wedding: (top) Brijesh singing with Asha;
(bottom) Sushil Bhai regaling everyone

(top) Two brothers and their father: my grandfather Manmohan Singh, his brother Sardar Kripal Singh and their father Sardar Ganga Singh; (bottom) My great grandather's house and courtyard in Peshawar

15

The Family Grows

BOTH SUNEET AND GEETIKA WERE BORN IN ALIGARH.

Suneet was born on 1 May 1962 and Geetika on my birthday, 10 October 1964.

I named Suneet after my dearest sister-in-law Sunita who was with me at the time of his birth in the Aligarh house with a midwife.

I walked through my labour pains in the vast garden outside. As the night drew to a close, I finally came inside. Suddenly, there was a storm. Lightning. Thunder. All the lights went off. The chowkidar brought the hurricane lamp.

Suneet was ready to come into the world. He did not need any artificial light. He was bringing his own light from God; and he has been shining ever since. He is one of the most religious young men I have ever known. A giver. He loves in abundance and invests in relationships. Many a times he keeps the Chalisa that means going to the Gurudwara daily for forty days; he regularly goes to Darbar Sahib every month. So much so that he became famous in America and the UK—all our friends know that if they want to visit the Darbar Sahib in Amritsar, they should get in touch with Suneet.

Suneet was a thinner baby than Vineet, with large eyes and black hair. He had sharp features like my father's and a cleft on his chin like Baldev.

He was a rebel from the beginning. Full of self-confidence. One of Baldev's aunts, Gwalior-wali Mami-ji, used to call him savy mirch (green chilli) and agg di naarh (a live wire). She would say in Punjabi, '*Indu, tu ai jins kithon paida keeta hai?* (Indu, what is this creature you have given birth to?)'

She was a fine lady. Suneet loved her and can still mimic the way she would speak till she ran out of breath.

If Suneet broke something he would shout to ask who kept it there! He was angrier than us.

He was an inquisitive child. While Vineet was happy playing with our dog Brownie or playing cricket with the domestic staff and their children, Suneet would stare into space or look at plants. He wanted to know about the inner workings of things. Once he put his hand into a boiling pot of water and burnt himself. We rushed him to the hospital.

He gave us major scares too—he contracted diphtheria, a life-threatening disease. My mother and I spent a week in the hospital in a Benzene tent with him. It was a miracle he was cured when the medical facilities were limited in Kanpur.

Whenever Suneet got his hands around a pencil, he started drawing and sketching. At six years old, as a child artist, he won the Save Venice award. He sketched film stars, artists and sportspersons on whatever kind of paper he could lay his hands on—sometimes this included the corrugated cardboard from biscuit tins. He still has sketches he made of Dimple Kapadia and Rekha.

Later, he would paint, sketch and design dresses for Geetika, apply Swarovski crystals on her cardigans, patch and embroider her clothes. The indication of his future interest was obvious. He also painted Vineet and Tinu as a marriage present, and Baldev and me, on our anniversary.

Geetika was the most beautiful baby I had ever seen. Baldev and I were looking forward to a girl. She arrived three weeks early. She was expected at the end of October but came on 10 October, unexpectedly. It was my birthday. I consider her to be the best birthday gift of my lifetime. There is a special bond between us, all mothers and daughters have it, and over the years I have come to find a lot of me in Geetika.

As a birthday treat, my parents-in-law had taken me to watch the morning show of the film *Anmol Ghadi* starring Noor Jehan and Dilip Kumar. It was running in the theatre Tasveer Mahal. I was once again with them in Aligarh.

There was Mata-ji, me in the centre and then Pita-ji on my other side. They bent over to talk to each other over my swollen tummy, recalling memories of Lahore in 1946 when they had first seen this film. Pita-ji used to call my mother-in-law Kunto, short for Shakuntala. '*Kunto, tenu ae yaad hai?*' he leaned across and asked a dozen times.

I found it so endearing, but I had also started to feel uncomfortable. I thought my labour pains had started. Though I knew it was early. But yes, I had to go home.

I whispered to Mata-ji, and she told Pita-ji that we must go home immediately. By the time we reached home I was running a high temperature too.

The doctor was called. Geetika had a cord around her neck, otherwise just the midwife would have been fine.

For the life of me I cannot remember the time she was born. It was recorded in a baby book but with the many houses we changed and our effects lying in godowns, it was misplaced.

It must have been afternoon, because Pita-ji had called my mother and Didi in Delhi to tell them that I had had a baby girl. They came immediately from Delhi and I could hear Didi screaming right from the gate, '*Aaj kis kis ka birthday hai. Ye kis kis ka birthday hai?*'

Baldev was somewhere still trying to re-establish the business. He was told that he had a new baby girl. He sent a telegram to Roopy in London at Dormy House. 'Girl born to Indira, mother and child fine. Father recovering. 10th October 1964.'

I was unwell for a month. The fever turned to typhoid, and I took twenty-one days to recover.

In any case, after the delivery Mata-ji tied a headscarf over my head and I was given special food to eat.

Mata-ji slept near my door and Mummy looked after Geetika.

Geetika was a demure and shy child. She had beautiful dark brown hair with a fringe and side curls. Roopy got her the prettiest bedding, a pram set, and frocks like I had never seen before. Tomato-coloured tricel, yellow knitted dresses, pretty doll-like shoes and socks from Marks and Spencer and everywhere else too.

We were in Amritsar when she was about one. She would sit on the wooden banni, a kind of a threshold, between two rooms, for long periods of times. I would give her cherries and other fruit in a glass. She would quietly sit and eat.

Once, we were in Delhi and Geetika must have been around five. It was Rakhi Day. It is our custom to feed the brothers khichdi and dahi. I sat Geetika on the table to run errands. When the time came for tying the Rakhi to Vineet and Suneet, we realised that Geetika had finished the khichdi and was sitting there as quietly as before.

She was a gentle child and the most pampered in the family. Vineet and Suneet were always very gregarious, obstinate and stubborn. I started to work when she was just five and was out of the house from morning to evening. My mother-in-law and mother were her caretakers. She followed her brothers around, especially Suneet, since Vineet had hit that phase in life where he preferred the company of his friends over his family, and often fought with his father and left home to be with them. But they were protective of her and very close.

For Suneet

Peheli May jab aati hai
Zindagi ke aangan mein
Khushiyon ki fizao'n se
Shukr ke hasee'n misrey … sajda rez hotey hain
Khush naseeb Betey ki … khush naseeb Maa hoon mein
Jisney farz se apney

Maamta ke rutbe ko
Aasma'n banaya hai
Taro'n ki numaish se
Motiyo'n ko chun chun ke
Qadmo'n mein bichaya hai

Seedhi raah par chalna
Papa ney sikhaya hai
Paak saaf dil mein ek
Narm narm gosha hai
Char chand rishto'n mein … har traraf lagaya hai

Uski nek naami ka
Sarey jag mein charcha hai
Fakr se merey lab par
Bas ye jumla aata hai
Ye to mera beta hai … Ye to mera beta hai

Apney Daata ke dar se
Ab talab nahi koee
Jis nay merey Bachhey mein
Qaynaat bakhshi hai
Merey ye sabhi jumley … Hain usi ka shukrana

16

Roopy Joins British Overseas Airways Corporation

Better on a Camel, that's what we called BOAC.

It was catchier than British Overseas Airways Corporation and often more accurate. Flights to India no longer took the four and a half months the first flight from London had taken in 1924, nor the seven days with twenty stops and four different means of transport that the first commercial flight had taken in 1929.

But travel took a lot of time, there were many stops, and sometimes you didn't land at the airports you were supposed to.

Our lives became intimately entwined with BOAC on 7 September 1964.

That was the date Roopy joined BOAC as stewardess.

That was the day our family crossed the line of poverty, silently and unknowingly.

It was as if the stars decided to uplift the three of us to a respectable human level. Magic had entered our lives.

Didi was already working at Cottage Emporium, I was between Kanpur and Aligarh, married with two sons, the third, a girl, awaited any day. Both of us had left home in 1959.

Roopy had just graduated from Kanpur Vidya Mandir Vidyalaya and turned twenty. She was very good-looking and slim. Gone were the days when she would stick cabbage up her nose!

We had reached a stage where we did not have to worry about our finances, though Papa had passed away in 1961. Didi would send money home, the house was ours and Mr Mitra paid us rent as well. The situation couldn't be called good, but it was manageable.

Roopy moved to Delhi after her graduation where she had been offered a temporary job at Cottage Emporium. She also moved into the Working Girls Hostel with Didi. There she would live for almost a year; Didi and Roopy became like friends and colleagues. Roopy started to call her Uma. I have never dared to call her by her name. It was always Didi and will stay so forever.

At Cottage Emporium she was spotted by the ad agency J. Walter Thompson and offered some very well-paid modelling assignments. I had done the odd modelling assignment too—campaigns for hair oil and for sarees at Cottage Emporium—so Roopy did not hesitate in accepting the assignments. We had learnt that when the black-and-white images were printed you could barely make out who the model was. Roopy's assignments helped her send money home to Mummy.

One ad agency told her to apply for a stewardess job in BOAC as they were looking for Punjabi-speaking girls. These were the days of mass movements of immigrants from Punjab to the UK for farm hands and other menial jobs.

The requirements for air hostesses would make feminists furious. Air hostesses were the supermodels of the day. You had to be good looking, single, between twenty and thirty years old, weigh between 47 kg and 63 kg in proportion to height, which had to be between 5'2" and 5'9", and have a good smile, no gums, all teeth. Plus, you could only fly for ten years, after which you were too old for the job, or if you married before that time, you had to retire.

Roopy applied but was underweight and was asked to put on five pounds. She came to me in Kanpur, and Baldev and I fed her beer, hot chocolate and parathas and her weight went up and up and up.

Roopy passed her test and it was soon time for her to leave for

London for her training. Fly and that too to London? To a country that had ruled over ours and had eventually left, partitioning our country and making our family homeless? My mother couldn't believe it. Never, she said. But when we told her the salary she was appeased. Seven thousand rupees a month with extra flying allowances. It was unheard of in those days.

The other girls who had been selected with Roopy also came to meet Mummy and she found them to be girls from good families, polite, good-looking, Punjabi-speaking, rajma-chawal-loving girls.

Roopy left on 7 September 1964.

And so a new era of our lives began.

Roopy posted picture cards from Britain every day, she stayed at Dormy House, Sunningdale, where the air crew was trained.

Training included how to mix cocktails, serve a five-course meal with wine, how to apply makeup, provide emergency medical aid, and be a good conversationalist. These were the days when flying reflected the luxury it was. Legroom was not an imaginary concept—seats stretched out. Food was served with silver-plated cutlery. And smoking was the norm.

Their instructor was a legend. Peggy Thorne had served on the first transatlantic flight. Roopy spoke about her so much that she soon became a part of our everyday conversation, almost a member of the family. How strict she was, how smart she was, how good she was, I could write paeans.

BOAC's centre of operations in India was Calcutta, and after returning from her training in London, Roopy moved into an apartment with her colleagues in 1965.

In the years to come she moved up the ladder from a stewardess to Route Steward, which meant that she made the rosters for the other air hostesses, assigning who would fly to Europe, the Middle East or the Far East.

Roopy's uniform was a silk saree in peacock and blue that would change every year, leggings, not very high heels, and she had to have her hair in a bun. You could also opt for skirts but since it was the India sector Roopy flew, she opted for sarees.

Then she was chosen Miss British Airways and was covered in the British Airways magazine. This was not a beauty contest but had it been one, she would have won hands down. She was awarded the title for being the most excellent worker and a role model.

Bahar aai to yaad aaye wo terey merey payam sarey,
Mahekte kagaz pay motio say likhey hue they jo naam sarey.

With the coming of spring I remembered those messages, yours and mine
And all those names written, like pearls, on fragrant paper

17

Roopy's Adventures in the Air

ONCE ROOPY STARTED FLYING WE SAW VERY LITTLE OF HER. SHE would fly for twenty-one days a month. If I wanted to meet her, I had to time my visit to Delhi to when her schedule would allow her a layover of a few hours or when she had an overnight stay.

If in case she could get a night in Delhi she would try and see Didi, Mummy and me, if I could make it from Aligarh.

Mummy had initially stayed on in the Kanpur house in Friends Colony. But very soon she rented the house out and moved to Delhi. She lived in the Constitution Club for a few months in a room allocated to Prithvi Uncle as a Rajya Sabha member and then shifted to the Working Girls Hostel at Curzon Road with Didi.

It was easy for me to come down from Aligarh to Delhi and I would do so quite often. A doodh-wali express, as Pita-ji liked to call it, started from Aligarh every morning and it took less than two hours to reach Delhi. It had a dining car, so most people bought a ticket, drank some coffee or tea and reached Delhi. It returned every evening around 7 p.m. and reached Aligarh by dinner time.

Roopy's base station was Calcutta, but she landed in Delhi at least once or twice a month as per her roster.

Every visit she came like Father Christmas, loaded with gifts for the children, Didi, Mummy and me.

I still have the bedding Roopy sent for Geetika: yellow, self-embroidered cotton, it was beautiful!

From that day till Roopy was married and settled in London, the presents never stopped coming.

She would send suitcases full of chocolates and fruit from Beirut, chocolates and shoes from London, clothes from Hong Kong, and cardigans and transistors from America.

My children never wore Indian-made goods because Roopy brought everything. Geetika wore the prettiest frocks of tricel, and knitted dresses from Marks and Spencer. Roopy even brought beautiful cardigans for both the boys. Turtlenecked pullovers, shorts and high stockings. Fancy socks, toys and painting material. Lip-smacking English biscuits. There was never an end. Scotch for my husband. Perfumes and powders for me. Sarees from Hong Kong.

Roopy sent me hundred-rupee notes in envelopes wherever I was because I never had any money.

Baldev was forever rebuilding his business and I always lived on the charity of my kind and understanding in-laws.

Those were the days of hysterical laughing fits with Roopy regaling us with hilarious immigrant experiences.

She recounted for us an incident where one passenger rang the bell for the stewardess multiple times. Roopy was serving another passenger and it took her some time to reach him. 'I've been fingering you for such a long time,' he shouted. Roopy gulped. It had taken all her training to keep a straight face.

'Sorry, Sir, I did not feel it,' she had replied, hoping it would pass over his head.

Another time, the bell had rung at 4 a.m. The plane was dark, quiet and everybody was sleeping. But as she neared the seat where the call light was glowing, she could hear something. A Sardar-ji was cross-legged on the seat, reading his Gutka Sahib aloud with great piety. His neighbours complained to Roopy, saying a few impious things about being woken up in the middle of the night.

Another family wanted ghee with every meal, and even wandered up the galley to check whether it was being hidden from them.

One person tried to have a bath in the washroom; Roopy saw

him enter with an armful of clothes and soap and had to rush to check. She politely asked him whether he needed anything and when he said that he would manage without a bucket, she had to tell him that he could not bathe.

Another passenger had to be convinced that the windows could not open and that he could not spit out of them—or in the aircraft.

Many of the families came prepared for the journey with large cans of ghee, gurh, sattu and even bedding.

There were sombre occasions too. Once, due to cross-border firing, Roopy's aircraft had to land in Lahore. The whole crew was allowed to disembark and make their way to the airline hotel. But Roopy had an Indian passport, and was not allowed. The captain intervened, but to no avail. Then Roopy suggested that her friend, a Pakistani crewmember, be called.

Her friend came with her mother. They put the Quran on her head and told the police and guards outside that Roopy was under their protection till she could fly back and took Roopy home with them.

The universe is full of good and friendly people.

There were numerous occasions of turbulence and nervous passengers, and Roopy led her brigade to calm them and be patient caregivers. She always told amazing, heartfelt stories, frightening and enlightening. All of us worried for Roopy and we would pray to Guru Nanak-ji to keep her safe.

There were many affairs of the heart on board the flights as well. Many of the girls married the captains. And we wondered whether that would happen to Roopy too.

One had seen enough romantic movies on celluloid to know that men and women have entirely different meanings of love and romance.

Women more commonly feel romance in words. They like to hear they are loved, cherished, valued but most definitely also respected if desired.

Roopy's way was entirely different. She had matured in all the hard times we had seen. She knew that any decision of hers would affect her sisters and mother for whom she was a big a pillar of support.

Over the years she had many admirers who wooed her, but she waited and eventually married Brijesh Mathur, a Doon School, St. Stephen's educated, good-looking young man.

He was known as the Lata Mangeshkar of Doon School because he sang so well.

They met in Calcutta, where he trained and later worked at Grindlays Bank, and then he followed her around the world, wherever she flew, till she agreed to marry him.

He would fly to Delhi if she had time off in Delhi, and since her base was Calcutta he would go to Calcutta and meet her. When she finished her twenty-one days of flying, she would have a week off and Brijesh would make a trip to spend time with her till they decided to get married. He wooed her ardently.

Roopy kay Naam Ek Nazm

Phir hawai'n mujhey sarhad say jaganey aaiyee'n
Ahed-e-mazi ke shabista'n mein bulane aai'n
Yaad aata hai mujhey ek ajab sa lamha
Jab merey kaan mein ek pyari khanak goonji thi
Jab kay mai khud bhi khanak say nahi waqif thi zara
Par merey ghar mein khushi khoob hui thi uss pal
Muskurati huee wo pyari hawa urh urh kar
Peeng lay lay kay badi hoti gayee himmat say
Uss nein murjhai huey phoolo'n ko kiya tha taza
Uss ko khud apni baharo'n ka nahi andaza
Wo hawa saans bani, rooh bani, jaan bani
Wo hawa aas bani, raaz bani, naaz bani
Us hawa nein kayee ehsan kiye logo'n par
Uss hawa nein kayee gham bhi sahey jeevan mein
Uss kay armaan ka jab khoon hua gulshan mein
Shaakh dar shaakh say dekha na gaya uss ka gham

Uss nay phir phool khilaya hai taro taaza sa
Uss hawa kay sabhi ehsaas ko hai mera salaam
Uss ka wo phool baney janey chaman, jaaney bahar
Uss ki khushboo say mehakta rahey uska dayaar
Wo hawa kaon hai kis rang mein chalti hai sada
Us hawa ka koi naam agar poochey to
Mai kahoongi ki wo meri bahen Roopy hai … Happy Birthday …

18

Cottage Emporium: The House of Romance

NOTHING EVER CHANGED AT CENTRAL COTTAGE INDUSTRIES Emporium, or Cottage as it was commonly known, no matter the hour, day, week or month. It looked like the set of a retro TV soap with many aunties, young behenjis and a few babus.

These were all counter staff and sales staff.

I am not referring to the sophisticated management and the buyers' team, the all-important names, who were friends of Indira Gandhi—Teji Bachchan, Teji Vir Singh, museologist Ratna Fabri, co-founder Sina Kaul, cultural czarina Pupul Jayakar, Lakshmi Chand Jain, K.B. Johar and the likes.

Cottage Emporium was on Janpath, originally called the Queensway. The now familiar wooden khokas or kiosks that define Janpath were also a means to rehabilitate the uprooted refugees from the then undivided India.

It should have been the happiest time for the country. India was free from British rule in the August of 1947. It, however, turned out to be a disaster. The country was divided into India and Pakistan on the basis of religion, followed by the world's largest migration. There was displacement, bloodshed, misery and absolute desolation. Artisans and artists also suffered due to loss of patronage from nawabs and rajas who took pride in supporting them and their families. Refugees, who were in the camps, temporary shelters of tents over their heads, took a long time to settle. Volunteers, society ladies and politicians came out to help them with cash, kind and service.

My sister Rajesh Nandini, who was teaching history in the Islamia College in Lahore, was asked to go back to Delhi. She decided not to follow a career in academia and worked for refugees instead. She started work in the Kingsway Camp. It was one of the many camps that had sprung up all over the city. A special ministry was created for rehabilitation.

Rajesh was given a group of student volunteers to assist her. These were the students who could not write their final year examinations for a graduate degree. They would be given a bachelor's degree if they served in the camps for six months. Kamaladevi Chattopadhyay joined them and so did and L.C. Jain, who gave up his studies to help those who had suffered.

The student volunteers were sent out in search of women who could embroider and those who could stitch clothes with the help of sewing machines. The idea was to give them work that would help them overcome their devastation both economically and emotionally. Truckloads of fabric was sent by Sardar Patel from the mills in Ahmedabad. The millowners were keen to donate this fabric. The sewing machines were provided by Sucheta Kripalani, from the All India Congress Committee. The student volunteers sorted out the fabric suitable for garments. Every day, Rajesh would cut about fifty garments, mostly salwars and kurtas, that were to be issued to the women who would stitch them. Each woman got 4 annas per garment. Whatever was stitched in one day would be sold the next day for 8 annas a piece. That gave the camp authorities enough profit to pay for next day's wages to the women. The women were able to buy suits for themselves and their families.

The casement fabric, suitable for embroidery, was given out to the women who could embroider. Mrs Vir Singh saw to it that the sizes were correct and that those with machines had stitched them correctly. Soon a formidable stock of embroidered linen was collected, which the refugees could not use. They had no homes. Mr Kaul of Pandit Brothers, who had a carpet and linen shop in Connaught Place, very kindly offered the women a counter space to sell the linen. So four ladies, Mrs Kitty Shiva Rao, Mrs B.K. Nehru, Mrs Prem Bery and Mrs Vir Singh, helped by many more, set up shop and invited people who were interested to buy the linen. Bedspreads, tablecloths, cushion covers, mats and serviettes. Lo and behold, the embroidery sold out in no time. Orders were booked for more and the women started getting regular work. By this time, Mr Kaul had become wary of women of such calibre sitting around on his carpets.

A shop was allotted to the Indian Cooperative Union on Barakhamba Radial Road and arrangements were made to shift the merchandise to this shop and also sell other items that were made by refugees. A whole lot of baskets came in from Faridabad. The shop was aptly named Refugee Handicrafts. By then most of the women had shifted to their own homes. A large number of cooperatives were made according to the areas where these women had shifted to, and regular business began from this shop. More women were employed: Mrs Hoon Padma Ahluwalia, Iqbal, Krishna Kapur and Motia Kaul are some of the names I remember. Swaran brought the baskets from Faridabad. Mrs Vir Singh was the manager of the shop.

The Department of Industries thus set up a shop in 1948 to sell handicrafts of artisans who had lost their patronage. It was called the Central Cottage Industries Emporium and was located in the Queensway (now Janpath) barracks. Pandit Jawahar Lal Nehru, the then prime minister, asked Kamaladevi Chattopadhyay to take over the shop, which was running at a loss. Refugee Handicrafts was doing so well that the Indian Cooperative Union decided to merge the two and move to Queensway.

Mrs Vir Singh, Krishna Kapur, Iqbal, Padma Ahluwalia, Motia Kaul and Mrs Hoon, not to forget Shakuntala, along with the staff from Faridabad, moved over to Cottage Emporium and started taking over the stocks from the government.

That was the flagship.

That was when I joined Cottage as a sales assistant, on 26 October 1952. I was associated with camp work because I was working in the Kingsway Camp after attending my MA classes in the University of Delhi.

Gulshan Nanda was awarded the Padma Shri in 2011 for promotion of handicrafts, a category created for the first time that year.

Being in Cottage Emporium felt like being in a time machine.

You entered and wished everyone. Some were knitting, some having tea, some just talking, and one lady used to sit cross-legged on her chair reading the Gutka Sahib.

Customers came and went, some bought handicrafts. Often dignitaries were escorted and you immediately recognised them from the eerie silence that would fall on the shop.

This was after all the flagship store of the country.

When you moved further in the same uninterested atmosphere greeted you. Only the product landscape changed, from sarees to shawls, jewellery, brass gifts and pottery from all over India.

You climbed a few dingy steps into a sort of alcove which was the display section. One lady would be sleeping at her desk, one haggling with the fruit-wallah over the expensive custard apples and tea would always be at hand. Regular intervals brought aalu tikkis and chaat from Janpath and delicious coffee from Depaul's.

If you were really hungry there was dal and roti from Kake Da Hotel or Chicken Curry from National.

Outside in the covered courtyard of the Cottage Emporium premises was the heavenly Bankura. It was an eatery managed by a Parsi lady called Mrs Kharas, who served the most delicious fare for one rupee or less. Rice and meat or meatballs, sandwiches, coffee, milkshakes … my mouth still waters.

Eating was the national past time. Knitting was the signature hobby. Heaters blasting in the winters, coolers in the summer.

My sister Uma sat here, looking like a model in her immaculately draped saris, cotton in summer and silk in winter.

This was the same staff that jumped to attention when the call of duty came. The very staff who created beautiful displays under the leadership of the famous Ratna Fabri and Sina Kaul.

The former managing director of Central Cottage Industries Emporium, K.B. Johar, recalls that after the demise of Ratna Fabri, Sina Kaul was asked to take over the responsibility of the display section in addition to her job of publicity and advertising where she worked with Som Benegal. Sina undertook the interior work of all the branches of Cottage Emporium at Kolkata, Mumbai, Bengaluru and Chennai.

Didi was hailed many-a-time by Sina Kaul for her displays and was asked to go around the country and set up displays for the other Cottage Industry centres.

If you moved to the right of Cottage Emporium, you would come across the most beautiful Kashmiri carpets, pile upon pile of richly hued, handwoven rectangles and many a time someone in deep slumber hidden behind a pile.

This is where my brother-in-law to be, Sushil Bhai sat, behind a Kashmiri wooden partition. A magician with words, who sang like Rafi, he held a daily durbar. The tabla was played on the table, there were mounds of cigarette butts and half-drunk cups of tea, paan was a constant; with him sat Sheetal and Ashok.

Sushil Bhai was an expert at everything he did—he sang, he was the union leader and he was exceptional at wrapping gifts. He had also been scouted for a few modelling assignments owing to his good looks.

Whenever the president of India or the prime minister had to go to other countries on State visits, Sushil Bhai would be called with his team to wrap all the gifts at their homes or offices.

Once a year, there was stock taking at Cottage for three days. It was closed to the public as the staff laboured away, hard at work with the auditors, making a note of every single article in the store.

At lunchtime working hard turned to playing hard. The staff would be split into two camps. I never quite figured out whether it was floorwise or counterwise … that was known only to the people who worked there. What ensued were three days of fierce competition or baint baazi of ghazal, poetry and song. It was a bit like antakshari, except that you used the last word rather than the last alphabet to begin the next recitation. There were also qawwali, mushaira, singing, acting and joke sessions. Sushil Bhai and Didi would recount what took place with such flair that it would almost feel like we had been there.

Cottage Emporium was a place where you also caught stars coming down to earth—Dilip Kumar, Nargis, Raj Kapoor, all with officers hovering around them.

Jacqueline Kennedy visited too, and both Didi and Roopy were on duty that day. She wasn't the most famous visitor either, Queen Elizabeth II and Queen Farah of Iran had also shopped there.

One of Didi's many roles was to man the ticket counter. The tickets for concerts, musicals and theatre were also sold at Cottage Emporium.

Didi was a very important person those days, since she was in charge of the seating chart. ADCs of senior officers would come for tickets, dignitaries would drop by and the phone would never stop ringing. Didi had learnt the art of having lunch in five minutes flat.

Unfortunately, there was one hurdle Didi could not surmount—she did not remember people and their names. Maybe it was due to the fact that she met hundreds of customers daily.

One day, a familiar face walked into Cottage Emporium and went over to Didi's counter for tickets. She couldn't remember his name, but she thought that it was one of my many devars. She chatted away with him, offering him coffee and her tiffin. She had just asked him about his parents, when one of the senior officers passed by.

Didi said she had never seen anybody move that quickly or announce a name so loudly. 'General Thimmaya! Sir! Have you got your tickets? Your seating?'

Didi felt that her breath had stopped—she had offered samosas to the war hero and Army Chief of Staff. Her face burning from the blunder, she quickly handed over his tickets.

Such things happened very often with Didi.

Cottage was one large family, and one large family meant affairs and heartbreaks, jealousies and camaraderie. If someone got married, the friends at Cottage were enough to form a baraat, nobody else was required.

In any case it was the perfect matchmaking site. Nobody could escape the romance. Whoever got a job there would only emerge after getting married. There were legendary romances, both among the management and staff, and numerous couples that began there tied the knot.

My Uma Didi and Sushil Bhai were one such example.

When Didi came to Delhi she was getting over a short relationship with a doctor in Lucknow. She was a romantic and had already had a few love affairs in Nainital and then in Kanpur.

Sweet dillagis or attachments you could call them.

Sushil Bhai was already working at Cottage. He was in the Carpets and Kashmiri Goods section.

He looked like a film hero, extremely good-looking with a mop of curly black hair. He was dashing and there was a swag about him. He had done many modelling assignments, and spoke impeccable English, Urdu and Punjabi.

Girls in Cottage swooned over him, especially when he sang. No one could ever get enough of him.

Like Didi, Sushil Bhai too had moved to Delhi to work at Cottage. Before this, he had lived in Ludhiana. His father was in the Railways till he got sick. They were so well-off at one time that he was taken to Doon School. He passed his exam and was ready to join when circumstances suddenly changed. Later he would study in the same college as my husband Baldev.

Baldev was two or three years his senior at Government College, Ludhiana. Sushil Bhai's Mama-ji was Chief Justice, a person of great reputation who had retired in Chandigarh. A few years after Sushil

Bhai started working at Cottage Emporium his mother and three younger sisters also moved to Delhi.

It was very obvious that Didi and Sushil Bhai were romantically inclined; they had eyes only for each other.

By 1964, after Geetika was born, I would travel to Delhi often. I stayed with Didi at the Working Girls Hostel. Sushil Bhai was a permanent fixture. He used to come and visit the hostel every evening and at times he would even eat with us in the visitors' room. When Mummy shifted there, they would all have dinner together.

I liked him from the get go.

Baldev liked him too—they had so much in common: the same language, the same college and Punjab.

Sushil Bhai was my closest friend because of our passion for Urdu poetry.

Whenever I wrote something I would read it out first to him and he would give me his opinion. In fact, both my brothers-in-law, Sushil Bhai and Brijesh, were my poetry and music buddies first and then brothers-in-law.

Over time, Cottage became central to my life. When I moved to Delhi, I was almost always a walking distance away. I could hop over to Cottage to have lunch with Didi or meet her for coffee.

Sadly, the old Cottage moved to a multistoried building at Jawahar Vyapar Bhavan elsewhere on Janpath. Now my only touchstone are three parking attendants whom Sushil Bhai hired when he was the union leader and fought with the management to make permanent staff. It was a struggle to convince the management, as the three attendants were deaf and mute.

I still meet them under the Indian Oil Bhavan where I go every year to buy chappals. They always find a place for my car, check on my children, their hands rising higher as they ask about all three.

I provide them with cardigans and blankets in winters and send them money. It's like meeting a part of your past, my connect to Didi and Sushil Bhai and to the many years of happiness spent on that piece of land.

The landscape may have changed, but the memories are vivid and fresh in my mind, like Peshawar, Nainital or Kanpur.

Tamam fikr zamaney ki taal deta hai
Ye kaisa kaif tumhara khayaal deta hai

Hamarey band kiwaron pe dastakein de kar
Shab-e-firaaq mein wahm-e-wisaal deta hai

All cares and concerns of the world are turned away
What is this headiness your very thought brings

Knocking on our closed doors, it brings
The illusion of meeting to our night of separation

19

A Brave New World

ARMED WITH JUST A SMILE, PRAYERS, DETERMINATION AND MY youth I travelled from Dehradun to interview for a job so that I could look after my three children.

My husband never stopped trying to put together his business. This time he was in Tanda, near Sitapur in Uttar Pradesh. It was predominantly a town of Muslim weavers. It was a great exporter of lungis. Baldev worked in liaison with the Weavers Cooperative Society and put up a textile finishing plant where the lungis needed to run through a finishing machine before being packed.

Unfortunately, like many of our other ventures, we could not depend on its success and we wound it up soon.

It was 1968, and it had already been six years since we had last had any success in business.

Pita-ji had retired and shifted to Dehradun. I lived there too, teaching PT at Welham Girls' School.

Roopy sent hundred-rupee notes hidden in folded papers inside envelopes. Even though every single piece of the children's clothing was from abroad—not because there was anything wrong with Indian clothes but because I had no money—much of it was threadbare.

God was waiting to give us better days and the opportunity soon came.

The ONGC chairman, Mr L. Johnson, who was very friendly

with Sunita and Virender Bhaisahib helped us. His son Christopher Johnson was with Citibank in Delhi, and he informed us that there might be an opportunity for me.

So there I was, being interviewed, almost at the doorstep of Citibank, 3, Jeevan Vihan Building, Parliament Street.

It was 1 January 1968 and the bank was closed for public dealings for the New Year. Parliament Street looked vast and empty, and the Citibank building looked imposing.

I was wearing my favourite green silk saree to give me courage; it flapped in the auto rickshaw that I had taken from Curzon Road. I wrapped the shawl tightly around me.

Mr Krishan Murari met me at the door and beckoned me in with a nod.

He read the papers of recommendation I had brought.

'Can you join tomorrow?'

Interview over.

'The appointment letter will be given later, and you will be confirmed in six months,' he said.

I walked out in a daze. Tears pricked my eyes.

I had a job.

Happy New Year to me.

My father-in-law came down from Dehradun and helped me find a small barsati in Defence Colony.

I was alone for the first few months—the children stayed on in Dehradun to complete their school year.

Soon I was confirmed and started to get a good salary. The children moved. Papsy's husband-to-be, then still the principal of St. Xavier's, came with me to the admission interview at Delhi Public School (DPS).

Baldev joined me in Delhi and he took up a job at a petrol pump. After years of living separately we became a family again. Our means were small but we managed. Between us we earned 600 rupees a month.

I cooked and cleaned and went to work. Mahesh Bhai drove

his scooter all the way from Kanpur and gave it to us so we could have transport.

Vineet was eight and he looked after Suneet and Geetika. The house keys would be hidden in a secret corner when we left in the morning; after school, Vineet would herd Suneet and Geetika home, lock the house from inside and make sure they were fed.

Yet, everybody flourished. It was especially clear when, in a matter of months, Vineet demonstrated his quick and sharp wit to President Fakhruddin Ali Ahmed and Prime Minister Indira Gandhi while showing them his creation in the science lab at DPS.

Another time, I was the lone woman standing among 500 people in junior school, clapping and crying simultaneously, when Vineet led the drill display parade for the NCC at DPS.

Some years go by and you wonder what happened in them, and some years come around where you wonder how so much could have had happened.

The year 1968 would turn out to be the latter. On one front, I started my professional journey, moved to Delhi, lived alone in a barsaati, then started to live as a family again, and later moved into a bigger place in Defence Colony. On another, I was to meet the person who fuelled my love for poetry, my appreciation of the ghazal and allowed me to give back to the genre that I loved so much.

Even though I wrote only a little during all those years in Kanpur, Aligarh and Dehradun, I never stopped reciting ghazals. Sometimes, their beauty consoled me, sometimes they were the expression of my grief and helplessness.

After starting work at Citibank, my love for the ghazal became common knowledge. I was invited to baithaks where the other guests also loved the ghazal as much as I did. They were learned scholars, authors and patrons. In one such baithak I met Koakub Durry Sahib. He was impressed with my love for the ghazal. I was in awe of his knowledge and the work he had embarked on. He was a renowned scholar of English, Persian and Urdu literatures. His day job was at Hamdard but he was putting together an anthology of ghazals, penning the meaning of the words, but also his reflection on the mood of the shair, matching it with a plethora of raags it should be sung in. It was a vast canvas.

He lived in Lajpat Nagar, I was nearby in Defence Colony.

When Baldev came to Delhi, they became very good friends, and Baldev often recited Sahir, Shakeel and Qateel.

Koakub Bhai would come by often. He was very concerned that the ghazal was losing its lustre, that it had taken on a jazzy pop style. In a shair, the first line points to something. The next line confirms it. He believed that if a singer spent a long time between the two, riffing on the raag or a word, nobody would remember the first line and the shair would lose its meaning.

He encouraged me to write. He instilled the essence of the ghazal form in me. The mood of the ghazal, the raag it could be sung in, the importance of talaffuz (pronunciation), the effect of opening the shair upon the audience—he taught me all this and more.

Somehow, over the course of that year, we started a society. Shaam-e-Ghazal was registered in 1968. S.M.H. Burney was president, Thakur Harnarain Singh was the vice president, Kaokab Durry was the general secretary, and I the treasurer. There are four other members in the executive committee, one of whom was the journalist and poet Noorjahan Sarwat.

Kaokub Durry Sahib, Noorjahan Sarwat and I would go on to present the traditional ghazal to the Delhi audience for decades. The India International Centre teamed up with us and gave us their C.D. Deshmukh Auditorium free for every programme. They wanted four programmes a year. We sent out joint invitations and the programmes became the celebration of the ghazal in Delhi.

We presented hundreds of artistes and the works of classical and modern poets at our public performances and soirees. Koakub Bhai knew all the artists and the people who promoted arts and leading exponents of the ghazal, such as Anil Biswas, Naina Devi, Hilal Ahmed Khan, Hafeez Ahmed Khan, Anjali Banerjee and Madan

Bala Sindhu. Chandan Das and Mazhar Ali Khan were invited to perform. Every visiting poet would be invited to talk: Faiz Ahmed Faiz, Ahmad Faraz, Zehra Nigah, Naina Devi, Shuja Khawar, Hassan Naeem and many more. It was the most popular idara in Delhi. Every show was packed to the brim, not even standing room to be found.

Because Shaam-e-Ghazal was a platform to revive the ghazal, the programme would always start with a short talk. We had a couple of rehearsals before each performance where we fine-tuned the talaffuz and the music.

Little did we know that we would soon be invited by President Dr Zakir Husain for a programme at the Rashtrapati Bhavan. Politicians like Uma Shankar and Atal Behari Vajpayee would come sit and listen to the performances, which were held at residences and at historical places like Ghalib's tomb.

The ghazal was presented through various forms—via kathak, through stage plays, through the mehfil and through the rich gharana forms. Many of these programmes are now available on YouTube.

For one memorable evening in 2009, on the ghazal in film at the India International Centre in Delhi, there were people waiting outside on the roads and on the lawns.

No money was ever given or taken. That was the beauty of music and Shaam-e-Ghazal.

At around the same time I met another person who was to become my guru. She was the poet Zehra Nigah. I'm not sure when her words first entered my consciousness, but I had heard her on the radio and at mushairas.

The first poem by her that I heard on the radio was *Aaj ki Baat*:

Aaj ki baat nai baat nahi hai aesi
Jab kabhi dil se koi guzra hai yaad aai hai
Sirf dil hi ne nahi, gaud me khamooshi ki
Pyar ki baat to har lamhe ne dohrai hai

Chupke chupke hi chatakne do ishaaro ke gulaab
Dheemey dheemey hi sulagney do taqazo ke alaa-o!
Rafta rafta hi chalakney do ada-o'n ki sharaab
Dheerey dheerey hi nigahoo'n ke khazaney bikhra-o

Baat ach-chi ho to sab yaad kya kartey hai'n
Kaam suljha ho to rah rah-ke khayaal aata hai
Dard meetha ho to ruk-ruk ke kasak hoti hai
Yaad gahri ho to tham-thum ke qaraar aata hai

Dil guzargah hai aahista khirami ke liye
Tezgaami ko jo apna-o to kho jaoge
Ek zara der hi palko'n ko jhapak leney do
Is qadar gaur se dekhoge to so jaoge

It remains my favourite even after sixty years.

I had an immense desire to meet this soft-spoken poet. Fate handed me the key when I was asked to interview her for All India Radio, for the overseas radio section. From 1966 to 1968, I came to Delhi regularly from Aligarh, to host programmes for radio.

Zehra Nigah would visit India for mushaira evenings, and after one of these I was to interview her. I clearly remember we discussed her nazm *Meri Saheli.*

Conversation veered from who the saheli was, the form of the khud kalami or monologue. It's not often that you know when somebody will be important in your life, but I could feel our connection from that single meeting. Ever since then we have been like family.

Over the years Shaam-e-Ghazal enriched me with more friends and artistes like Radhika Chopra, Sudeep Banerji, Shoma Banerji, Rekha Bhardwaj and Shubha Mudgal. Salutations.

Meri Saheli
by Zehra Nigah

Zaheen aankhey, kitabi chehra,
wo sanwli ek udaas larki
Safed aanchal se tan ko dhanpey
merey darenchey me jhaanki hai

20

Around the World with Didi and Roopy

IN SENIOR CAMBRIDGE WE HAD FOUR BOOKS IN LITERATURE: *Travels with a Donkey* by Robert Louis Stevenson, *A Midsummer Night's Dream* and *Twelfth Night* by William Shakespeare and *Lays of Ancient Rome* by Thomas Babington Macaulay, the last a collection of narrative poems written in 1842.

Travels with a Donkey was indicative of what I would be doing for a career, which would be the source of accolades and achievements for over forty years. I could not travel with a donkey but came very close, I sent a bear to dance at the India France Festival Mela on the Champs-Élysées in Paris. I made a passport for him, and we called him Munna. He entertained the Parisians to no end with his dancing, handshakes and by folding his hands in a respectful namaste.

But my first travel abroad was an around-the-world trip with my sisters in the autumn of 1969.

Roopy was to be married in December 1969 and would need to resign from the British Airways, so she decided to avail the 10 per cent fare ticket offer—where we only needed to pay the tax on the tickets and take a trip around the world. Our fare was a princely sum of 1,207 rupees for each ticket.

It had been a little over a year after I had joined Citibank that Roopy proposed the idea. Could we do it? Didi and I were excited at the idea. So were Sushil Bhai and Baldev when we discussed it with them.

I got a month's leave with much difficulty. Didi, too, took leave from Cottage Emporium.

Roopy had planned the trip with destinations where British Airways, or a sister carrier that would honour the discounted ticket, could fly us. She had also made arrangements for us to stay as paying guests where needed and otherwise with close friends.

Our trip would take us from Delhi via Tel Aviv to London, New York, Los Angeles, Hawaii, Tokyo, Osaka, Hong Kong, Bangkok and back.

Baldev and I had recently moved to a bigger house in Defence Colony.

Baldev rummaged through his books and bookmarked information and kept aside a stack of reference books and a mini atlas for me. He told us what all we must see, what trains we could take and bus routes too. My children were so excited when Baldev showed them all the tourist destinations we had planned to visit in London: Buckingham Palace, The Tower of London, Trafalgar Square, the British Museum, Big Ben, the Houses of Parliament, the Victoria and Albert Museum, the National Gallery, Hyde Park and Covent Garden.

When it came to the non-touristy, Roopy was a London expert. During her five years with the British Airways, she had been to London countless times, and had stayed and trained there as well.

First stop, London. Obligatory photos were taken in front of Buckingham Palace, gawking at it and thinking of Mummy. We saw plays, street theatre and roamed the Oxford Street daily. We licked ice creams and bonded like we were children once again. We were together and supporting each other's joy. We ate at small cafes and Roopy spoilt us rotten.

We reunited with Shamim and Patto who now lived in Wimbledon. They had moved to the UK in 1965 and we spent two nights with them. I had met them the year before on their annual visit to India but you can never have too much of a good thing. It was with a feeling of homecoming that we met them in a foreign land. We hugged each other tight, and they fed us all the ghar ka khaana: dal–chawal, bharta, bhindi, saag gosht. We Indians start to miss our dal–chawal the moment we step into the aircraft. They also took us around and showed us Oxford, Cambridge and Bath.

By this time, I had already faced a lot of grief at airport immigration. They would let Didi and Roopy pass the gate but hold me back. We looked so different they refused to believe that I was their sister. How could I avail the 10 per cent fare ticket which was only applicable to family?

It was painful and harassing for me but fun for Didi and Roopy and I got a new nickname on that trip: 'Steppy', short for stepsister.

In New York, wherever we went, people turned to look. We heard lots of whistles. Women in sarees were still an uncommon sight. At the Statue of Liberty, strangers took photos of us. They wanted to know the length of material that was draped around us. Was it a stitched garment? Was it a slip-on? Some people asked us if we lived on trees in India. Others asked us if we came from the country of snake charmers. They were shocked that we spoke English and that too proper Queen's English. Some had no clue that there was a country called India and were most surprised about our knowledge of the history of the UK and the USA.

In New York, I visited the Citibank main office and met my friends DP and Chander Ahuja. DP came to receive me at a tube station waving a toothbrush. I was going to their house straight from sightseeing and had no time to go back to my host's house to pick up my toiletries.

After New York we went to Los Angeles, looking out to catch sight of Hollywood stars. I hoped I might run into my heartthrob Rock Hudson, who was single again after his marriage to Phyllis Gates, but I had to make do with the Hollywood sign, the Hollywood Boulevard and the Walk of Fame.

We stayed with the warmest of hosts, Roopy's close friends Kish and Naresh Kriplani, two bachelor brothers who lived in Calcutta during her flying days. They drove us around for ten days, taking us on day trips to San Francisco, Disneyland, Redwood City and Beverly Hills. I was reminded again of how much fun it was to be with my sisters.

We spent two days at Disneyland and stayed in a small and quaint cottage nearby. We took a few careful rides—no roller-coasters for us. We got our chills and thrills from the haunted mansion and from going into caves where I felt like I might die. We ate ice creams and shook hands with Mickey, Minnie and Donald Duck.

Kish and Naresh took us to casinos, to Rodeo Drive, the Beverly Hills Hotel and the Beverly Gardens Park where we admired the rose gardens and fountains. Here a mini crowd surrounded us, mainly students wanting to know about Gandhi. This was the decade of the civil rights movement and the anti-war protests and the new generation was hungry to know the history of a country that had won its freedom with non-violence.

I had a burger for the first time. I ate Mexican curry and rice, and was very happy to eat rajma again. But each helping was a huge mound of food, the portions in America were so large that we could never finish them.

On 8 October we flew to Hawaii. It had been bitterly cold in America, and we had worn socks, pants, cardigans and coats. We reached Hawaii at midnight, and the next morning, we put on all our layers of clothing again and went to the beach for breakfast. Didi even carried a pink umbrella.

What we saw around us were people in bikinis or no clothes at all. We looked like we had come from an alien planet!

And then on our flight to Japan, sometime during the night, I lost my birthday when we crossed the International Dateline. It was suddenly 11 October when we reached Tokyo.

Osaka, Hong Kong, Bangkok—these were adventures of the nose. Everything smelled unfamiliar, fishy and oily. We bought electronics and sarees; my big buy was a stereo player that I knew the children and Baldev would love.

And just like that we were home.

Abhi suroor fiza mein hai kainaat mein hai
Abhi ye hath hamara tumhare hath mein hai

Zara bhi khauf nahi hai kisi bhi manzil ka
Mere naseeb ka tara tumhare saath mein hai

The air is still heady, so is all creation
My hand is in yours, still

There isn't the slightest fear of any goal
The star of my destiny lies in your company

21

Didi and Roopy Get Married

DIDI AND ROOPY BOTH GOT MARRIED IN 1969, DIDI IN MAY AND Roopy in December.

Didi's marriage took place at the Arya Samaj Mandir in Lajpat Nagar in Delhi.

Didi and Sushil Bhai had been in a relationship for ten years. Didi had fretted often about getting married, but in the way of traditional family hierarchy Sushil Bhai couldn't marry till his sisters did. The years passed, the questions from Didi became more frequent. 'When are we getting married?' 'Have you set a date yet?' There were no answers and the tension increased.

At the end, Didi and Sushil Bhai decided to forge ahead with their marriage even though two of his sisters were still unmarried. His family was displeased. This was a break from tradition and so they decided not to attend the wedding.

Neither Sushil Bhai nor Didi had enough money for an elaborate wedding and so a simple ceremony was arranged at the Arya Samaj Mandir. It was a pretty little standalone mandir with a large garden in front. The date was set for 15 May. The ceremony was to take place in the afternoon with a high tea afterwards.

Or that was the plan.

Roopy was flying back for the wedding from Hong Kong. Her flight was to land In Delhi on 14 May. Except the flight flew over Delhi and went to Calcutta.

Confusion and tension were abound.

Should we postpone the wedding?

Didi didn't even have to think about it. Of course. Both her sisters had to be present for it.

The wedding was deferred to 17 May. My sister-in-law, Urmill Behen-ji, and her son, Anil, made all the eating arrangements.

There were around forty people at the wedding. Sushil Bhai walked in with a few of his Cottage Emporium friends. There were Didi's friends, Roopy, Mummy, Baldev and I.

Didi wore a rich red saree and looked beautiful. Sushil Bhai wore a grey striped suit and looked dapper even without the customary pagri and sehra. They wore rose garlands and looked very happy.

'The mood was infectious. After the wedding everybody sat around for a long time, talking and laughing.

Naturally at some point Sushil Bhai was requested to sing. Everybody turned to him as he stood at the centre, his eyes trained on Didi, sang:

Jo bhi gulcha tere hoothon pe khila karta hai,
Woh meri tangiy ka dama gila karta hai.

The smile that blooms on your lips
tells me how little I have to give to you.

Had he practised this song by Qateel Shifai before? Had he just found it? I had never heard him sing those words. Everybody was moved by the silence he sang into, his voice had been laden with emotion which made Didi tear up. I, too, had a lump in my throat.

Both my brothers-in-law sang beautifully. My best collection of music is full of tapes with their recordings, which I painstakingly converted to digital files later.

An amazing relationship grew amongst the three brothers-in-law. They were hum zulf in every sense. In Urdu, hum zulf means husbands of sisters. In Hindi, it means sandus, sagi behno ke pati. They sang together, ate together, teased the three of us, and adored the children collectively. They had their own secret jokes, most of them dirty Punjabi ones.

I could predict that Baldev and Sushil Bhai would get along, but Brijesh? His upbringing was totally different. Born in an elite Mathur family from Lucknow, the only pampered son, he studied in Doon School with Rajiv Gandhi as a classmate. It was a joy to see the brothers-in-law together, especially at family functions, marriages and the musical soirees we would have at home.

Brijesh would make a trunk call to me from wherever he was posted to know the next shair or the lines of a particular ghazal.

He would say, '*Saali, jaldi se bata is ka agla shair kya hai, mujhey khat mein bhi likh kar bhejna.*'

There was no STD then, no mobile phone, no messages and, of course, no WhatsApp. The world has shrunk into our palms these days, everything we need can be acquired with the touch of a button. What is there in the world that cannot be searched for on the internet?

But those were fun days too, to wait at a PCO for a loved one to call. To have neighbours who owned a phone!

Savouring good poetry and reciting it with relish is a tradition in my family. Brijesh and Sushil were the ones who encouraged this tradition the most, even staying up all night long for our sessions of poetry and ghazals. Somebody once said, '*Yeh family badi FMM hai*—family much music-minded.'

There was plenty of music at Roopy's wedding too.

If Didi's marriage was a simple affair in an Arya Samaj Mandir with no band baja baraat, Roopy's was a lavish affair that became the talk of the town.

Roopy married into a very rich and land-owning Mathur family from Lucknow whose clan members were spread all over Meerut and Delhi.

Roopy's father-in-law was Gangeshwar Dayal Mathur, who established and was later the chairman of the State Bridge Corporation, India. A brilliant man till his last days. It was a family

Uma Didi

Uma Didi and Sushil Bhai

Tanuj, Pooja and Mehak

Ruhi and Rohit

Queen Elizabeth and Prince Philip at Cottage Emporium

Jacqueline Kennedy at Cottage Emporium

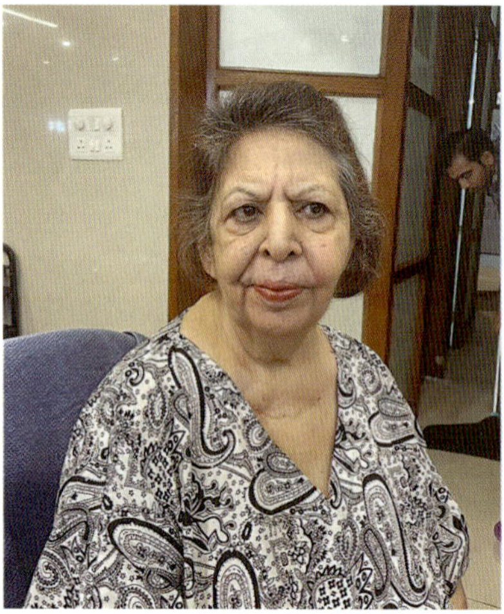

Roopy

Roopy and Brijesh

Siddharth, Batasha, Leela and Deviki

Siddharth and Batasha

Roopy, Hiroo and I

Vineet and Tinu

Vineet, Tinu, Rhea and Aria

Three samdhans, Balwant-ji, Sushma-ji and I, with Arun and Angie, Tinu's brother and bhabhi

Geetika, Kavi, Tarika and Nainika

Geetika, Kavi, Tarika and Nainika

Tarika and Nainika

Dhruv Bhai-ji and Baldev, who spent hours drinking imaginary tea from little plastic teacups with Tarika. Hysterical grandfathers, both devoted to their granddaughters.

Suneet

Suneet with Prince Charles

One of Suneet's fashion shows

Suneet at one of his fashion shows

Suneet once made me walk the ramp too!

Vineet, Suneet and Geetika, in Aligarh, 1964

Vineet, Suneet and Geetika, in Amritsar, on Vineet's sixth birthday

Vineet, Suneet and Geetika, celebrating Suneet's 25 years in fashion

Clock tower, Peshawar

Presumably our childhood house in Peshawar

In Karachi

At Khan Club in Peshawar

At Government House, Lahore

At Shalimar Gardens, Lahore

The IVS team

The ambassador and his deputy decorating me

The day we signed the agreement

The first IVS brochure

CM Shiela Dixit and my artists, Radhika, Sudeep and Shoma, at the release of *Hum-Umr Khayal*

At the release of my book *Hum-Umr Khayal*; to my left is Ahmad Faraz Sahib

With Jagjit Singh at the release of my book *Shafaq ke Rang*

At the release of my book *Dosti ka Ek Samandar*

My book *Romancing Tagore* being released by PM Manmohan Singh in the presence of my family and close friends

Faiz Sahib at my house

With Gulzar Sahib, Pawan Varma-ji, Sukrita Paul and Zehra-ji

Farida Khanum-ji at my house

The melodious Shanti Hiranand-ji, the first shishya of Begum Akhtar

M.F. Hussain, Zehra-ji and I

Lunch at Sid and Batasha's house

All the boys gathered in honour of Sunita's visit

Family at my house

Bunty, Poonam and I

My grandchildren and a great-grandchild with me

Sushma-ji and family at my house

The frequent foursome

Anoop Mami and Amrik Mama-ji

Minni Maasi-ji, Gurdeep Jija-ji, and the three girls, Raveen, Saveen and Meenu

Balo Bhapa-ji and Todo Bhabi

Dolly Mami, Bholi Didi, Todo Bhabi, Balo Bhapa-ji and Billi Mama-ji

With my friends from Citibank days, Pullo, Rumjhum, Renu and Vibha

On the cover of *Eve's Weekly,* during my Citibank days

Asha, Veena and I

Vibha, Renu, Manju, Abha and I

Veena, Asha, Achla, Geetika and I

Rama, Dhira and Priya

Neethi, Bindu, Rama, Asha and I

Tasmima, Sakina, Priya and I, in Dhaka

Madhu, Ratan and I

My children

And their children

Mahesh, my Rakhi brother, with my sisters and me. We grew up together in Kanpur. He left us too soon.

With our Rakhi brother, Ibrahim Khan, and his lovely wife, Najma Bhabhi. He presented me four volumes of poetry on my thirteenth birthday. He sends us Rakhi gifts a month in advance. They live in London.

With my goddaughter, Leena Diwan, with whom I share a very strong bond from my travel days. She lives in Nice, France.

Rakhshanda, my daughter in every which way, with her husband Justice Waziri and her mom Mahajabeen-ji when Zehra-ji and I visited her beautiful house. I am Ina Nani to her children.

My colleagues from Thomas Cook: on the left is Radhika, who I have known from my Kanpur days, when she was two or three years old; our families were friends. On the right is Serena, who is also from Ramnee Park, Nainital. She now lives in the USA.

My family. Missing from the photograph are Kavi-ji and Rhea.

Our husbands, Baldev, Sushil Bhai and Brijesh

Uma Didi, Roopy and I

full of IAS and IFS members. Roopy's mother-in-law was from Kinnaird College, Lahore, and her brother was a General in the army.

Roopy's parents-in-law, Daddy and Jijja, lived in a beautiful house called Chhoti Chhatar Manzil in Lucknow. They owned agricultural lands, houses and a large kothi in Nainital.

The date of her wedding was set for 3 December 1969.

We hired the Munna Lal Manzil, a sprawling bungalow at 20, Shahjahan Road, and the family shifted there for a week. The lawns were decorated with fairy lights and a pandal of flowers and festive paper was created. It took two days to put up.

Such decorations were not usual in the Delhi of the late 1960s.

The caterers were from the famous Greens restaurant from Jalandhar. They specialised in non-vegetarian food.

Roopy's in-laws were Kayasthas and famous for eating rich non-vegetarian food. We served quail and partridge, chicken and pork, and so many different tandoori fish dishes. The Chinese and Thai food, that is so popular today, was not so easily available then or, more accurately, nobody had heard of them then.

There are many stories of that food which Sushil Bhai and Baldev would regale us with years later. How one guest demanded chicken breast after chicken breast, who demanded what alcohol and who ate only the sweet. We call it the Chesta Breasta stories.

The baraat was elaborate, about 200 people, including many foreign guests who were Brijesh's bank colleagues and friends. Brijesh came in a beautiful convertible decorated with flowers but, as custom demanded, got on a horse a few feet away from Munna Lal Manzil.

The reception of the baraat was very Pishori. All my Mamas and cousins including Amrik Mama-ji and Prithvi Uncle did the luddi dance, where the men of the family dance in a circle waving their handkerchiefs.

It is a common sight in all Pakistani dramas.

A special Military and Police Band was sent in advance, arranged by Brijesh's uncle in the army, and they played all evening much to everybody's delight. There were also bhangra dancers and our family men dancing to the luddi. It was a sight straight from a Sooraj Barjatya film.

I have never seen such a display of jewellery as I saw that night. Roopy got twenty-one sets in her muh-dikhai rasam. That Rani Haar went back generations, and we heard many stories about it.

There was more glamour than we had ever seen. All Roopy's British Airways friends, our childhood friends from Kanpur, my friends from Citibank and Didi's friends from Cottage Emporium had come for the wedding.

There were some very cute customs too. Vineet and Suneet had to wash Brijesh's feet before the wedding. It was December and bitterly cold, but rituals are rituals and they are to be followed. For this Jijja gave both the boys beautifully tailored suits, checkered coats with grey trousers, shirts, ties, socks and shoes.

The bidai was as dramatic, with the shehnai players and a decorated car.

The reception was held in Lucknow with a qawwali evening. Shankar Shambhu, the famous qawwals, sang for the guests, many of whom were government officials and included the chief minister.

Sar-e-guroor ko sajda naya sikhaya tha
Kis ehtmaam se tumko khuda banaya tha

Buss itna yaad hai pabose ho gaee thi nazar
Phir uss ke baad paristish mein rang aaya tha

A new prostration was taught to the haughty head
You were made God with such pomp

All I remember now is how my gaze had kissed your feet
And how colour then seeped into my worship of you

22

The Citibank Years

I SPENT TEN BEAUTIFUL YEARS AT CITIBANK.

I could drive to 3, Parliament Street blindfolded from Greater Kailash—past Lady Shri Ram College, past Defence Colony, Golf Club, India Gate, Ashoka Road, the Post Office and on to Parliament Street. It would take just fifteen minutes to reach work.

The challenge was to get inside Citibank before its gates closed for the daily transfer of cash to the Reserve Bank of India (RBI). Being even a minute late meant standing outside till the whole process, which included guns and trunks, was over. A sort of changing of the guard ceremony, daily.

This is when the bank deposited the money from the day before and got new money for the new day. The bank counters opened at 10 a.m. sharp.

There were not many cars then; Kaka Nagar, Sunder Nagar were all green fields. Except for Lady Shri Ram College there were just tall weeds in Greater Kailash. I saw the Oberoi come up as I went to work every day. My mother-in-law was worried when, at times, I came home late and had to pass through desolate and deserted areas.

People said that wolves roamed the streets freely at night.

Baldev got a job with the garment export division at Escorts. His job involved overseas travel and Escorts even gave him a car.

We went through the most beautiful years here. Stable, good jobs, children in good schools and later, good colleges.

A new lease on life had started.

But before that we had to deal with the loss of Pita-ji. He passed away on 2 May 1970, in my house in Defence Colony.

A well-read man. He complained of a bit of chest pain the evening before and had a massive cardiac arrest the next morning at 7 a.m.

Of Human Bondage by William Somerset Maugham lay open on his pillow, at page 81.

We wound up the house in Dehradun and Mata-ji came to live with us. My mother too would come to live with us later.

We shifted homes once again and eventually moved to an independent ground floor house at Greater Kailash-1. We lived there for thirty-four years. It became the adda for all our family get-togethers. It was the maika for my sisters as well as my mother.

The driving part did not last long either. Since the price of petrol suddenly shot up to three rupees a litre and we could not afford to take the car out as often as we had earlier, I joined the chartered bus service that had mushroomed overnight.

After putting aside money from our salaries for household expenses, the children's schooling, their clothes and other miscellaneous expenses, I would get a pocket money of 200 rupees per month from my husband.

Of that, forty-eight rupees went to Omi-ji who owned the chartered bus, fifty rupees to Mummy for her maid, and I was left with about a hundred rupees to indulge in paan outside the bank or buy a bag of peanuts, which we ate while sitting in the beautiful YWCA garden or the roundabout outside the RBI. Madhu would join me almost daily from the Doordarshan complex on the opposite side.

I got to work in many different positions during my time with Citibank: at the telephone board, Opening and Closing of Accounts, head of Traveller's Cheques, Credit Analysis, Trading and as key holder of the vault. As the key holder, I opened the vault every day with the combination I held alongside another person. I was also platform officer, PRO. And I even worked at the Stationery department.

There were hundreds of forms needed in the bank daily. Each position taught me so much and gave me a lot of exposure to public dealings.

There were no machines in our bank, no calculators and no computers. Everything was maintained by hand. Ledgers, cash registers and foreign exchange were all tallied and written by hand. Only then could we go home.

As soon as you entered the bank you saw a huge hall. Bang opposite were the cash counters: the Fixed Deposit Receipt counter and the Foreign Exchange counter.

At the entry, on the right side, were the two Opening Account desks where I sat. At the back of the hall was the Platform where four people sat. That is where I sat when I became the platform officer and when I looked after traveller's cheques.

Those were the days of the hippies; every day, we had scores of them walking in. Ninety per cent brought fake cheques, had 'lost' their cheques or had faked signatures. Dealing with them was a regular drama. They would shout, scream and lie down in front of my desk, threatening to die. We had to take the help of the police on numerous occasions. Often Tara Singh, a seven-foot-tall Sardar guard, would just pick them up and hurl them outside.

On one of these days, in walked a scraggy looking woman with a scraggier puppy tied to a string. She looked as if she hadn't eaten for days, her hair looked matted. She presented a cheque to Vibha, a dear friend, who was at the Foreign Exchange counter. The cheque was drawn on Citibank New York for a staggering amount. Vibha, taken aback, looked disbelievingly at the lady. Should she call Tara Singh? The woman tapped on the counter impatiently.

'Come on, woman, I don't have time to play tiddlywinks with you,' she said.

Some moments later, one of our senior officers walked out and realised that she was the wife of the bank's vice president in New York.

Such incidents were an everyday affair. They kept our spirits high and encouraged a tremendous camaraderie amongst the staff.

I was the married one with three children and thus a safe elder, so my desk was a gathering place to discuss daily happenings, the food we ate, but especially the love affairs. My desk would be abuzz with all kinds of chatter: who was going out with whom, who was seen with whom and where, unrequited love, double and triple dating.

When a lovesick staff member would enter the bank with a forlorn look, R.L. Seth would say, '*Indira-ji ai gavachi gau di tarah kyon paya phirda?* (Why is he looking like a lost cow?)' Knowing very well why.

Citibank had some very famous love affairs, some of which ended in marriages and some in heartbreaks.

Plenty of weddings took place.

When Vibha married Sunil, the whole bank went, dressed in their finery, for the wedding which took place was at the Chunna Mal Haveli in Chandni Chowk that belonged to her father.

Viju, another colleague, married Sunil's younger brother Gogi. They were in the fertiliser business and are very close to me even now.

Renu and Rohington too married.

Rumjhum and Bharat's love also culminated in marriage. An elegant reception followed at IIC.

Rumjhum was our femme fatale of the bank. As soon as she walked into the bank with her beautiful cotton saree, her hair well beyond her waist and her anklets tinkling, all the Cash counter staff would stop whatever they were doing and stare. I knew a remark would come from Seth Sahib: '*Kyon, Indira-ji, ai mausam barha khush gawar ho gaya hai na* (Indira-ji, the weather has turned pleasant).'

No one in this world is rich enough to buy his or her own childhood or the past. Only friends can recreate those memories at no cost. My Citibank friends are like fairy tales, they have been there since ... once upon a time ... and will be there forever after.

My friends from Citibank and I still meet often and share our happiness and sorrows. All the NRI colleagues come once a year and a get-together is a must. Rumjhum, Pullomaja, Vibha, Renu, Abha, Manju, Edu, Niru and Vinay are on a Citi chat and that's our comfort zone. We are friends on Facebook and regular on WhatsApp too. We lost DP Ahuja, Rajesh and Renu Kapoor.

The Citibank building was surrounded by interesting areas. On the left was our competition, Bank of Tokyo, and right across the road was the Sansad Marg Police Station where a busload of women from the red light area were brought every day for haziri, much to the amusement of our clients. On the right was the most famous chhole-bathure-wallah. If you opened a window the tempting aroma was enough to drive anyone crazy.

That is what used to happen to Pullo, Pullomaja Atal, whose very beautiful and caring mother would pack a tiffin of boiled vegetables and dahi to help her lose weight. All that Pullo had to do was open the window, put her hand out and say, *'Ek plate dena.'* Nothing was lost, a lot was gained.

Citibank was never at a loss for dramas. Once I had to sit inside the vault for eleven hours while the auditors counted every penny, every department was thoroughly checked. I sat on a mountain of currency notes since there was no other place to sit. Hence I know what millions of dollars and rupees look like and also how uncomfortable they are to sit on.

There were reasons to rejoice and reasons to be sad.

Sad when we came to work to find out that Mr Shafi who left the bank with all of us the evening before, hale and hearty, had passed away at night.

Horrified when the two children of Sara and Chris Johnson—whose father Leslie Johnson had helped me find this job—fell down from a balcony and were spiked to death.

Shocked when our colleague who seemed so holy and pious, so friendly and full of fun was imprisoned overnight for fraud.

Chagrined that some officials hid porn magazines in their desk drawers. Once when some of the younger staff stole the magazines, the officer, red-faced, was desperately searching for them. And though all of us knew we kept asking him what he was looking for.

'*Arrey, kuch nahi. Kuch nahi. Tum log apna apna kaam karo na.* Thank you for your offers of help.'

We could have died laughing.

We had some colourful and illustrious managers in the ten years that I worked there: Promodh Malhotra, Ashish Bannerji and more. My longest tenure was with Lorenzo Roncari, an Italian who used to call me IV. He spoke English with an Italian accent and I could mimic him very well.

I was given the task of sending the RBI returns which went fortnightly. After the Account Opening counter closed in the afternoon I would work on the returns. Four large colourful sheets had to be completed with precise details and figures.

All through my time at Citibank I would write and recite poetry for friends and colleagues.

One day suddenly something came to my mind and I started to scribble it on the sheet, above the column for returns. Just then Mr Roncari walked into the bank and saw what I was doing.

'Oh my God, IV! What are you doing? What are you doing?' he shouted. 'The RBI is going to kill us!' He was absolutely aghast, his hands gesturing wildly.

I started laughing. 'Don't worry, Mr Roncari,' I said. 'These are just the rough figures,' I reassured him.

Personally, I had some exciting adventures in the bank. I was featured on the cover of *Eve's Weekly* magazine.

Once I even took a morning off to play the Maharani of Patiala in Richard Attenborough's *Gandhi*. 'Just wear a saree and come, you only need to look elegant,' I was told by my school friend Dolly Thakore. I don't even know if the scene made it to the final cut of the movie.

I was also featured in the Citibank magazine with Tara Singh, our guard.

Customers would recognise me.

I opened about 14,000 accounts, I was told.

Once a very handsome officer who I worked with asked me if I would spend a weekend with him in Nepal. I politely declined.

There were very few diplomatic missions then in India and I looked after all of them. Most of them opened their accounts with us.

One day Mr Roncari called me to his office and said, 'IV, we have liberated a desk and from today you will be the platform officer.' Later in the day we came to know that our friend and a colleague was sacked.

When Rajiv Gandhi, Sonia Gandhi and Sanjay Gandhi came to open an account, they were handled by my neighbouring desk officer Amir Kidwai, the beautiful Salma Sultan's husband.

Festivals and Independence Day were celebrated with great enthusiasm and Ashish Banerjee, the then manager, came in a spotless dhoti kurta and sang the National Anthem with us.

Those were the days of Union strikes. Suddenly we would be told 'Pens down, pens down. Come outside there is to be a dharna.' This was a serious matter but with so many fun elements. All of us giggled and joined in the slogan shouting: '*Tanashashi nahi chalegi nahi chalegi*' and '*Jo hum se takrayega choor choor ho jayega.*' We women used to quietly say chipak chipak jayega. Then Kasturi Lal would have a closed-door meeting and would be called back to work.

Voluntary retirement or a golden handshake was quite the norm in America and it came to Citibank, New Delhi too.

We were all offered jobs in the Middle East that had just risen like a sphinx on the atlas. Riyadh, Bahrain, Muscat, Qatar and UAE. Many of our colleagues went and earned the petro dollars, as they were called then. I was offered a post in Muscat, which I promptly refused. My husband and children were settled in Delhi and there was no point mulling over it.

I took voluntary retirement in December 1977 after a stint of ten years. It was a great learning experience and a foundation for the sixty years of my professional life.

I got a fantastic offer from Thomas Cook to become the head of their Business Travel Unit and a new adventure started.

~

THE EARLY YEARS OF CITIBANK

Krishan Murari

(Krishna Murari interviewed Indira Varma for the job at Citibank.)

National Citi Bank, New Delhi was established in November 1963 at Jeevan Vihar Building, Parliament Street, New Delhi. Initially, it had about ten employees.

As a foreign bank we had quite a few problems because of extreme shortages of even basic utilities like telephones, computers, power and transport.

Despite this, through intensive staff training and employee relations our staff had become quite a committed team. Once during inspection of the branch by a team from the USA, there was a difference of ten paise in balancing the savings ledger and we all worked through the night to find the difference and balance the books.

Another time, when the cash vault located in the basement of our office could not be opened because one of our officers had forgotten the combination, we had to get a team from Bombay to cut open the vault. They drilled a hole in the steel wall working the whole night to get into it.

We had an American manager once, who after getting drunk, misbehaved at a diplomatic party and therefore had to be replaced immediately by another from Bombay.

But eventually things settled down and the operations and the business began to grow and we established our reputation as the best foreign bank in town mainly because of the training and commitment of the members of the team.

One morning, a young and a beautiful lady walked into our

bank asking for me. She introduced herself as Indira Varma and said she had come looking for a job.

I found her keen, committed and very intelligent. I hired her straightway. And that is how she started her career in banking even though she had never worked before. Soon she became one of the best employees of the bank.

We have been in touch ever since though I have worked in ten different countries since.

~

ON THE OTHER SIDE

Kasturi Lal Malhotra

One of the most beautiful young girls with grey green eyes entered the premises of Citibank at Parliament Street, New Delhi on 1 January 1968. It was Indira Varma, who also held some beauty titles. Her entry as staff member of First National Citi Bank added creditability and charm to the working atmosphere for staff as well as clientele of the bank.

The popular song of the day, *Eh sonehri kuri kithoo ayee ae,* was a query by one and all at that time. Always on time, her elegance, sweet words and sympathetic nature attracted everyone.

She recited poetry often, which added to her popularity. She was also a sincere comrade and responded to all the calls given by AIBEA or Citibank Staff Association/Federation.

She created new records and made history by introducing many thousand clients. She was very active in Citibank club activities. During the celebrations of Independence Day when Humayun Kabir, the minister, was the chief guest, she brought her three children in Bheel dress and participated in fancy dress show.

We met her husband Baldev Varma when he sometimes picked her up from the bank. With his support, she would arrange a mushaira at her residence every month. She never ran after popularity, but popularity followed her.

She is committed to a powerful language, Urdu, and its literature through the ghazal, nazm and other forms of poetry and she has perfected the art of adab as her way of life, from how she addresses people to her relationships.

~

Lau de uthi hai shamma badi muddaton ke baad
Rang layi hai umeed badi muddaton ke baad

Palkon pe deep jalne lage hain visaal ke
Aane se phele dhoom machi muddaton ke baad

The candle has given off a flame after ages
Hope has borne fruit after ages

The lamps of union have been lit on eyelashes
A celebration has broken out even before the arrival after ages

23

Bonds of a Lifetime and Beyond

C-90 GREATER KAILASH 1 AND 3, PARLIAMENT STREET. TWO ADDRESSES that would come to contain a multitude of happiness.

C-90 was a three-bedroom house with a small but beautiful garden, a large courtyard inside where we did our daily living and eating, and a terrace that could accommodate 200 people, which it did for Vineet's and Geetu's weddings. It was bigger than any of our previous houses in Delhi. It was almost always full.

Mata-ji lived with us. After spending her life in huge railway bungalows with an army of staff, she had to adapt to our much smaller house, our food and our way of living. Despite being a person set in her habits, she adjusted with Baldev, me and the children.

Mata-ji was a stickler for appearances. She would only ever emerge from her room fully groomed, powdered and perfumed. She wore Banarasi sarees and even slept in them. She believed your spouse should only see you at your best and drilled that into me. She loved compact powder; Baldev and I, as well as Mata-ji's other children, would get it for her from all over the world.

Besides Mata-ji, Baldev's younger brother Bunty and his wife Poonam lived there too. Bunty got married from my house, and their children were born there too. Before they left for Fiji, soon after their wedding, Mata-ji went to stay with them in the house they had set up.

Mata-ji's food preferences were totally different from ours. She liked pickles with all her meals. The only problem was that they were detrimental to her health. Of course, that never stopped anybody from eating what they want. Baldev would be angry every time he caught her, which resulted in teary scenes. She also liked to add ketchup to dal; if you gave her saag and makki ki roti without a substantial amount of garam-garam ghee with it she would say, '*Mere kolon ai randa saag nahin khaaya jaanda* (I can't eat these dry leaves).'

Mata-ji's unhappiness came from another source too. Vineet had brought home a monkey. It was named Tinker. My house suddenly saw a spurt in popularity in the neighbourhood. Children came with their nannies early morning to see Tinker or they wouldn't have their milk. They said Jai Hanuman-ji. They fed Tinker dozens of bananas and Tinker was very happy.

But unhappy, very unhappy was Mata-ji. Tinker would tear up her petticoats that had been put out to dry on the terrace and throw them strip by strip down to her. She would shout and scream not knowing whether to laugh or cry: '*WE MAR JAANYA THEHAR TU! MAIN TENU WATTE MARANGI!*' She would throw her chappal at Tinker. Tinker would catch it deftly, chew it up and throw it back to her.

Once he pounced on Vineet's childhood friend Amita and yanked out a chunk of hair from her head. Amita still has a bald patch there, I believe. The Tinker chapter soon ended when he ran away one day. Vineet looked for him all over Greater Kailash. Mata-ji may have prayed vehemently that he never be found.

Mummy would also come to live with me in a few years. She shared a room with Suneet. He was his Nani's favourite child. My mother and Suneet would go and see films together; he would then buy her a pastry, which they would share. She loved pork chops, so he would buy them and eat with her.

Still, it was a balancing act to live with both mother and mother-in-law. Mummy was fashion conscious. Mata-ji was regal in her old-world style. My mother would sit and pluck her eyebrows and my mother-in-law would ask her, *'Behen-ji, tussi ai ki karde ho?'*

But they wanted the best for the family. They had reached some sort of unspoken agreement that their issues would not spill over to our lives. Sometimes they would laugh and have a good time together, at other times they would not even talk—it was as families are.

Mata-ji died on 24 October 1990. At that time, she was living with Poonam and Bunty in New Friends Colony. Baldev and I had gone to see her a couple of days before she passed away. Karwachauth and Diwali were not too far away, and she told me with her very beatific smile, '*Aitki ta mein Sàuth di saree leni hai* (I want a saree from the South)'. Who would have thought that that would be our last exchange?

Mata-ji was eighty-three. Baldev would die a mere nine years later, in 1999, at the age of sixty-seven.

With Mata-ji's death, another story came to an end, the life she had lived as one of the three survivors in her family of the plague of 1897. She had lost her parents and almost all her siblings in it. Only she, her brother Satdev Nayar (who was more important to her than all of us put together) and her sister's son Bir had survived.

~

In the little turns of luck that define lives, Didi, Roopy and I had found husbands who, like us, passionately loved Urdu poetry and music. Didi married Sushil Bhai, whose singing bore an uncanny resemblance to Mohammad Rafi's, and Brijesh, Roopy's husband, was known as the Lata Mangeshkar of Doon School.

In Greater Kailash, we started what would become the tradition of the house. Evenings of baithaks and singing soirees. Sushil Bhai and Brijesh would sing all night and we would join in, unaware of the outside world. They sang individually too. But when they sang together it was sheer ecstasy. Their friends Sheetal, Ashok and Gyan made my house a music haven. Our friends would join in too.

Dil laganey kisi se ye saza payee k buss
Aisi aisi ishq mein iss dil pe ban aayee k buss.

Aaj ki raat gam-e dost mein
Shiddat hai bahut
Jinse ulfaat thi bahut unse shikayat hai bahut

Tu jo nahi hai tto kuch bhi nahi hai
Ye maana ki mehfil java'n hai hasee'n hai

Those nights were endless. Endless.

When it came to friendships, Baldev and I were very fortunate in life. Childhood, school, married life, all the different places I worked—the friends I made at all these places are still with me every step of the way.

In Greater Kailash, we became friends with a few couples who lived nearby. One of them was Madhu Raja who worked at the Doordarshan complex on Parliament Street too.

Madhu Raja was a well-known face of television; she did many programmes and plays. A born actress who after her retirement as station director of Doordarshan Mumbai started to work in Indian soaps. I met her in Delhi when I was invited to do some work at Doordarshan—I did a children's programme called *Gudiya Ghar* and also the popular *Mirror of the World* under the famous producers Sai Paranjpye and Mazruddin Sahib. I used to do a lot of TV work but left it because it took up a lot of time. I had a job and a family to look after.

Madhu and I discovered that our husbands also knew each other. Baldev's office was in South Extension and so was Raja's. Raja was a manager at Govan Travels and every day at lunch time the two had juice together and a paan each. I have never met a man so full of life and laughter, and with such excellent culinary skills.

When the price of petrol suddenly went up to three rupees a litre, our husbands refused to drop us to Parliament Street. Madhu and I then joined the chartered bus service that had mushroomed overnight and would go to work together.

If he was around now, Omi-ji, as the owner was called, would make for an excellent stand-up comedian. He had us in splits most of the ride even though I tried to catch up on my poetry reading or watch the beautiful trees of amaltas lining the then clean, wide roads of Delhi.

Madhu and I would meet every day at lunchtime and sit in the RBI garden or the YWCA next to Citibank. In winters, we would eat a bag of peanuts and watch the world go by. There was hardly any traffic on Parliament Street then.

Madhu sang and so she automatically became a part of the family singing sessions.

They lived nearby and it was understood that we would have dinner together as potluck at my house every day.

Raja and Madhu both had tambaku-wala paan, many a day. They both carried their potlis with them wherever they went. They spoke and sang with the paan tucked in their cheeks. It reminded me of Girija Devi-ji and Begum Akhtar who sang for hours with their paans safely lodged in their cheek.

The last programme of Begum Akhtar before she passed away is often shown on Doordarshan. In the audience, one can see Madhu and me as well as the one and only Salma Sultan with her signature rose and dimple.

I opened an account for Neethi Ravindran at Citibank in the early 1970s. That's how we met. She was a very well-known face on television, a very popular newscaster who read the English news for many years.

I met Achla Dhawan during the course of business. She was a manager at Campa Cola. Achla was married to the all-powerful Congress politician R.K. Dhawan and has a daughter, who is now a pilot with Indigo.

Then I have friends who are part of my life's percussion, like the three arms of a triangle that produce the best music and harmony when together.

In European classical music, the triangle has been used since around the middle of the eighteenth century. Its bars are made of steel like my friendships. My friends are like pieces of a jigsaw puzzle. When together, we form a treasure box.

Like Priya Gupta, Rama Gujral and I.

Like Asha Cariappa, Veena Bahadur and I.

Like Madhu Raja, Ratan Laul and I.

Like Tasmima Hossain, Choti (Sakina Miralli) and I.

Our husbands were just as friendly. One had to see them to believe that they were grown men. When they got together, they were like schoolboys.

Priya is a homemaker. She dabbled in a bit of journalism but that was before I met her in early 1969. She had also come to Citibank to open an account. She was wearing a white saree, satin, I think, with lots of bangles, and a gajra round her bun. She had probably attended a function before she walked into the bank. There was a trail of henna in the air when she sat across me.

She would visit often as she was building her house in Friends Colony. When we started talking, we discovered how similar our interests were. We loved Urdu poetry and music. I have attended many soirees in her beautiful house, evenings with the giants of music such as Aziz Warsi, the Dagar Brothers and Munawwar Ali Khan Sahib, son of Bade Ghulam Ali Khan Sahib. We became friends. We would go to mushairas together, eat at Pandara Road often and would follow it up with paan. She would tell the paan-wallah outside the bank, '*Miyan, tumhara paan kha ke paseena nahi aaya tto paan bekar.*' He probably broke out in a cold sweat whenever he spotted her.

The Dagar wives and Munawwar Ali Khan Sahib's wives were Bhabis to us and they treated us to fabulous biryanis, kormas and fish curry.

Priya now lives mostly in Montreal in Canada but I am very close to her younger sister Dhira and keep up with their family through her. Dhira is a beautiful soul whose concern for me is extraordinary—she calls and drops by very often.

Priya's husband Bhushan Kumar Gupta had the Midas touch, turning to gold every one of his ventures. In the travel trade we referred to him as Billy King Gupta because he travelled first class often. They ran the most sophisticated solar energy factory.

Rama worked in export all her life, wore the most beautiful clothes, and was a fabulous cook. Her yakhni gosht was always a sought-after dish in our friends' houses, which she would send by the deghful. Her husband Ravi ran the most famous Gujral Press, a family business, and he was a chess champion.

Asha Cariappa carried a very famous name on her shoulders. She was the daughter-in-law of General Cariappa and was married to Nanda Cariappa. She was a buyer at Cottage Emporium, and we were introduced by my son Vineet, who was two years old then. He mistook her for Didi and ran to hug her when we got off an auto rickshaw. Later, Asha also joined the travel trade and we would meet often. She would drive me to work every day as we lived and worked close by. There are dishes Asha makes which are incomparable: brain curry, gurde kaleji and baigan.

Veena worked with Swiss International Air Lines and was known as the human computer. No one could calculate fares like her. No one can cook sarson-wali fish like her. She loves classical music and comes from the famous Bahadur family in Civil Lines. These are the real Dilli-wallahs.

For years she lived in Defence Colony and would give a lift to Didi and Sushil Bhai who worked at Cottage just across from her office.

Our friendships in Delhi were formed in the 1960s and have endured ever since. Our families too have intertwined.

Ratan came from a well-known family of Khatters from Dera Ismail Khan. She was married to Sudhir Laul, an engineer in CPWD. I met them in Dehradun on one of my long stays with my parents-in-law.

Once when Baldev was visiting, there was a taash party at Krishna Puri's house. Baldev was playing, so was Sudhir. Sudhir had an uncanny resemblance to Dilip Kumar and kept his hair like him with a few locks falling on his forehead. It is here that we met.

I never played but sat around and watched the games. A round of Flash was dealt out. I happened to be sitting behind Sudhir and saw that he had three aces. The only other player left in the game was Baldev who continued betting at every round.

Sudhir kept asking me '*Kyon, Indu-ji, ki kariye?*' My heart was in my mouth, but I dared not look up or at Baldev. A game is a game when it is fair and played with a sportsmanlike spirit.

When Baldev finally asked for a show, his hand had an ace, king and queen. Naturally, Sudhir won. Baldev lost heavily. But I got a great cheer from everyone. A new lifelong friendship was born that evening.

Ratan and I soon became like sisters and her parents treated me such.

Ratan also sang, which brought her ever closer to our family. Each one of us had a vast collection of music.

A bachelor, Chander Sahdev would join the singing sessions many an evening. Every time he was accompanied by a different blonde draped over his arm, much to the delight of all our husbands. He called Madhu, Rani Sahiba. One evening he kept requesting Madhu to sing a song but couldn't remember the words. He could only describe it, his description was: *wo darwaza khula hai khula rahega.* All of us laughed till we realised it was indeed a beautiful song from the film *Purab aur Pashchim.*

Koi jab tumhaara hraday tod de
Tadpata hua jab koi chhod de
Tab tum mere paas ana priye
Mera dar khula hai, khula hi rahega, tumhaare liye

All four couples, sometimes joined by Neelu and Vijay, my colleagues from Citibank who lived nearby, would get into one Ambassador car and go for drives, to have paan or watch a movie.

Those were the most joyful years, with friends like family.

Maya Angelou writes, 'Don't trust people who don't laugh.' We laughed like there was laughing gas around us all the time. We grew together, helped each other grow, learnt from each other, and became mothers, then grandmothers and, in some cases, great grandmothers.

We are friends of sixty years, and sometimes we still get together. Madhu Raja comes to stay—to charge her batteries, she says.

Nostalgia of husbands, children, mothers, films and music all take centre stage and the powers of memory are tested.

'Arrey wo kaun sa gaana tha?'

'Arrey hum sub gaye they yaar ...'

'Golcha Cinema ...'

'Arre tumharey paas uska 78 ka record tha ...'

And I rack my brains and google to save my reputation. Because I am the one famous for having an elephant's memory.

'Yaad aa gaya! Iqbal Bano. *Ulfat ki nayee manzil ko chala.* Lyrics: Qateel. Film: *Qatil.* 1955.' Google Kaur, memory booster.

We miss our third singing partner, Ratan, who lives in Vasant Vihar and cannot join us daily for these brainstorming sessions in the pre-breakfast hours.

And amongst all this bhoojo, gaao, question hour I almost always find a way to my favourite song, sung by Nirmala Arun (actor Govinda's mother) and written by Shakeel Badayuni:

Bana bana ke tamanna mitaai jaati hai,
Tarah tarah se wafa aazamai jaati hai,
Jab un ko meri muhabbat ka aitbaar nahi
To phir nazar se nazar kyo milaai jaati hai,
Hamaare dil kaa pata vo hame nahi dete,
Hamari cheez hamin se chhupai jaati hai,
'Shakeel' duri-e-manzil se naa-ummeed na ho,
Ab aa hii jaatii hai manzil ab aa hii jaatii hai.

Madhu sings it beautifully. So the mornings merge into afternoons and the afternoons into late evenings, remembering days gone by, beautiful melodies and loved ones lost.

Life always moves on, as it is meant to—with joys and sorrows. But the older I grow, the more the Partition haunts me. I am old now. I am a woman who has read so much about the Partition. I have also seen the world, and killings and atrocities. I am sure millions more like me are as haunted. I have nothing against politics or politicians but the decision to split the country was taken by just a few. It was a decision in which women had no voice.

It is one of those decisions that makes you question whether it was taken in the best interests of people or was merely a way to satisfy the egos of a few—one will never know. Why were a handful of minds given the responsibility—and the authority—to decide what happens to millions? Millions of people lost their roots. It was not genocide as the Nazis had wrought on the Jews but it was no less painful for those who were affected.

The loss of home was the loss of identity, of roots, of a way of living, of language, food, culture and traditions. For people like my grandparents, it was also the loss of self. Who they were was wiped out and they struggled throughout the rest of their lives, not able to accept the new selves created by the act of partition.

If even I am unable to say whether I am poor or rich, whether I'm a refugee or an aristocrat—and I was just a child—I can only imagine how they must have felt.

Even the children have noted how the Partition has come to invade my thoughts with age. Vineet once asked me, 'Mom, I notice you now talk about the past more than before. About the Partition, about your losses Why? Why don't you celebrate the present, your well-placed children, grandchildren, and every luxury?'

Suneet, on the other hand, has always heard me out. Many times, he has also asked me questions on his own. Recently, at the Colombo Fashion Week, he met some designers with roots in Pakistan. He asked me to send pictures of the clock tower in Peshawar and our connection with it. Maybe because he had heard even more stories from his Naani. He spent a lot of time with her as a child and even later in life.

All three of my children have been very encouraging about this memoir. When Geetika heard a Sardar-ji read out a poem written by his father about Gujrawala, it moved her immensely. She said, 'Mom, you must call him for your book release. They, too, left behind everything like your family did.'

But let me get back to my thoughts on friendship and bonds beyond family. Later in life, around the year 2000, with much trepidation, I joined the governing body of the Sarvodaya International Trust. The aims and objectives of the Trust were to revive, invigorate and spread the moral ideas and action programmes of Mahatma Gandhi, nationally and internationally. It was something I believed in. It was the need of the hour.

Albert Einstein wrote about Mahatma Gandhi: 'Generations to come, will scarce believe that such a one as this, ever in flesh and blood walked upon this Earth.'

I joined a very august team and have been the chairperson of the Trust for many years now. Each member of the trust is famous and socially and culturally prominent. It astounds me that I could be amongst them with only a Senior Cambridge to my name. They call me their mentor.

It is said in Vedanta that you have to be like a lake and gather knowledge and wisdom. People will come and take it from you. Just as people come and draw water from the lake without the lake publicising itself.

Through all my friends, my karma of learning, humanity and humility has been enhanced manifold. My naman to them.

Dost jab ziwaqar hota hai
Dosti ka mayar hota hai

Ab tasawwur ki suni wadi mein
Roz jashn-e-bahaar hota hai

When the friend is dignified and honourable
Friendship is the hallmark of dignity

Now, in the desolate valley of the imagination
The festival of spring is celebrated everyday

24

Baldev's Illnesses and Travels around the World

BALDEV'S MANY SICKNESSES STARTED EARLY IN THE 1970S.

While I also had my own crosses to bear, my ill health was not in the same league as Baldev's. In 1970, I had fallen down in the bathroom. I suffered from a slipped disc and my back became the bane of my life. I underwent physiotherapy, I wore a belt, I avoided steps, I even gave up driving for long periods of time when the pain was acute.

Baldev, on the other hand, had to put up with much more. I don't glorify his ill health, nor blame Baldev for being unwell so often. Baldev was heroic. Despite falling sick so many times, he travelled extensively to places known and unknown.

Baldev started travelling overseas after he joined Escorts. He travelled to London, Dubai, Dhaka and Damascus but his main destinations were East Europe, Russia and Africa. He would go on twenty-day trips, and sometimes would be gone for up to three months when he was based in Angola.

He went to Khartoum and witnessed a coup there. There, he got shot in the leg when he tried to run away from the hotel.

Indians were rescued and sent to Bahrain. He was operated on and the bullet removed. We had no news of him for six months. My mother-in-law went crazy asking questions, but I had no answers. Eventually, he was brought to India on a stretcher in August 1970.

He visited Bangladesh often, to supply the Madras check cloth for lungis that were popular there.

He went so often that our friends Madhu, Raja, Ratan and Sudhir made up this song for him: '*Papa jaldi aa jaana, lungiyon ke bazaar se chhoti see gudia laana, Papa jaldi aa jaana.*'

From there he brought meningitis and was in the hospital for a month. His screams of pain could be heard all over Holy Family Hospital.

Before that, quite early in our marriage he had jaundice twice. My in-laws would wet his hand with a layer of choona (lime) and the choona would become yellow.

His heart problem began in 1973.

We had gone to Kashmir for a holiday and on our return, Baldev had a minor heart attack.

Then followed many attacks.

So many Januarys were spent at Holy Family Hospital. Outside the ICU. I would wrap the kids in my shawl and we would sit huddled together on the steps facing the chapel, not knowing what the morning was going to bring us.

Once he was there for a month, and I stayed with him. He had had a massive heart attack and we almost lost him. But Baldev bounced back, he had amazing resilience.

I took the voluntary retirement scheme from Citibank in December 1977. A new scheme was floated. There were options to be transferred to the new world that had come up in the Middle East with petro dollars. Dubai, Abu Dhabi, Muscat, Bahrain and Saudi Arabia were all offered as transfers and lots of my colleagues took that route. D.P. Ahuja went to Bahrain, Chris Johnson went to Muscat and Ranjit Chatterji, with whom I spent the last year in the bank assisting him as Trader, went to Saudi Arabia. But it was obvious that I could not go, leaving Baldev and the children behind. The voluntary retirement was a very good offer too with a lump sum plus pension for many years. My good friend Pullomaja Atal and I retired together.

Baldev and I invested the money in a 500-yard plot in Gurgaon. The Swiss Air staff had started a colony, so I invested there, knowing most of them. It was our first big purchase.

Soon thereafter, I started getting job offers. Ten years in Citibank had given me good experience, especially with traveller's cheques. At Citibank, I would beat the travel giants Thomas Cook at sales of traveller's cheques every month. It wasn't long before Thomas Cook approached me. They wanted me to join as the head of the Business Travel Unit, a new concept for corporate travel. I told them that I had absolutely no knowledge of travel, ticketing or sales. They said they would train me.

So, on 1 April 1978, I joined Thomas Cook.

A new world lay before me. I decided to trust the process and dive into it.

When I was at Thomas Cook, Baldev's work took him to the remotest places, places unheard of in those days, like Maputo, Lilongwe and Lusaka. Baldev was with Mohan Exports then.

He supplied army software to the armies of different countries against tenders.

He could look at a beret, a badge, a belt and tell you which country's army used it. He would do third-party exports, have goods manufactured in Sri Lanka and export them to Angola or have the goods manufactured in Seoul and sell them to Algeria. Camouflage fatigue suits, beds, chairs, mugs, mosquito nets, belts, he supplied them all.

Those days fares had to be manually calculated. There were two popular people in the travel industry who were wizards at it, my dearest friend Veena Bahadur in Swiss Air and S. Mathur in Air India.

Mr Mathur would tell me Baldev's ticket was always the most difficult to issue because often he would go to places that had no air connectivity.

Baldev also travelled all over Russia and even to new countries like Azerbaijan, Kazakhstan and Dushanbe. He went to Iraq, Iran and Syria too. I accompanied him often when he we went to Syria.

We would pass through Dubai, a Dubai that is unthinkable today. The airport was a small strip of tarmac with sand all around. The only two buildings that one saw from the aircraft while landing were Jumbo Electronics and Sony. The flight halted for about twenty minutes, and we had to run across the sand to the duty-free shop. It was a small room, just twenty feet wide, with one counter selling things like Cross pens and wallets. After the discovery of oil, this old image of Dubai is almost unimaginable.

I loved Damascus, which felt ancient but alive. The traces of three—maybe five—millennia of people that have lived continuously in the city lend it a weight that is as intangible as it is real. When you are said to be the centre of the Earth and have seen Alexander the Great, the Romans, the Crusaders and the Ottomans, the result is both depth and lightness.

Damascus was always fun. Its ancient buildings and narrow lanes, bustling bazaars and the warmth of its people called to me time and again. I spent hours in the Mariamite Cathedral of Damascus, believed to be the oldest church in the world.

The food was another attraction—the cardamom-scented coffee, the grilled meats, the hummus—some of the best I have ever eaten. Baldev's buyers were very hospitable, and I was invited to meet their families ever so often. We made lifelong friends there. My Syrian friends presented me with beautifully zari-embroidered, kaftan-type long robes. I bought a lot of handcrafted cutlery from there that I still use.

Dhaka, on the other hand, was like home. Two of my best friends, Tasmima and Sakina, lived there, and we experienced the best of their hospitality in beautiful palatial houses, clubs and restaurants.

Tasmima Hossain, or Tiptip, came from a political family. When she got married, her doli went to the house of Bangladesh's founding father, President and Prime Minister Sheikh Mujibur Rahman. Mujib, as he was popularly known, treated her husband

Anwar Hossain Monju like his son. The main Parliament Road is named after Anwar's father Tofazzal Hossain Manik Miah, popularly remembered as Manik Miah.

Baldev had been doing business in Bangladesh from his days at Escorts and was very close to them. Whenever I would visit, which was quite often, Tasmima's mother-in-law would personally cook a vegetarian meal for me despite having about twenty domestic staff in the house. They lived in a palatial home in Dhanmandi.

Our relationship endures even today. Tiptip's four daughters are very close to me and my children. Her sisters and mother visit me and we have travelled together too.

Sakina Miraly came from one of the richest families in Dhaka. They had only about seventeen cars standing in the driveway. Whenever they came to drop me at the airport it looked like a car rally or a VIP convoy. Her family too visited me often, especially after we started a collaboration with them for manufacturing garments to export.

When we visited Dhaka after signing on the dotted line, we found the road to the city peppered with big hoardings of our collaboration. Sakina's wedding to Nasurullah Miraly from Kenya, one of the most prominent Aga Khani families, was like a fairy tale. I listened to Mehdi Hasan sitting together in a room at the wedding in Dhaka. Music was always a constant.

Jo khayal unka aaya to ghazal kahi hai maine
Kahin phool muskuraya to ghazal kahi hai maine

Woh khushi ke ya dukhon ke hon zamanay koyee lekin
Kabhi dil nay ghum chupaya to ghazal kahi hai maine

I thought of him and wrote a ghazal
I saw flowers smile and wrote a ghazal

Whether it was a time of joy or sorrow
Or when the heart hid sadness, I wrote a ghazal

25

The Generous Mathurs

Roopy quit BOAC as she got married. Even as I set up base in Delhi, Brijesh and Roopy moved around the country—Delhi, Kanpur, Bombay and Calcutta—due to Brijesh's postings with Grindlays Bank.

In Bombay she was united with our childhood friend Hiroo who was by then married to Yash Johar and had a little boy, Karan. Karan would later create history in the world of cinema. I made many trips to Mumbai, so did Mummy and Didi. The children grew up as almost one family.

Didi and Sushil Bhai already had a son, Tanuj, who was born a year after their marriage in 1970. In 1975, Tanuj was followed by a daughter, Ruhi, who was known as Poppins by everyone. Didi and Sushil Bhai lived in Defence Colony. His family had reconciled with him and the children were even looked after by Sushil Bhai's sister while they were at work.

In 1975, Roopy was about to have her first child. Just before the delivery, Brijesh was posted out of Delhi and Roopy came to stay with me. On 11 October, her son Siddharth was born.

He was a highly awaited child as Roopy had had two miscarriages earlier. I had prayed to God and made a mannat for a child to be born to Roopy. After Sid's birth, I left for Vaishno Devi shrine the same evening.

Some years later, Brijesh was transferred, as a director on the board of Grindlays Bank, to London. They got a standalone house at Knightsbridge, 1 Monrpellier Road just opposite Harrods. Then they lived for two years at Ennesmore Gardens with Ava Gardner as their neighbour. Eventually they bought their own apartment on De Vere Gardens in Kensington; the vast and beautiful Hyde Park lay across the road.

Roopy would entertain lavishly and served the most fabulous meals in beautiful porcelain, cut-glass dinner and tea service sets. Soon their house became a gathering place for the crème de la crème of the Indian society that visited London. They would go to the races, they would be at the casino every night, and they partied with the richest of the rich.

There was never a single digit number in Roopy's vocabulary when she went shopping, her counting started from twelve. If she bought chiffons, then a dozen was the minimum. If she was at a store and liked something for her kitchen, she would order for me, for Didi, and a few of her friends as well. She was the soul of generosity, as giving as our grandmother.

We went on holidays dozens of times, and my children Geetika, Suneet and Vineet even studied in London. While Suneet shared a flat with Ravi Bajaj, and Vineet only went for short courses, Geetika stayed with Roopy for five years, from 1983 to 1988, while she studied hotel management and computers.

We sisters shared our happiest days with Roopy and Brijesh in London, a far cry from the Kanpur days of hurricane lamps, no money to pay fees, and the odd jobs we did to make money. But we never forgot those days or our grandparents.

Shabnam bhi baharon ka bharam khol rahi hai
Phulon ki tarah aankh se dil tol rahi hai

Karti hai hawa jab sar-e-gulshan tera charcha
Gul kehtey hain hans hans key ye sach bol rahi hai

The dew is breaking the illusion of spring
Like the flowers it is weighing it with its eyes

When the wind talks of you in the garden
The flowers laugh and say she is telling the truth.

26

New Job, New Adventures

THOMAS COOK WAS A NEW CHALLENGE AFTER A VERY SUCCESSFUL tenure at Citibank.

As a travel agent I learnt that I must first establish trust with my clients. It was very easy to sell a ticket, we just had to write it, raise a bill and send it. But a successful sale had to be a circle, where you collected the money after selling ticket. This was where smaller agents failed.

I built a roster of some of the best corporates in India as my clients. Lurgi India, Jagatjit Industries, DCM, Bharat Swatantrata Mills, Airport Authority of India, Khemkha's, HCL, Cimmco International, Escorts, Indian Council for Cultural Relations (ICCR) and the breakaway faction from DCM that later became HCL were amongst my clients.

I have to my credit many firsts at Thomas Cook.

I ticketed the first-ever labour movement from Delhi.

In the late 1970s, large numbers from the Indian workforce started to be sent abroad—to countries like Iran, Israel, the UK, Canada, Australia and New Zealand, from Libya, the UAE and Saudi Arabia—for manual labour, to make buildings, lay roads, drive taxis, to work in the fields, in hospitals, hotels and airports. This was known as the labour movement.

I was in charge of arranging the travel of the first six potato sowers from Patiala to Iran for which I drove down to Patiala with a colleague, Rajan, had lunch with the Maharaja and was absolutely dazzled with his palace and charm.

Later, Sri Lanka, the Philippines, China and Nepal started to send people from their countries too.

I undertook full recruitment for the Marriot Hotel, Dubai. This included arranging hotels for the Marriot officials to interview applicants, getting group visas for the people that were hired, taking care of their health requirements, their travel and, many times, their passports too.

I also helped send about 200 people to Jeddah, in collaboration with Pankaj Khemka who ran a recruiting agency, and hundreds to Tripoli, Libya and Sana in Yemen for the Airports Authority of India.

One of the largest groups we promoted from Thomas Cook did not speak a word of English, but I had never seen such enthusiasm and such high spirit.

~

THE LARGEST GROUP PROMOTED AT THOMAS COOK

Loveleen Sapra

I met Indira Varma in 1979 when I joined Thomas Cook in the Commercial Sales department, which she headed.

She taught me how to interact with various kinds of people and to respond to the queries generated.

She had a vast knowledge of the world as she had travelled extensively; it gives you an edge to preach when you have practiced.

In my memory I still remember that she had executed the ticketing for a group of 117 members belonging to the cloth merchants of Old Delhi; 80 per cent were illiterate. We had to go to a park opposite the Old Delhi railway station for a couple Sundays to explain to them how to make their passports and also the etiquette for travelling abroad. We got seventeen visas per person and every staff member in Thomas Cook helped fill up the forms. It was a mammoth task. After office hours we got children from all the staff families to help too.

One Dhappal Devi, about eighty years old, was the heroine of the group. At the airport on their departure the group was garlanded so much that one could not see their faces. The airport floor was a carpet of marigolds, till the authority had to forcibly remove the guests who had come to see them off.

This was one of the largest groups ever promoted; other reputed travel companies were engaged in group travel not beyond a busload, which was perhaps a maximum of thirty-two people.

Handling this group was a learning experience for me as it taught me patience, tolerance and an appreciation for their ingenuity. When the group returned their clothing had been radically urbanised from a rural Indian style to Western wear.

Mrs Varma accompanied the group till Paris from where our colleague Gopal Khindria was to assist them.

While she was in Paris, at 4 a.m. there was a huge commotion with whistles and fire alarms going off. There was loud knocking at her door. It was the hotel authorities. They wanted her to look out of the window.

Outside was a sight to behold. Our Vayam Vikas Kendra Group was on the road doing yoga and exercises in short pants and topis, blocking all traffic and even police vans. It was utter chaos.

Mrs Varma had to rush out and speak to the group leaders Mr Bhagmal and Mr P.D. Gupta. They stopped and she apologised and explained to the hotel staff till they were pacified.

~

Though the incident has been beautifully narrated by Loveleen Sapra, she forgot to mention one very amusing thing. How this group used to bring money to my office in a cloth bag full of vegetables, which when emptied on my table elicited not only paalak, methi and mooli but bundles of notes as well.

Our managing director, Sunder Gidwani, who was based in Mumbai, used to call me his Woman Friday in Delhi.

I developed the greatest admiration for two giants of the travel industry: Inder Sharma and Kapil Bhatia.

Inder Sharma founded Sita Travels, The Select Hotels and the Select City Mall.

Kapil Bhatia became a general sales agent for multiple airlines and a chain of hotels in collaboration with Accor. They have about forty hotels now named IBIS.

From them I learnt many things that would help me when I later became an entrepreneur.

Their magic was in their humility. Their quality to treat everyone with respect, be it a driver or a peon or a travel agency representative like me.

I made some enduring friendships too: Radhika Ralhan, Serena Mehra, Loveleen Sapra, Supriya Sharma, all of whom I am still in touch with.

There were many perks too. Free travel, FAM or familiarisation trips, the privileges of AD75, which meant that I only had to pay 25 per cent for my own ticket or those for my family. I sent my three children for holidays to London while in school—I could finally afford it.

I also got to travel a lot. Citibank had given me a lot a domestic travel for training and management courses, but Thomas Cook showed me the world.

I took many groups to the East, for example a twenty-one-day trip for Escorts Dealers, to visit all the Yamaha factories, their collaborators in Japan. We travelled extensively in Japan—Tokyo, Nagoya, Kyoto, Kobe, Osaka and more—by train and special tourist buses. Japan was beautiful, their small towns are like miniature gardens, but it is also very expensive. The precision, timing and speed of their trains and the disciplined queues at the stations surprised me.

On an Air India FAM I visited the East again—Bangkok, Hong Kong and Japan—and discovered the Tom Yum soup which is my favourite till date.

On our way back we stopped at Manila, which was then a small fishing village. No roads, no hotels, just shacks as overnight stays and we were rowed over to them. The airport was a small patch of land. There was no line for immigration and no visa was required.

Two of my favorite FAM trips were to Europe. One by Lufthansa to Seeheim, Germany, and the second to the Scandinavian countries at the invitation of the government.

Seeheim was the Lufthansa training school. It was an hour from the Frankfurt airport, and huge. I attended these courses with a group of six or seven other travel agents from India. My first trip was in 1978. I did two courses at Seeheim—basic and advanced—and my second trip was in 1979.

But my first trip still stands out. I knew everybody from various training programmes or meetings. There was easy camaraderie amongst all, even while there was intense rivalry to do well and beat each other at sales. At Seeheim, we forgot about work and became students who had day-long classes and even exams. Just like students after school we had lots of fun.

~

SEEHEIM AND THE INDIAN TRAVEL INDUSTRY

Kumar Baveja

Lufthansa developed a unique concept of training all their staff members—not just management, but every single member from Reservations to Baggage Handling. They then went a step ahead by starting basic trainings even for travel agents.

Due to the paucity of space at Frankfurt airport in the 1960s, Lufthansa started the basic trainings for its employees from the barracks of the airport at Hamburg. Realising quickly that this was not enough for a growing carrier like Lufthansa, they found a place up on the hills of a village called Heppenheim, approximately 40 miles north of Frankfurt airport; by early 1970 they had built a state-of-the-art facility there called Seeheim. This training school was specially designed to undertake all trainings required to run the airline professionally.

This school had around 400 rooms for the students and about fifty classrooms for training. Since the Germans also believed that all work and no play made Jack a dull boy, they built a massive restaurant, six bars, a bowling alley, table tennis rooms, a disco (for use every Tuesday), a sauna, two swimming pools, about ten TV lounges and a lawn tennis court. Free bus service was also provided for airport transfers on arrival and departure.

Initially, when important travel agents were sent to the Seeheim School, they were also subject to written tests, which they had to pass with a minimum of 80 per cent marks and the result reports were sent to the owners of the travel agencies. This practice was later discontinued. Ms Indira Varma was one of the lucky students to have attended two trainings—basic and advanced—during her tenure with Thomas Cook, which was one of the best travels agencies for Lufthansa. Very few travel agency staff were fortunate enough to have attended two or more training courses.

~

Seeheim felt like a city in itself. I had not been exposed to such dining rooms before. At any given time, there were about 200 people eating breakfast or lunch. Dinner was optional, we could eat outside in the town or eat in Seeheim by 8 p.m. We would run down to Frankfurt via a mountain track, go pubbing, and eat Pakistani food. No one in Germany used to, at that time, serve water with food; they served beer. Once we walked into a small Pakistani restaurant and I said in Hindi, '*Hai, ek glass paani mil jaata …*' and from under a counter a bent head replied, '*Lijiye huzoor*' much to our delight. It was a young Pakistani boy from Lahore. We sat talking for a long time. He almost cried when I told him I was from Peshawar.

On the last day of our stay, after the results, we were taken for a cruise on the river Main in Frankfurt. The view of the city's skyline was spectacular, we saw the pubs of Sachsenhausen, the European

Central Bank, jumped off at Gerbermühle and learnt about the poet Goethe.

From Frankfurt I took a one-week holiday and flew to Montreal to see my friend Priya and her husband. I stayed with them for three days and took a train to Toronto and spent time with my Mama-ji, Diljit, and his wife, Gulshan Mami.

They lived in a luxurious house with a private lift opening to their bedroom. Diljit Juneja was the eldest member of my family and the president of forty insurance companies.

I also visited my nephew Karan and his wife Vijay in Toronto. Karan was the elder of my sister-in-law Vimla Behen-ji's children; his younger brother was Arun, who had studied hotel management in Lucknow and worked with various hotels as a chef, and whom I helped send to Jeddah when we were recruiting for hotels at Thomas Cook.

My gift for everyone was the LP record of *Unforgettable*, the first album Jagjit Singh and Chitra Singh brought out. It was a landmark in the timeline of the ghazal and remains one till date.

On my way home I visited my sister-in-law Urmill Behen-ji and Prakash Bhaisahib in Brussels; Prakash Bhaisahib was posted at the High Commission there and they drove me to the Hague.

Two years later, in 1980, I went to Denmark, Sweden and Norway. Six travel agents had been invited by the Scandinavian Tourism ministry; I was the only woman. I knew the others from travel meets and we were friends, but being the only woman gave me a great advantage. I was always seated next to the tourism officials and had great conversations.

We travelled to Copenhagen, Stockholm and Oslo. In Copenhagen we went to see the statue of the Little Mermaid and roamed the pubs in the daylight till 9 p.m. We saw Tivoli Gardens and its many palaces.

We had the most delightful day trips by river, including one to Swedish tennis legend Björn Borg's house.

Norway's landscape was another highlight, with the fjords,

mountains and the Northern Lights, but I also learnt for the first time about their philosophy of capitalism with a conscience.

Nuggets of trivia I learnt during that time stayed with me. The world's longest road tunnel is in Norway. Denmark is made of over 400 islands. Copenhagen is the world's happiest city. Norway is home to Hell, a small village near Trondheim's international airport. Hell even has its own train station. Sweden is the third largest exporter of music to the world—there's a lot more than ABBA. Norway introduced salmon sushi to Japan. Carlsberg beer was founded just outside of Copenhagen. Norway is actually called Norge or Noreg by its residents.

I learnt new ways to eat fish and my children tease me till date reminding me of the fish stories I told them on my return.

At one of the official State lunches, I was seated next to the president of Tourism. I was nervous looking at the set table. There were seven knives and seven forks on both sides of the plate and a few assorted spoons in front. I thought it best not to pretend, so I whispered into my host's ear that I would follow his way of handling the cutlery as I did not know how to handle so many. He was totally charmed by my honesty and throughout the meal we exchanged secret smiles while he indicated which course to handle with which cutlery without anyone catching on.

Iss tarha roz-o-shab guzarey they
Gham ke toofan humse haray they
Khwab mein gulshanon ke manzar they
Khushnuma har taraf nazaray they

And so the days and nights passed
And we defeated the storms of sorrow
In my dreams were visions of gardens
And the sights all around were pleasant

27

London and a New Lease of Life

TIME PASSED, BRIGHT, SHINING, LIGHT.

As I turned forty, the ghazal also grew with me. I learnt Urdu again. Dr Ajmal Ajmali from Hamdard University would come to teach me. He was a very learned professor. Baldev would pick him up on alternate days and bring him home. Lessons were divided into two: Urdu learning and poetry analysis.

He would give me themes on which to write, and then he would help me correct the thought or find the best words for it.

To understand the ghazal more, Dr Ajmali suggested I also learn how to sing it, as every poem has a metre. I found another teacher, M.A. Qadri. He was a radio artist and a harmonium and sarangi nawaz. I spent two years learning bhajans and geet. He would teach me the lay or the rhythm of words put together.

But this rhythm was shattered in January 1983 when Baldev had a massive heart attack. He had had two minor attacks already, the first in 1974, another a few years later. He spent a month in the Holy Family Hospital recovering; it was a miracle that he was saved. Even after he was discharged, he was short of breath most of the time, more so after a meal. He was prescribed blood thinners. Additionally, after eating he had to keep Sorbitrate under his tongue. He had to sit awake all night as he could not breathe if he lay down. He could barely walk a few steps and not climb any stairs.

The heart specialist as well as Dr B.B. Mathur told us that his only hope was to have bypass surgery. In 2023, heart surgery is still serious but safe, common and mostly affordable. In 1983, a bypass surgery was unheard of. It had only been fifteen years since the surgery was introduced in America, and it was not yet available in India.

Roopy and Brijesh checked in the UK and found that it was being done there. We took Baldev to the Harley Clinic in London.

The surgery cost an arm and a leg. It took us six months to arrange for the money: we sold a plot of land we owned, borrowed money from friends, got permission from the RBI, and transferred money to the Harley Clinic. The date of the surgery was set, and is branded in my memory: 6 August 1983.

Dr Ronald Ross was our surgeon at Harley Clinic. A kind, soft-spoken doctor with amazing patience who answered all our questions and reassured us.

Baldev was admitted the day before the surgery. I stayed the night with him. Neither of us got much sleep.

I was so nervous the next day that, despite being a brave Pathani, I fainted!

The surgery had gone on for four hours and still there was no sign of it ending. I was waiting with the family in a lounge designated for visitors. Only one attendant was allowed, but we were Indian and there is no concept of one when it comes to family. Sushil Bhai had come from Delhi, Brijesh and Roopy were there, and so were Suneet and Geetika.

Suddenly my name was called out over the loudspeakers.

'Oh my God,' I thought, 'Baldev is gone.'

I walked in a daze towards the telephone booth, Roopy just held my arm and pushed me in. I picked up the phone and heard my name ... The next thing I remember is two nurses trying to revive me on the carpeted floor. Cold water trickled down my neck.

The concerned faces of Roopy, Suneet, Geetu, Brijesh and Sushil Bhai looked down at me.

The phone call was from my friend Priya Gupta, she had called to check if the surgery was over, Roopy quickly informed me.

She forestalled my question. 'It's not over yet.'

In the end, Baldev was in the operation theatre for eight hours. And I was not prepared for what I saw when they took me in to see him after the surgery. He was hanging upside down mid-air from the machines with his tongue pasted on his cheek.

Baldev was in the Harley Clinic for ten days, first in the ICU and later in a special cardiac care room. He had had four blockages and that too near the aorta. The surgeons had taken a vein from his leg and made several bypasses or new channels for the blood to flow.

The doctors told him his heart was absolutely new and if he looked after himself, he could have another ten years.

It was hard to believe them given the state Baldev was in. I don't think I slept peacefully for even one single night during that time. I would wake up several times to see if he was breathing. His snoring was the most assuring sound then, it meant he was alive. Strange are the trappings of fear. His snoring used to bother me so much and now it was what I wanted to hear.

Even after he was discharged from the clinic, he had to go there for fortnightly check-ups. His diet had to be controlled, he had to start walking again and follow his exercise schedule.

We ended up staying with Roopy for three months.

I pushed on. I had got through the stress of preparing for the surgery and now it was a matter of post-operative care. Baldev was the patient but there and some days I wanted to curl up in a room all by myself. But I carried on, leaning on Roopy, Brijesh, Suneet and Geetu when possible.

In this time, I received a phone call. It was my friend and guru Zehra Nigah who had come for her annual visit to London. More than me, Roopy was overjoyed to have her there and used her as an excuse to push me out of the house so I could get some fresh air and time away from my convalescent duties. Zehra-ji would drag me away to Hyde Park for walks and sometimes to her house, where we would talk of many things, cabbages and kings included.

Often Zehra-ji would accompany me home to borrow or return video tapes of Hindi films and Pakistani plays from Roopy.

Her good friend, the famous poet Faiz Ahmad Faiz was also getting treatment at nearby Cromwell Hospital and often Zehra-ji would bring Faiz Sahib along to sit with Baldev. One evening, I invited Faiz Sahib, Zehra-ji and her husband, Majid Ali Sahib, who was advisor to the king of Abu Dhabi, for dinner at Roopy's. By chance, Koakub Bhai was also in London for a two-day stay and could come over. It became a beautiful evening, a Shaam-e-Ghazal in London.

Brijesh entertained everybody by singing Faiz Sahib's *Mujhse pehle si mohabbat.*

Little did we know then that Faiz Sahib would be no more in a year's time.

One night, Brijesh and Roopy came to pick me up after dinner at Zehra-ji's house. Farida Khanum, Iftikar Arif who looked after the Urdu Markaz in Piccadilly, and Faiz Sahib were there for dinner. Brijesh could not let such an opportunity slip by even though Roopy was waiting in the car downstairs.

'My wife is going to be very upset with me, but I must request you to sing a few lines of *Aaj jaane ki zidd na karo,*' Brijesh said to Farida-ji.

Farida-ji was charmed and complied.

The doctors there had given Baldev's heart a new lease of life. But old habits are hard to give up. Baldev went back to smoking, drinking and tedious travel. And in a few years his health began to deteriorate again.

Hum ne to wafao'n ke deep yu'n jalai hai'n
Pattharon ki basti mein aaine sajai hai'n

Kah do apni khushio'n se door hi rahe hum se
Lab huey bahut zakhmi jab bhi muskurai hain

We have lit the lamps of loyalty in such a way
And adorned mirrors in the valley of stones

Tell your joys to stay away from me
My lips have been wounded whenever I have smiled

28

Our Mother Fades Away

LESS THAN A YEAR LATER, MY SISTERS AND I WERE DEALT AN unbearable blow.

It was 13 April 1984. Baisakhi.

Didi, as she had done every year since her marriage, had come with jalebs, a large jalebi which is part of traditional Pishori Sikh celebrations. It was especially good to see her since all three of my children were no longer at home and festivals had lost some of their shine in their absence. Now there was only Mata-ji, Baldev, Mummy and I.

Vineet had joined Grindlays Bank (now Standard Chartered) and he was posted in Mumbai. By his late teens, he had been certain that he wanted to be a banker, and had enough examples since we were a house full of them. I had worked in Citibank, Brijesh was with Grindlays Bank, my brother-in-law Bunty, Baldev's younger brother, was with Bank of Baroda. He had also met many dynamic bankers through Roopy and Brijesh, including Mehr Mehta, our very dear and brilliant friend, and Ashok Hoon who later would be Vineet's first boss.

Suneet was studying fashion design in London. He had made up his mind to go abroad after graduation. We could not afford Fashion Institute of Technology, New York, so he went to the American School of Fashion in London. Even that was an enormous amount of money for us and we had long discussions about it. Finally, we sold the plot that I bought from the money I had received from Citibank.

The extended family had already had a designer—Rohit Khosla, my sister-in-law Usha and Kanwal Khosla's son. Considered pivotal to the establishment of the fashion design industry in India, Rohit had already won fame and recognition and so a career in fashion designing was not entirely a new concept to our family, especially to Baldev who was so immersed in the arts himself.

But it was not the same for people outside the family. At that time, the only acceptable courses of work were medicine and engineering. At the most, you could do management, join a bank or the IAS or IFS.

When it was time to go to London, we had to take permission from the RBI to send Suneet for further studies, to remit the fee and his boarding and lodging. We had an appointment with a deputy controller, Mr Khan.

We had all our papers in order and put them before Mr Khan. Suneet did all the explaining.

'You are spending your parents' hard-earned money to go become a tailor?' he said, shocking Suneet.

But he granted the permit and we thanked him profusely. Suneet was to return in 1988. This Baisakhi he was preparing for his final graduation exams.

Geetu was in London too, where she was pursuing a course in hotel management and computers, and staying with Roopy and Brijesh.

That Baisakhi, 13 April, was also Mummy's wedding anniversary. We mentally marked the day, though we had never celebrated it.

Mummy was unusually restless.

A little while later, she hesitantly told us that she was passing blood in her urine and had been doing so for a few days. She had hoped that it would get better on its own but it seemed to be getting worse.

Didi and I looked at each other. 'Dr Mathur,' we said in unison.

Dr Mathur was not only Baldev's doctor but our family's guardian angel. He treated Mummy like his own mother and Mummy, who had suffered years of UTI, always looked forward to her check-ups with him as it would lead to much banter and some light-hearted gossip.

Dr B.B. Mathur sounded worried. 'Rush her to the hospital. Something sounds very wrong.'

Tests were carried out and she was admitted and put on a catheter. Didi and I were called to Dr Mathur's office.

'She has severe infection and is hemorrhaging internally,' he explained.

Didi and I waited for him to prescribe the treatment. Random thoughts of dealing with another surgery had barely passed through my mind when Dr Mathur spoke again.

'I think you should tell Roopy and Brijesh to come see her,' he continued.

For a moment, I could not grasp what he had said. I looked at Didi. She was already protesting. 'There must be some treatment we can try!'

Dr Mathur shook his head. 'It could be stomach cancer. That would require a major operation and we can't be sure that it will help. It's too late. The way things are, your mother does not have much time left. A week at the most.'

I shook my head. This couldn't be right.

He explained that Mummy would live till she was able to pass urine, even if it was drop by drop. She already had a catheter in place. The moment that stopped she would go into a coma and the end would be near.

The most difficult thing in my life was to go back to Mummy. Her eyes were closed, and I was intensely grateful, as mine were full of tears. I looked at her beautiful face and was overwhelmed by the futility of her life. She had had the world at her feet in Peshawar—rich, beautiful, married to a law student with great prospects, and then she had withered on the vine, a single mother, living in difficult circumstances in Kanpur, and then dependent on her daughters and their husbands for much of her life. The regrets flooded my mind and my eyes. I turned away.

Didi came in later, her eyes and nose red.

Baldev and Sushil Bhai informed the family.

Vineet came down as soon as he could for a day's visit.

All of Mummy's cousins in Delhi from Papa's side came: Amrik Mama-ji, Anup Mami, Raj Maasi, Mummi Maasi, Bachiter Mama, Billi Mama. Even Amrik Mama-ji's sons, the film producers Toni and Tito flew in from Mumbai. She saw them and smiled. Gave her blessings to Toni and Tito. Minnie Maasi, our kindest family member, Mummy's first cousin from Naani's side, came down from Jalandhar to be with us.

Roopy booked her ticket immediately and arrived soon. She came to the hospital straight from the airport. 'I've got your favourite candy, Mummy.' She tried to feed Mummy the chocolate. Mummy opened her eyes and looked at her and tried to smile. Eating was out of the question.

As if it was too much effort, she closed her eyes. We just sat there helpless, huddled together on the sofa in the Holy Family Hospital. We watched her fade slowly over the next ten days. It was torturous for the three of us. In the beginning we tried to speak, to exchange news about each other and our families, in order to maintain some feeling of normalcy, but our voices kept cracking. Maybe Mummy could hear, but she had stopped responding.

Some moments bring home the absolute ruthlessness of life. The death of a parent surely must rank as one of life's biggest tragedies and yet, life continued. The sun did its twelve-hour stint and night fell, and yet morning came again. We ate, we slept, we brushed our teeth, we worried about our children, we made conversation with friends and family, we were even pleased to see them. And all through time Mummy's life was ebbing away, painfully. How could these two realities play out alongside each other?

Morning came again, cruelly bright. It was 25 April, almost two weeks since Mummy had been admitted. Early in the day, Dr Mathur told us it was a matter of a few hours.

Mummy passed away in a coma with Baldev and Sushil Bhai reciting the Gayatri Mantra near her bed.

Suneet's cries of 'Nani! Nani!' echoed through the corridor of the hospital.

Didi, Roopy and I were distraught.

My Mamas and Minnie Maasi took over. Minnie Maasi called my father to tell him about Mummy's death and asked if he would like to see her.

He said no.

They dressed her as a suhagan with bindi, lipstick and sindoor in her maang with a pink dupatta on her head.

Amrik Mama-ji called the best ragis from Patiala, and we did her Chautha at the Pahari Wala Gurudwara in Greater Kailash.

Now the fight to survive and hold up each other was left to the three of us.

Ye shafaq shafaq udaasi sar-e-shaam chha chuki hai
Dil-e-ghum zada ki hasrat bhi lahu baha chuki hai

Wo jo rait per bana tha ik umeed-e-dil ka manzar
Usey aaj dasht-e-jaan mein ye hawa udaa chuki hai

The sadness of the twilight has spread across the evening's cheeks
The yearning of the sorrowful heart too has spilt blood

The scene that was created on sand by the yearning heart
Today it has been swept away by the breeze into the desert of life

29

Taking India to the World

Life limped back to some semblance of normalcy. Almost nine months later I was offered a job with the Ministry of External Affairs through the Indian Council for Cultural Relations (ICCR) as Honorary Director, Travel for Festival of India. ICCR had been one of my major accounts at Thomas Cook.

It was a prestigious offer, and I did not have to think too much about accepting it. I joined them in April 1985.

It was to be a short but intense journey. I was there for eighteen months before the long hours became too much for my back to handle.

But those eighteen months were so enriching and opened up so many different vistas of art and music that to this day I cannot comprehend all that I learnt. It was as if I had entered one of the most beautiful, award-winning garden shows. The hues and colours and various strains of music, dance, and the cultural heritage of our country lay before me to assimilate.

It all began when I met the stalwart Pupul Jayakar, commonly referred to as the czarina of Indian culture. She was instrumental in promoting Indian arts, culture and heritage by organising Festival of India abroad.

It led not only to the recognition of Indian culture and heritage abroad and the revival of several dying art forms but also the spread of cultural knowledge of India within India itself.

She headed the Indian Advisory Committee for the Festivals, consisting of distinguished personalities from the intellectual and artistic worlds.

The Government of India organised these festivals in the USA and France during 1985-86. The year-long festival in France was inaugurated by the then prime minister of India, Rajiv Gandhi, and the president of France, François Mitterrand, on a pleasant, sunny day on 7 June 1985. A week later, on 13 June 1985, Prime Minister Rajiv Gandhi and American Vice President George Bush inaugurated the longer eighteen-month Festival of India in Washington, DC.

This soon became the starting point of many an artist's journey, a starting point which transformed their lives and brought for many of them high acclaim.

Pascal Alan Nazareth and Mr S.K. Mishra were the able administrators who implemented the vision of Festival of India and played a major role in their success. P.A. Nazareth, director general, ICCR and S.K. Mishra, director general, Festival of India, asked me to head the travel and logistics cell of the Festival of India.

Working at ICCR was like whirlwind. We were constantly in touch with Chérif Khaznadar of the French team and Patrice Fusillo on the US team as well as the team of Gautam Mukhopadhaya and Harsh Vardhan Shringla at the High Commission of India in Paris. Shringla would later become the 33rd Foreign Secretary of India.

We collaborated with Krishna Menon, the technical director for the mela, and Ahmedabad-based designer Dashrath Patel, along with Sita Murari.

Holding the inaugural event of the Festival of India in France was an incredible idea. It would be a mela, a mela held at the Jardin du Trocadero, under the Eiffel Tower. An esplanade of one-and-a-half kilometres was transformed into an extravaganza, with twelve massive gateways—colourful triumphal arches—made of Indian textiles, pith and bamboo, several stages for the performing artists, and innumerable food and handicraft stalls. The Eiffel Tower itself was draped with two 100-metre-large flags of India and France. The charismatic Rajiv Gandhi kicked off the festival by presenting the French president with a baby elephant, brought all the way from India. This is where Munna the bear also danced.

This concept would later become a template for numerous events being showcased in India and abroad.

The arrangements for the 200-odd artists participating in the mela were all made from the one room on the ground floor in ICCR. For many of them the Festival of India signified many firsts: the first time out of their villages, their first time in Delhi, on a plane and in a foreign country!

We were completely caught up in their excitement.

The beginning of their journey with Festival of India started at a nondescript hall on the ground floor of ICCR. This was the Festival of India cell I was heading. They were briefed about the country they would be visiting, and the itinerary, travel plans and performance schedules. There were several apprehensions which we undertook to assuage with advice and pre-departure briefings.

The nondescript room was more often than not in a mayhem of hectic work, with colour-coded lists, plans and colourful labels for all the equipment and teams.

It was all about colour. Even the lists of performing groups, schedules, name tags and baggage tags were colour coded and tied with colourful ribbons. It felt like the festival had begun right there in my office itself.

It's a wonder that it turned into a comprehensible organised process filled with anticipation and excitement.

The festivals were far more than a showcase of folk and tribal dances. It was a year-long experience of meeting accomplished and gifted people, most of whom became masters in their respective fields of work, making waves in the cultural, artistic and literary worlds, not only in India but renowned worldwide.

I was introduced to forms of performing arts seldom heard of outside their villages or districts, from folk artists from the Langa and Manganiyar communities, the Chhau group from the east, to

Kutiyattam, a Sanskrit theatre form from Kerala, which ultimately was recognised by UNESCO as a masterpiece of oral and intangible heritage of humanity, and the martial arts of Kalaripayattu and Thang-ta from Manipur. My world was a symphony of sounds, languages and dialects.

I met Bansi Kaul and his theatre group and Teejan Bai, then an unknown solo artist of Pandavani, a single performer of Mahabharata. She told me how she had been married at the age of twelve and about her life in general. She is now a well-known name and a Padma Bhushan and Padma Vibhushan awardee.

I arranged for several young and upcoming dancers to travel, from the beautiful, doe-eyed Malavika Sarukkai—who received rave reviews in the *New York Times* for her beautiful performance—to the young and talented Aditi Mangaldas, the beautiful niece of Pupul Jayakar, and Saswati Sen who performed along with Birju Maharaj's group from the Kathak Kendra in Delhi.

I also sent the mother-daughter duo of Mrinalini Sarabhai and Mallika Sarabhai to France.

It was humbling to meet the many accomplished classical musicians who were part of the festival: shehnai maestro Ustad Bismillah Khan, Indian classical vocalist Pandit Kumar Gandharva and dhrupad legend Rahim Fahimuddin Dagar.

The list is endless.

Romila Thapar, the renowned historian of ancient India, met us in the office before going for a seminar as did some scientists participating in the Science exhibition at the Museum of Science & Industry, Chicago and thereafter travelling to other cities in USA.

Richard Kurin was the mela programme coordinator for USA and Rajeev Sethi was the programme adviser from the Indian side. Sethi was also instrumental in conceptualising and organising the Golden Eye Exhibition, a collaboration of international designers and traditional Indian crafts and Indian craftspeople.

The Festival of India left me breathless. It was an explosion of learning and awareness. How little do we know about our own country, what a wealth of things it has to offer, even if you were to try and listen to all the music or the languages the country holds, we might never finish them all. India is multiplicity, and it is this multiplicity that has attracted the world to come and learn from it. This is why there is no corner where you will not find Indian music or dance and teachers to teach it. I thank God every day for it.

Kitni noorani banaee hai mere malik ne
Din mein suraj ki chamak shab mein hilali duniya

Khud se mujhko mila hukm-e-safar ye kehkar
Arz pe jao sanwaro'n ye niraali duniya

My master has created such resplendence
In the day the sun's brilliance, at night a luminous new moon world

The order to travel came to me from heaven, saying
Go to the earth, adorn and refashion this peerless world

30

Vineet's Wedding

IN THE MIDDLE OF THE MAYHEM THAT WAS THE FESTIVAL OF INDIA, Vineet's marriage was fixed. He was twenty-five, working with Grindlays Bank. Tinu, his wife-to-be, was born in Rhodesia (now Zimbabwe), schooled in India, China, Pakistan and Switzerland but mostly in Stockholm. Her parents were a wonderful Sikh family, very religious and from the Foreign Service.

Vineet had met Tinu in college. He had studied in Shri Ram College of Commerce and Tinu in Miranda House and must have met through their friends. Tinu's family also lived in Greater Kailash. They had dated for a few months before Vineet had got a job at Grindlays Bank in Mumbai and had gone away for training. When they met again a few months later, they decided to get married. We had absolutely no objection.

The wedding was set for December. Family members from both sides arrived in Delhi for the joyous occasion.

One week before the wedding, we started singing. This continued day and night, this included Tinu, my daughter-in-law to be, her parents, her brother Arun and his fiancé Amrit.

Almost three generations of every family unit participated. My three beloved sisters-in-law and their husbands, Vimla Behen-ji and Baijnath Bhaisahib, Urmill Behen-ji and Prakash Bhaisahib, Sunita and Virender Bhaisahib to their children and even grandchildren. My brother-in-law and his wife, Bunty and Poonam, and their daughters Meghna and Shibani were all a part of it.

The dancing and singing was led by Minnie Maasi, a trait passed on to her three daughters, Raveen, Saveen and Meenu. No family function is complete without them. Lilly and Bublee danced at my wedding and now Meenu and Bublee were dancing at Vineet's wedding.

One can write reams about Minnie Maasi. She was Badi Mummy's sister's daughter. A classic beauty. Didi was her little lamb. She married Gurdeep Jija-ji, a good-looking Sikh who owned many cinema halls in Punjab, Srinagar, Karnal and other places. He financed films and was very friendly with the filmy crowd. He even did a friendly cameo in Raj Kapoor's *Around the World in 80 Days* in 1967.

Both husband and wife supported many families. They placed her brothers in jobs, had an open house in Jalandhar, and looked after my sisters and me right from my marriage onwards.

Just about everyone sang. There was nonstop dancing. Suneet's glamorous friends added colour. Madan Bala Sindhu-ji sang Reshma to pin drop silence. My glamorous, always beautifully dressed Minnie Maasi, who had been taking care of us three sisters after our mother passed away, sang all the Punjabi wedding songs and made every member dance.

We sang so much that on the day of the puja and marriage no one could even speak. We were hoarse from all the singing.

In all the mayhem, our Irish Setter Bonzo went missing on the day of Vineet's wedding. We called for him and searched for him, but he was not found anywhere. We made a police report and gave them a picture of Bonzo lolling on the sofa.

Then we got busy with the wedding. It was the most joyous of affairs.

And a week later Bonzo strolled in with a policeman in tow. He had been recovered from poachers who were breeders and had stolen Bonzo for mating their bitches. So much for being a good breed.

Pyaar ki sari misalon pay tera naam likhun
Ji mein aata aai ke palkon pay tera naam likhun

Jab khayal aata hai jaltey hain umeedon ke chirag
Kaash main sarey chiraghon pay tera naam likhun

I will write your name on every example that is given of love
I wish I could inscribe your name on my eyelashes

When I think of you the lamps of longings are lit
If only I could write your name on those lamps

31

Becoming an Entrepreneur and Being Decorated

FESTIVAL OF INDIA MAY HAVE BEEN PROFESSIONALLY CHALLENGING, culturally enriching and personally satisfying but physically it was very taxing. The long hours of strenuous work affected my back and led to a debilitating attack.

I underwent traction, learnt how to sit and walk again. It was a very painful period. I was in bed for over six months. Taking the stairs was banned, long journeys by car too.

My term at Festival of India finished and I was a free bird after many years, but my seniors in the industry would not let go of me. They insisted I start something from home, something related to travel. They suggested a visa service as it was the need of the hour.

Gone were the days when families travelled to their grandparents' homes for their yearly holidays; now attitudes were changing and so were latitudes. Incomes were rising, both partners worked and saved for a holiday. People had started to travel for nightlife, for cruises, for sports, food tasting, adventure, and more. New destinations were emerging: Thailand, Singapore, Malaysia, Japan, East Europe, and the newly opened Russia.

In the late 1980s, approximately 7,000 passports came to Delhi for visas every month. There were hardly any diplomatic missions elsewhere in India. There were only honorary consulates in the metros that did not issue visas. So, anybody applying for a visa either had to courier their passports to the embassies, had to come themselves, or send their passports through relatives. The visas then had to be processed and sent back. The safety of these passports was important.

So, I became an entrepreneur in 1987. I called it International Visa Service.

I hired just two people at first. Eric John, whose mother worked in the Holy Family Hospital, and Eric's friend Lance Miranda.

I was the first ever visa service provider in India, advising travel agents on documentation. I went to every embassy and gathered complete information. I stocked visa forms. I joined hands with Blue Dart and sent forms and passports through them. It became a relationship that would last over thirty-five years, turning from using them for work to using them for personal items and urgent documents.

Most embassies knew me, either from banking with Citibank or from working together for the Festival of India where we had handled thousands of passports and visas.

The first ever passport we processed was from a travel agency in Chennai, Vayu Yatra. Soon we were representing agencies in Cochin, Bangalore, Bombay, Patna, Trichy, Calcutta and Hyderabad.

The best part was that I was working from home.

I converted my large living room into a beautiful and comfortable workplace. If I was tired, I would get up and rest a bit.

We even started a newsletter and culminated in a publication called *Source*, which ran into ten editions.

The industry hailed *Source* as its travel Bible. It won every possible award that is considered prestigious amongst the travel fraternity in India.

In 1990, we were selected as 'Role Models' amongst 2,000 travel agents at the Mosaic Conference in Barcelona.

With the advent of the Central Reservation Systems (CRS), which came to India in 1994, our publication was programmed as an electronic visa package 'Source' software that was distributed by Amadeus and Galileo.

Our data was beamed from Nice in France for Amadeus and from Swindon, UK, for Galileo.

It was designed as a one-stop shop for all your visa worries. All you had to do was log on to the website to gather all relevant information about your travel, from car rentals to hotels, insurance and airlines.

Most importantly, you could download visa forms for every country (IVS was the only software from where every embassy accepted the visa forms; I had letters from every one of them that confirmed their acceptance), get help in submission of forms, and track your applications.

Soon, we added an outsourcing unit as well, the IVS Visa Application Centre. The embassies of Spain and Greece outsourced their visa to us.

We opened a beautiful office at Mathura Road with the help of Inni Bawaji. We are one of the oldest members of TAAI, TAFI, IATA/UFTA.

The year 2012 was a golden year for me.

I was decorated on behalf of the King of Spain by their embassy in New Delhi with the Cross of the Order of Isabel La Católica, the highest civilian honour in Spain. This was in recognition of the work my team and I did when they outsourced their visa process to IVS Visa Application Centre. Along with me, they also decorated Ankush Sharma, the head of my team and manager.

The ceremony was awesome. About thirty of us from the travel trade, our family and friends were invited by the Ambassador. At the Investiture Ceremony, a citation, signed by the King of Spain, was read, and a medal was pinned to my grey and green silk saree. The Ambassador spoke, I spoke, and then the champagne flowed.

This is a very long story of forty-three years, which ended in 2020 because of the pandemic when no staff could come to work, and travel came to a standstill. My company is still alive, but I have sold my software to InterGlobe Technology Quotient, a strategic business unit of InterGlobe Enterprises.

IVS Global and IVA World Visa Guide exist till date. IVSource.com is a household name.

My partners from Mumbai have taken it to the world and IVS has footprints in eighteen countries. I am not an active part of it anymore.

I wish it success forever.

It is a very proud feeling that one woman working from home started a totally new vertical for our country.

India now has a ministry involved and each year tenders are invited from bidders to start an outsourcing unit in other countries. There are over fifty Indian Visa Outsourcing Units across the world and more are being added every year. It has become a multibillion rupee business.

Zikr aisa sar-e-anjuman keejeye
Ek chaman ko mukammal chaman keejeye

Mushkilei'n saari asan ho jaingi
Bass zaroori had dil mein lagan keejeye

Talk in such a way in that assembly of assemblies
Turn this garden into a garden complete in every way

All the obstacles shall become surmountable
All you need is perseverance in your heart

32

Life, a Story of Losses and Gains

PARTING. SUCH AN INNOCUOUS WORD TO HIDE SUCH A TROVE OF emotions. Pain, love, and maybe even a bittersweet happiness, the kind you feel at the weddings of your children.

Partings are not just a physical cleaving of loved ones, they can be mental too, like the pain of letting go ideas and thoughts that one is attached to.

The pain of parting is often considered a measure of love. And the depths of my love were tested in 1989.

Suneet had returned from London where he had interned at Yves Saint Laurent and Nicole Farhi at French Connection and was already making a name for himself in fashion, an industry India was still getting used to. He had had a small fashion show and was designing clothes under the label Carma. He had set up a studio in Hauz Khas Village.

One day, he took me aside; he had something important to tell me. It took me some time to comprehend what he was trying to tell me about his sexual preferences. Initially, it was hard for me to understand, but with time I did. I also made the effort to educate myself, so I could support him.

Baldev was a very erudite man and knew it without even being told. Baldev and I never discussed this topic, but it was very clear and a silent understanding became apparent by our love and constant support.

Suneet is our beloved son, and we will always stand by him. His private life is private, and no one has the right to interfere.

Geetika had spent the past few years working with the Taj Palace. In 1989, Geetika's marriage too was fixed. She married Kavi Seth in October.

Kavi is the son of Sushma and Dhruv Seth. We knew Sushma-ji only from the big screen and the small screen as one of the most famous and loved stage and cinema artists.

Geetika returned from London in 1987. The next year, on a visit to Vineet and Tinu in Calcutta, she met Kavi, who was also a friend of Suneet's. They started to write to each other, and fell in love.

Kavi-ji was a tremendous sportsman, playing every sport known to man, from squash to football, both within and outside the country. A Liverpool fan since his teens, he grew up listening to their games on the radio before the television became commonplace.

After marriage, everybody was taught and often sang the Liverpool anthem *You Will Never Walk Alone*. Their daughters say their earliest memories are of watching games from his lap; he would later take them to Anfield—the mecca of Liverpool fans—to watch the games. In 2020, their devotion led them to be the only family selected from India to be a part of Liverpool history in the official documentary *The End of the Storm*, which tells the story of the Reds' first-ever Premier League triumph in 2019-20. It was directed by Emmy-nominated James Erskine.

From the beginning, my son-in-law and I shared a beautiful equation, full of respect. I always called him Kavi-ji and never Kavi. We discuss markets and shares, children and family. Suneet calls him Setha, since they have been friends for a long time, Vineet calls him Kaubi-da taking on the Bengali way of addressing others.

If Vineet's wedding was a weeklong riot, Geetika's had elegance and charm, all planned by Sushma-ji. The Sangeet was like a film set, artifacts were strewn all over the massive garden. There were ornamented doors with beautiful flower arrangements, including a flower strewn jhoola for Geetika and Kavi-ji to sit on.

All week we were served food from Moti Mahal. Pishori food brought to India and made famous by Kundan Lal Gujral. It was the heyday of Moti Mahal and their signature tandoori chicken and chicken butter masala. Our guests were appreciative, but for me it was a bittersweet reminder of home.

~

MOTI MAHAL: THE ORIGIN STORY

Dr Ali Jan on the Pishoris

Kundan Lal Gujral, who was working the tandoor ovens in a sweet shop in Peshawar (in what is today Pakistan), eventually bought the place from his ailing boss, renaming it Moti Mahal.

A Hindu, Gujral closed his Peshawar restaurant and relocated to Delhi during Partition. It was a journey that millions of others made, in one direction or the other, depending on one's religion, sense of nationalism or fearfulness about personal and familial safety as communal rioting and murders escalated on the cusp of independence.

In Delhi, Gujral reopened Moti Mahal in Daryaganj, an area close to Old Delhi's walled city, which was founded in the 1600s by the Mughal emperor Shahjahan when he relocated his court from Agra.

The newly installed Moti Mahal was where, one evening, scanning the drying-out pieces of unsold chicken tikka hanging on seekhs above the tandoor, Gujral is reputed to have struck upon the idea of enlivening them with a sauce, rather than throwing them away or selling them tough the next day.

Gujral is said to have added butter, cream, tomatoes and more spices to the tikka marinade, to create a sauce that, when added, returned moisture to the unsold chicken, and a new curry was thus born.

Moti Mahal is proud of its history, and its popularity among celebrities and politicians, especially in the 1950s when it attracted people including the Shah of Iran, India's first prime minister,

Jawaharlal Nehru, US president John F. Kennedy and latterly, Indira Gandhi, the first woman prime minister of India. More recently, celebrity chef Gordon Ramsay filmed a cooking show in the restaurant's kitchen.

~

The wedding was not without its share of challenges. Roopy too was unable to attend as Brijesh was down with bronchitis and was not allowed to fly.

Baldev too started to feel unwell. On the day when Geetika's Choora ceremony was to take place, Baldev's health took a turn for the worse and we had to call in the doctor. He had come after a very strenuous trip from South Africa and was not feeling well. The doctor ordered an ECG be done immediately. We took it in our bedroom.

Neither Baldev nor I could sit at the havan. I made Bunty and Poonam take our place and my friends Asha and Veena took over all the work of putting on the pagdi and sehra.

Our side wore bright saffron and the Seth family wore bright magenta pink pagdis.

Asha and Veena also sat in Lajpat Nagar and had the special flower baddhi made, a very Mathur and Dilliwala tradition. It is a garland of motia buds sewed crisscross which the groom wears over his sherwani.

I have never seen a more beautiful baraat, all the men in magenta pink pagdis, the ladies dressed to the nines, Sushma-ji and Dhruv Bhai-ji resplendent in gold. Kavi-ji arrived, a very handsome dulah on a white mare. Geetika with the radiance only a bride has, her happiness shining so bright that we were bedazzled.

Chashm e purnam se huess thi Geetika ki rukhsati
Duaaon se bharhi Geetika ki rukhsati
Aankh mein sabke they ansoo har koee tha udas
Phir bhi dilon mein khsushi thi Geetika ki rukhsati

~

A month later, I received a call from my cousin, Balo Bhapa-ji. My father had passed away. He had gone to Jaipur to plead a case and had suffered a heart attack there.

What to feel for somebody who was my father and yet a stranger? Whose loss was heartbreaking because I was now an orphan in every sense of the word. He may never have been around but there was some comfort in knowing that he existed somewhere. Now even that nominal connection was denied to me.

I grieved for the time I had never known him and the finality with which any hope of ever knowing him had been shattered. I was angry too. I had always been angry, I realised. Why had he abandoned his children? Why had he broken off all relations with us? Why had he never cared for us? Why had he never looked to see how we were doing?

And I would never be able to say any of these things to him, not even that I loved him and I missed him and had always wanted him in my life.

I called Vijay Mehta, my stepsister's husband. I wanted to see my father off, to help with any last rite, to bid goodbye, to mark an end to this important part of my life.

But I was told that I would only be able to see him like any other visitor, not as his daughter.

I was not welcome, I understood.

I would not be able to see my father's face one last time. I consoled myself, after all, I had barely ever seen him. It was perhaps apt that we parted this way.

~

Roopy came to Delhi in December on her annual Christmas visit. Siddharth came with her. Though Brijesh had recovered from bronchitis he still had to wind up some work and was set to join us before Christmas.

They had just bought a new house at De Vere Gardens Kensington, a street across the beautiful Hyde Park.

Roopy's visits to India were like clockwork, twice a year, for one or two months, and she would stay with me.

The family was gathered at home. Didi and Sushil Bhai had also come over and Baldev was playing carom with Sid, Poppins and Tanuj. Geetika had moved to Calcutta after her marriage, transferring to Taj Bengal, and Vineet had moved to Dubai. Only Suneet still lived in Delhi, but he was out with his friends.

Roopy had just washed her hair and was sitting on the carpet. I sat on the sofa behind her, drying her hair. We were arguing about *Sholay*. Roopy wanted to watch it and I didn't because I found it violent.

'No, I can't watch it,' I said. 'I'll dry your hair, you watch it.'

The phone rang. I got up to answer it. Brijesh was flying out that evening, it must be him.

It wasn't. It was Sukku Nayyar, a colleague of Brijesh's.

'There's bad news,' he said. 'Brijesh is no more.'

'What?' I couldn't comprehend what he was saying. I turned to Roopy and beckoned her. 'It's Sukku Nayyar. I don't understand what he is saying.'

Roopy took the phone. I watched her dazedly as her face crumpled. The words I had heard on the phone finally sank in. Brijesh had died.

Brijesh had been sitting at his desk, working. He had just lit a cigarette, and in a split second had had a massive heart cardiac arrest. He was gone with the cigarette still in his fingers.

He was only forty-six.

23 December 1989. Our world had turned upside down.

Within two hours my house was full of people: Roopy's in-laws, friends and family from every side.

I didn't have the STD long distance calling service, so Brijesh's cousins went to their homes to make the phone calls. We booked as many calls as possible. Brijesh's parents had to be informed.

By the morning, Hiroo and her cousin Pappu had arrived from Mumbai, Brijesh's best friend Deepu (Pradeep Narang) had arrived from Puducherry, Geetika flew in from Kolkata and Vineet came from Dubai. There were countless people and the sounds of wailing all around.

It was heartbreaking to watch Jijja and Daddy, Brijesh's parents, trying to cover those ten steps from the gate to Roopy.

Siddharth would not come out of his room.

What we did not realise was that we would not be able to see Brijesh for another two days.

Meanwhile, Didi and I brought some semblance of order to the house. We emptied the living room and made seating arrangements on the floor for people.

All those who had been close to Brijesh arrived; his banker friends, shikari friends, the Thapars, the Singhanias, his business associates and the whole of Grindlays. Meher Mehta arrived. Even Mary, who had worked with Roopy and Brijesh right from Siddharth's baby days in Mumbai and then in London.

Countless people came. We waited for the body to arrive.

Two days and two nights came to pass and no one slept a wink.

And then on 24 December, at around 11 a.m., the coffin arrived.

People cried unabashedly. Roopy, Jijja and Daddy were inconsolable. I saw Vineet hide his face near the window, his body shaking as he wept.

It was difficult to get Siddharth out of the room and then to get him to wear the kurta pajama required for the puja the pundits were waiting to perform.

Brijesh lay in a suit, as debonair and handsome as ever.

We cremated him that afternoon and by the time we reached home Deepu had arranged for the Mata-ji of the Aurobindo Ashram to come and conclude the Chautha.

Four days had passed.

Roopy stayed on in London for a year after Brijesh died. In that time Roopy decided to move back to India with Siddharth, even though they had the option to reside permanently in the UK. But since Brijesh and Roopy's families were both in India, Roopy made the decision to return. London had been a world that Roopy created with Brijesh, it was incomplete without him. How could she live there alone?

I was reminded of Heidi Priebe's words: 'As long as there is love there will be grief because grief is love's natural continuation.'

Grief and love, both intertwined, poured out in spaces that Brijesh once occupied, in smells and sounds, stores and clothes, movies and jokes.

Siddharth was still in school and the lifestyle Roopy was used to, despite the pension she was to receive, was no longer possible. India was more economically viable.

We all helped her pack up. She had to sell the house that they had bought in Kensington, and tie up all sorts of loose ends.

She returned to India at the end of 1991. She stayed with me for six months before getting a spacious, four-bedroom flat of her own. Siddharth joined The British School after getting a transfer certificate from England.

Eventually, he went back to London and worked in a bank but returned to join a chain of restaurants as food was his first love.

He is happily married to Batasha, the lovely daughter of Renu and Pavan Varma, former ambassador to several countries, Rajya Sabha member and author. Siddharth and Batasha have two daughters, Leela and Deviki.

~

A LIFE

Siddharth Mathur

I was born in Delhi in 1975, and after spending a few years between Mumbai and Kolkata, moved to London in 1981. I joined Hill House School, the most sought-after prep school in London, and whose alumni included Prince Charles (now King Charles), the Brunei Royal family and Lily Allen.

Growing up in London during the 1980s was fantastic. I was

surrounded by culture, trends, art, diverse people, food, fashion and music. Being the son of one of the most successful investment bankers meant having a houseful of guests. I can barely remember a week where there wasn't a dinner hosted by my parents, or people staying with us. Our home was always warm, always buzzing. My parents were constantly entertaining guests, whether at home, at London's best restaurants, or at the London Park Tower Casino.

In 1989 tragedy struck, and my father passed away. He was an only child. My mum was one of three sisters, so growing up I was very close to my cousins and my mother's side of the family. This played an important role on the decision of moving back to Delhi, as that was where the family was.

After ten years in London, we moved back to Delhi, where I joined The British School, New Delhi. My passion for sport really kicked in during these years, and I went on to captain school teams for athletics and football. During one week in school, students were were asked to join music appreciation class. I asked my teacher if I could skip this, and she jokingly said only if you are going to represent the school for Delhi State Athletics trials that week. Not knowing my own speed but knowing I didn't want to spend a week in music appreciation, I went to Nehru Stadium, wearing my Bermuda shorts and long T-shirts (it was the 1990s). After a week of races, I came fifth in all of Delhi for the 200 metres race!

After The British School, I followed in the footsteps of my father and great grandfather, and joined St. Stephen's College, Delhi.

Right after college, I ventured into private banking, working with Citibank and ING Barings. In 2005, I moved back to London and continued eating my way around the world while spending another five years with Citi Private Bank. However, when the epicure in me refused to be content, I returned to India and made my foray into the F&B industry.

On my return to India in 2009, I partnered with Impresario Entertainment & Hospitality Pvt. Ltd and came on board as Director, and Head of Food. The group has reputed names such as

Social, Smoke House Deli, Salt Water Café, to name a few. Today, Impresario has expanded its F&B portfolio across thirteen cities with close to seventy restaurants.

I also founded Secret Ingredient, a hospitality and food consultancy, one of the leading food consultancies in the country. We specialise in providing solutions for new and existing restaurants, while extending advisory services towards FMCG, hotels, malls and schools. We have advised some of the biggest names in the food industry, and our clients include Jubilant Foodworks, Select Citywalk, Ambuja Neotia Group, Ikea, The Park Hotel Group, Swiggy and The British School, New Delhi.

I married Batasha Varma in 2011. Born in 1981 in Bucharest, Romania, Batasha is the daughter of former diplomat, best-selling author and politician Pavan K. Varma and Renuka Varma. She spent her childhood oscillating between travelling the world and being ensconced in the cultural milieu of New Delhi. She studied in New York, Moscow, Cyprus and London, graduating with a BA in communication and visual culture from the London Metropolitan University. She has written for publications like *Hindustan Times*, *The Cyprus Times* and *The Sunday Times*, England. These days she is a full-time mom, a talented home cook and owner of condiment company Sam & Pups.

Pavan Varma's last post as a diplomat was as the Indian Ambassador to Bhutan, and this is where I proposed to Batasha. In fact, after our wedding in Delhi, we had a small reception in Bhutan, as well as an intimate lunch with their friends and the King of Bhutan.

Three years later, on Valentine's Day in 2014, Leela Mathur was born. Today Leela has followed in the 'foodsteps' of her parents and loves to cook and loves to eat. Apart from making recipe videos, her other hobbies include reading, swimming and painting.

The family loves to eat and travel.

With the launch of Khoya Mithai in 2016, we set a new benchmark in the Indian mithai market. I believed the gifting market in India had been long dominated by chocolates and international confectionery, while the traditional box of mithai often didn't make the cut. Khoya has its flagship store in Chanakya Mall, Delhi, a presence at The Oberoi, New Delhi, and their clients include Louis Vuitton, Karan Johar, the Ambani family, Lexus and many more.

~

Ishq ka rang kisi taur badalne na diya
Mujhko Yadon ke hisaron se nikalne na diya

Zabt karne ka saliqa bhi diya hai uss ne
Meri ankhon se kabhi gham ko pighalne na diya

He did not allow the colour of love to change any how
He did not permit me to leave the circle of memories

He has shown me the art of endurance
He has never let sorrow melt from my eyes

33

Searching for My Father

A FEW YEARS DOWN THE LINE, AFTER THE RELEASE OF MY FATHER'S book, I found within myself a hunger to know him.

I begged distant senior relatives for photographs. There were only a few relatives left, and fewer photographs. I found no photographs of my parents together or of my father from his youth. Finally, I found some and saw, for the first time, what my Dadi (Sona Devi) and my aunt, uncle and cousins looked like.

Unexpectedly, I found him on Google under *Famous Sikh Personalities*. The article referenced works like *A History of Punjabi Literature* and *Punjabi Sahit da Itihas.*

My father, who I had known to be a lawyer, was also a poet. A poet influenced by Saadi and Hafiz, Mir, Ghalib, Iqbal and Faiz, knowledgeable about the Vedas, Upanishads, Ramayana and Mahabharata. A poet who wanted to take his reader closer to nature, to lie on a riverbank, sing with birds or swim with fish to shake off the dust of modern life.

A poet about whom Amrita Pritam had written 'Anoop Singh has found his "self". It's a state where there is neither want nor is there prayer for more. It's like a reliquary full of the holy water from the Ganga where the water has flowed out. The mind is in a questionless state. For this questionless state, I pay my respects to Anoop Singh.'

Anoop Singh was born 3 February 1910, to a prosperous

Peshawar family, and came to Delhi during the Partition and started practising law again. He was considered an authority on trademark, copyright, design and patent related matters in the Commonwealth area.

Yet, his inner poet could not be denied and his first collection of poems in Punjabi titled *Roop-Anoop* was published in 1981. His creativity seemed to flourish and he soon published a handful of poetry volumes: *Akkhar-Birakh, Indestructible Full, Anant Nain, Sixty Eight Tirath* and *Adi Aneel*. He was hailed as a philosophical poet, rejuvenating Sufi ideology.

He wrote in Gurmukhi, Hindi and English. I believe he spoke Farsi and Pashto as well. And his love for Ghalib was legendary.

He had been seventy-nine when he died. I had met him twice. But I now knew why I wrote. And why I had been writing poetry compulsively for so many years.

I knew now why I have been able to live through the adversities of my life with the help of my poetry and music.

I knew now why I had steered Shaam-e-Ghazal for so many decades. I only wished I had spent more time with my father and learnt from him.

I see so many similarities between us and so many coincidences too. His book *Kavya Yatra* was to be released by the then prime minister, Dr Manmohan Singh, but the prime minister was rushed to the AIIMS for a bypass that day.

A few years later, Dr Manmohan Singh released my book *Romancing Tagore*.

After his death, my father's book *Kavya Yatra* was released by the senior lawyer Arun Jaitley, who had worked with my father for many years.

I was shocked to hear all that he had to say: My father loved Ghalib and Faiz, so do I; his favourite actor was Sanjeev Kumar, so is mine. He loved the songs of the film *Aandhi*, so do I. He would sprout a shair at any given moment to make his point, so do I. Many-a-times arguments in court take help from poetry to explain their point.

A chance incident brought me and my half-sister Manju Mehta together at a dinner. Manju's husband was an exporter. My husband Baldev also worked with an exporter, Ashwini Puri, and we met at Ashwini's house.

Ashwini's wife Neeru told Manju about my poetry. Manju, in turn, told me about the many books our father had written and published. We sat together all evening discovering each other.

Manju sent me five books through Neeru. And I have read them every day since then.

I wanted to translate them, to make known his very unusual thoughts to the Urdu-speaking public.

But Gurmukhi is difficult to understand, and to translate it all into Urdu is hard and time-consuming work.

But I started.

With the help of Balo Bhapa-ji and his wife, my beautiful bhabi Todo, I first understood the Punjabi meaning. Then I began to translate them into English. So many words had me perplexed: winga tinga, hularey, what did they mean?

The online Punjabi dictionary was difficult to operate. But I did not give up. I will continue till I can.

It is also an emotional journey. I often cried while translating my father's work. His thoughts and words were so beautiful. And through his work we were finally close, my father was finally speaking to me.

My thinking is so much like his, my poetry too like an echo.

Some of my father's poems and my translations in English

Mera Roop Anoop

Kise samay main Brahma barhya'n
Kise samay main hoya Mahesh
Kise samay main Vishnu hoya
Kise samay main Gunrhi Ganesh
Merey roop anoop badalde
Aih vi meri maya hai

Sab vastu han asthir ithhey
Srishti supna chhaya hai.

Sometimes I became Brahma
Sometimes I became Mahesh
Sometimes Vishnu I became
Sometimes the learned Ganesh
My incomparable changing guise
Is also my Illusion
Every object is but a fleeting
The Universe just a shadow of dreams

Maut

Jis din da main janam liya hai
Terey val paya aava'n
Tu vi khadhe uddekei'n kidrey
Payee hularey bahva'n
Pata nahi'n taitho'n kyo'n dardey
Iss dharti de lok
Dukhha noo'n aih kismet kehendey
Tainu'n kehendey MAUT!!
Lai Maa jholi paa lai mainu'n
De ik lammee lori
Neend sukha'n di main sau java'n
Torh k jeevan dori.

Ever since the day I was born
I keep coming back towards you
You are also standing somewhere
Swinging your arms enticing.
I do not know why they fear you
The people of this earth
They call their miseries destiny
And you they call MAUT!

Take me mother in your lap
Sing me a long lullaby
Let me sink into a peaceful slumber
And break this thread of life

Pardarshini

Dil vich main pardarshini laee
Navein puranrhey chitr
Koee madham koee ubhrey
Kuch nindak kuch mitr
Ai hai chanda oh hai suraj
Tarey vich nishitra
Sab tto'n uchha sab tto'n suchha
Mata chitr vichitr

In my heart I etched an exhibition
Of photographs old and new
Some faded, some bright
Some critics and friends a few
This is the moon and that the sun
But the jewel amongst the hue
Most honoured, most loved
The loftiest and the purest
Is a picture my mother of you

Momin

Jyot ghati main nirbal hoya
Jharh gaye merey pattey
Raati mainu neend na aavey
Tarhpa main din sattey
Main tta chanarh wal ha'n turya
Deevey kahnu baley??
Aadar naal karo mainu vidiya
Chalya momin macce

The light has faded
And I have become weak.
Devoid of all my foliage.
At night I cannot sleep
I am agonised all seven days.
I am walking towards light,
Why are you lighting diyas?
Bid me farewell with respect,
A worshipper is going back home

34

A Visit to Kanpur

I SETTLED MYSELF ON THE BERTH. DIDI WAS ALREADY TAKING OUT food to eat even though the time taken by train from Delhi to Kanpur was only about six hours. More if the train was late, which was almost always the case.

Even though it was late at night, Roopy was trying to spot a chai-wallah. No train journey was going to come between her and her endless cups of tea even though the last time she had travelled by train may have been at least a decade ago.

'What are you smiling at,' she asked suspiciously.

I shook my head. 'Just happy to be travelling with both of you.'

It was true. The last trip the three of us had taken had been around the world. Now we were going home. Was Kanpur home? I wasn't sure. Delhi perhaps had become home now. Definitely for Didi and me. It had only been five years since Roopy had returned from London. I wondered what she considered home.

'Is Mahesh coming to pick us up?' Didi asked.

I nodded. Mahesh had become my rakhi brother when I was thirteen. Now it was the wedding of his nephew Thoma, the son of his sister Sweety, and he had insisted that the wedding would not happen without my sisters and me. As is often the case with pet names, we had forgotten what Thoma's real name was and when we had received the wedding card for Amit Bakshi, it had taken a few minutes to figure out whose wedding we were being invited to. We have always called his mother Sweety and father Indu. His sister was Gudia.

The date was fixed for 24 October 1996.

Didi, Roopy and I had decided to go.

We hadn't taken a train journey in years and the nostalgia of Kanpur and our parents was enough of a pull.

Did we want to reconnect with our childhood? Recapture memories? Did we want to revaluate how we had developed our principles and what led us to make the decisions we made? Had we made the right decisions in our lives? It was confusing, emotional.

Was the romance still there? Mummy, Papa, the backyard, the guava tree? The all-important green rose?

It reminded me of an article I had read in a magazine on one of my flights. The experience of visiting a childhood home works wonders if you're angling for a trip down memory lane. It brings fuzzy and disjointed memories into focus.

But a house is not static—tiles change, walls come down.

If you walk into a house that has been radically altered since you lived in it, those changes may leave you feeling like someone erased you from the picture, especially if you were the one who had made those earlier design decisions.

The overnight train journey was difficult. We hardly slept. We talked of our past. We talked about our marriages. Were we happy? About our husbands, children. So much time together. Where were we now? We laughed, we cried. We ate moongphali. But we talked as one and not as three. Our lives were so entwined, maybe we had been one soul in another birth.

Our oldest memories were our treasures, our oldest friends and companions had stayed in our hearts and minds through the ages.

Our earliest parties, our first fall, a dog bite. The first taste of something that still brings water to our mouths even now or a scent that surrounds us with nostalgia for a person one hasn't met in years.

A tree that one sat under, the neem buds that got crushed under our keds as we hurried about in school. That smell.

A whiff from the kitchen.

Sometimes memories are built around old pictures, albums, cousins one grew up with, siblings, warmth of parents, holiday trips and much more.

Later in life there are cue memories recalled like a word or a thing can conjure up childhood all over again. Though there are many factors included it is mostly emotion or episodic.

Researchers says that a child starts to store memories from the age of two, like I remember Roopy's birth, the doctor and the smell of Dettol. I was just three or so, but it is so vivid. And there's also a gender bias. Women have more elaborate memories than men because mothers are freer to emotionally express themselves and reminisce with girls.

Morning came.

The station seemed familiar though very crowded. We stepped off and were engulfed in so many welcoming arms.

The wedding was a grand affair with great Mughlai food and snazzy people. Thoma had become a successful founder of the pharma company Eris Lifesciences and the wedding befitted his status.

Mahesh had booked us into Hotel Meghdoot. The hotel was new but the road was familiar. Opposite the Reserve Bank and Grindlays Bank.

The next morning, we decided to go and visit our old house and school.

41, Friends Colony. Each one of us was full of emotions.

The lane to our house seemed narrower now. Had the wall always been this high? We looked at each other. We touched the wall and I think we washed it with our tears.

Where were our loved ones who had fed us with their hands, washed our uniforms, polished our shoes?

The owners were very kind, they offered us water and tea. Mr Mitra came to meet us. He was still a bachelor though greyed.

He said Didi had not changed at all and looked the youngest

out of the three of us. Roopy and I had put on weight. Didi never went above 50 kg all her life.

The yellow rose creeper was still where Papa had planted it. It almost touched the terrace now. Beyond Mr Mitra's window and onto the verandah on the first floor.

It touched us like a gentle breeze with its fragrance, as if telling us: I'm your friend, I remember everything too.

We stayed there for an hour. Not much had changed inside the house. The rooms and the kitchen were the same, and the verandah still had a takhtposh. I wondered if it was the same Mummy used to sit on and have her tea. The bathroom had been modernised a bit.

We thanked everybody and left.

We did not talk for a long time. The silence was comforting. The three of us were in sync like a heartbeat. We were each trying to control our emotions to help each other. We held each other's hands tight. As if to say, yes, I felt that too.

We were in front of the gate that made us who we are. It stood proud, down the mall past Kwality Restaurant, past Regal Cinema and Phool Bagh and Dr Kalra's clinic and onward to Cantonment.

We looked around, the weather was gorgeous, November at the threshold. Roses in full bloom greeted us.

I recalled all the matches I played. The last room of Senior Cambridge where we mugged up all our textbooks.

The car stopped at the porch and we went to the principal's office. The first thing I noticed were the large pictures all over the walls. Gold House, 1958. There I was standing tall with my team. Captain of the Gold House.

We went to the chapel and knelt at the pew. We prayed in the memory of those who were not with us anymore. This chapel used to hold our exam papers at one time. The nuns met us. Not one was familiar. But they were kind and tried to console us. God and kindness are universal.

On the drive back, we got off near Phool Bagh and told the driver to go to the hotel.

The three of us hired a rickshaw and went to Shivala in Meston Road. Didi remembered the shops. She bought bangles and bindis for all her friends. She was like a little girl, crazy, buying little trinkets everywhere. It was hard to believe that she was the mother of two grown children.

I always thought it was because she had to grow up too soon, to shoulder the responsibility of our family at such a young age, that it was only when she was older that she could indulge in the fun of childhood.

From there we went back to the hotel giggling together and then back to Delhi with baskets full of the most famous mithai of Kanpur—the Galori Paan. It was made of khoya and wrapped in a pan shape with dried fruit inside.

Ek marhalla aur paar hua.

Jo girafta dil hai mera sanam yeh toh aashiqui ka nizaam hai
Yaha mantiqon ka guzar nahi yahan falsafa bhi haram hai

Huwa sajda paye sanam pe jab toh suroor had se guzar gaya
Sar-e-bandagi yeh pata chala ki sanam khuda ka he naam hai

This captive heart of mine, my beloved, follows the rule of love
There's no place for philosophers here, even philosophising is excluded here

When I bowed in prostration before my beloved, my intoxication crossed all limits in the course of my devotion I discovered that the beloved is the name of the almighty

35

January Becomes the Cruelest Month

ANYONE FROM DELHI WILL TELL YOU THAT WINTER IS THE BEST TIME in the city. Gentle sunshine warms you in the day and at night, there is the cosiness of the razaai or lihaafs.

It was a beautiful crispy cold winter's day that January. The date was 17th. It was a perfect Sunday. We were celebrating Siddharth's return from London after working in Citibank for a few years. He had just joined a bank in Delhi and was already looking ahead to the next New Year and how going into the new century might affect banking. It was the first time we were hearing about the Y2K effect that might follow at the end of the year.

Baldev, the children and I had had a fabulous lunch with Roopy, Siddharth and Roopy's in-laws. Roopy's cook, Bishan Singh, who had been with their family for almost seventy years, cooked everything possible. He was excellent, unmatched by anybody who came after.

Baldev had indulged in all that he shouldn't. Mutton, rasmalai and even gulab jamun.

When we were home, we were so drowsy from the lunch that we promptly went to sleep.

Thoma was coming to dinner that evening. He had an interview in Delhi the next morning. Baldev was looking forward to meeting up with him. Thoma seemed to be late, and I had my Reiki to do.

Baldev said he would wait to eat with Thoma. So I had a bite and was ready to retire to my room.

Thoma arrived just as I finished my meal and the two of them sat down to eat.

'You go, I will watch some more TV,' Baldev said. CNN had just become available in India and Baldev was planning to watch the news on it.

Those were his last words to me.

Around 10 p.m., Bahadur, our trusted cook of many years, came running to me. '*Sahib gir gaye*,' he said, panic in his voice.

I ran to the bathroom.

Baldev was sprawled across the bathtub and his head was on the white tiles. There was blood on the tiles. We tried to lift him.

'Raj-ji! Raj-ji!' I kept calling out to him (he used to call me Rani and I called him Raj-ji).

Finally, we managed to move him to the bed.

'*Doctor ke paas bhago!*' I told Bahadur. Some part of me noticed that he ran without wearing his chappals.

Thoma came to enquire about the disturbance. We tried shaking Baldev to rouse him. The doctor lived across the street and arrived in no time. Suneet came as well.

Baldev was gone.

Baldev, where did he suddenly go?

How do you deal with grief? Grief again?

This incessant flow of dull pain, a constant unbearable weight which you cannot share with anyone. Yoga, meditation, music, I've done it all and yet every January I still have nightmares. We had gone through so many bad Januarys with Baldev's sicknesses that I have come to fear the month.

My goddaughter Leena Diwan, who lives in Nice, France, had once gifted me a book called *Simple Abundance: A Daybook of Comfort and Joy* by Sara Breathnach. It describes a day in every month with a quote. I have read it many times and found new meanings every time but would end up going back to the 17 January page again and again.

'Harmony: Achieving Balance in our Lives' is the heading, and it goes on to quote Arthur Schnabel: 'The note, I handle no better than many pianists. But the pauses between the notes … ah, that is where the art resides.'

A Chopin piano nocturne played by a novice musician and by a virtuoso will not sound the same. That is because one of the two pianists has had a lifetime to practice the music as well as learn when to pause in order to colour the notes with passion while the other has not.

So it is with the concerto of our lives. Individual notes must be learnt and played and practiced before we achieve harmony. And above all, we must learn how to pause.

And my time to pause had come.

No more waiting for Baldev anymore, no more worrying for him day and night. No more constant checks to see if he was breathing. No more of telling him not to eat this or that. No need to watch him with his table full of medicine, to ensure his every pocket was packed with a Sorbitrate.

He was only sixty-seven.

I was fifty-nine.

The Harley Clinic had given Baldev a new lease on life. But the Supreme had other plans.

Those few days were heartbreaking for everybody, the children, the grandchildren and Baldev's family.

Tarika left small notes in front of his picture every few minutes.

'*Nanu! Kheera aur hai, aur hai!*' said Nainika one day, when asking for more cucumber. My eyes flooded with tears. Nainika loved cucumber and sometimes, when she had eaten too many, Baldev would hide the salad plate from her. And she would demand more from her Nanu. She still remembers that. Vineet's children were too young; Aria even came later.

The entire family from both sides showed their support on the Chautha. They stood beside me like a wall. It took an hour for people to give their condolences and leave.

My two sons, Vineet and Suneet, stood beside me holding me

strongly. They were now the head of our family and they have done me proud at every step.

How was I to move on? How do I get past this grief?

I don't think anyone is really prepared for such a loss. Baldev's health had been going downhill for the past two years, but I was unprepared for this.

Papa, Badi Mummy, Mummy, Brijesh, Didi, Sushil Bhai, Mahesh, all of them have left too. Yet we live.

There are so many theories of internalising grief. But is it really possible to celebrate someone who you miss so achingly?

We all know that endings are as natural as beginnings. Birth and death, the eternal cycle. Why then do memories bring tears and smiles? Is this karma? Is this another way of grief?

Grief is a journey that everybody has to traverse alone.

I don't believe in rebirths, of meeting again in some life somewhere. I believe that you can keep a person alive as long as you want, in your heart, in your smiles, in your pain, in your writing, in your poetry and in conversation. For me they are living within me and I often talk to them as I have conversations with my God.

They are indelible.

Baldev is present with me and in the three beautiful children we bore together.

Sometimes I think about how much he would have enjoyed the joys of having grandchildren. He and I used to go to the India International Centre for lunch every Sunday. Now Suneet takes us to the Oberoi hotel for their famous brunch. Baldev would have loved being pampered by the children, their visits and their academic achievements.

But his travels had ended that day in January 1999. And that was something none of us could change.

Her dam firaq mein sanam umr ke din guzar gaye
Tu bhi bikhar ke reh gaya hum bhi bikhar bikhar gaye

All the days of my life passed in waiting for union, my dear
In the process, you got scattered and so did I

36

A Trip to Pakistan in Search of My Roots

I STARTED TO TRAVEL ONCE AGAIN IN THE YEAR 2000.

Baldev had passed away and my children had moved out. IVS was running well with an able and trusted staff.

My back was better, and I could sit for the long periods of time required for international flights now. My first trip from that time was unforgettable, a journey on the Orient Express. I felt like I had been reincarnated as a royal, living and travelling in luxury that was seen only in films and magazines. But that journey would pale in comparison to the one I would undertake the next spring.

I had spent almost my entire life wanting to return to Peshawar and finally, in 2001, I got the chance. Two of my close friends, Tasmima Hossain, or Tiptip, and her sister Lotun from Dhaka, were planning to visit their cousin Meeta, who was married to the chief of the IMF, in Islamabad.

They asked me to come along as I would have diplomatic immunity and we would be able to go wherever we wanted. A ten-day trip was planned; our base would be Islamabad and we would take day trips to other destinations. The two sisters and I went on this well-planned trip. My visa came with difficulty. But it came and I did not have to report to the police station.

It was the middle of February. Tiptip and Lotun landed in Delhi.

The days of Delhi's good weather were upon us. The skies were blue and the air had a chill, but it wasn't cold enough to bother us. I had been packed and ready for a week. Years of travel had given me a method—take as less as possible!

If only my feelings could be so neatly compartmentalised. I had already written, called and mailed all my family members. Where was our house? What were the landmarks? Did anybody remember a house number? I had received landmarks and directions from my uncle, aunt and Didi. I was as prepared as I could be.

We flew to Lahore.

The Afghan war had ended but there was still some fighting between the Taliban and the Northern Alliance. The Kargil conflict between India and Pakistan had taken place eight months ago.

For whatever reason, when we got off the plane it was oddly frightening to be confronted with what seemed like scores of tall burly policemen, Pathans perhaps, with huge shamlas. I wondered later whether it was their size or a perception of the land that had made me fearful, or whether it was just the anxiety of what I would find in the place of my birth.

Still, we had diplomatic immunity and people came to the aircraft took us to a secluded lounge from there we boarded another flight for Islamabad. A few hours later we were there, being received by Meeta.

We drove through the neat geometric roads of Islamabad, Pakistan's modern capital city built as late as 1960s. The city was designed in a grid pattern with sectors for government, commerce, residential, recreational and industrial use. In sharp contrast, Rawalpindi, Islamabad's twin city, is a sprawling, congested, chaotic, and typical South Asian city.

We stayed in a beautiful house with vast gardens and many rooms. Meeta was a splendid hostess, one could see that she entertained a lot, her table groaned with load at every meal. A Bengali, she cooked the most delectable dishes for my friends and me. Her two daughters and son were loving children, and I could never forget her maid Hafeeza who kept my room fragrant and beautiful with arrangements of fresh irises and daffodils every day. In Islamabad, and everywhere I visited in Pakistan, glorious flowers were on sale in every market.

Meeta and her husband took us everywhere we needed to visit. From our base in Islamabad, we made several day trips and two-day excursions by car.

One of the first was to Lahore.

The M2 Motorway to Lahore was a modern six-lane highway. At my age and with a bad back I could not have prayed for a smoother journey. There were mobile workshops, mobile hospital vans and radar systems. It was punctuated with clean elaborate rest stops every few miles.

On the road to Lahore, we passed the salt range that lies between the valleys of the Jhelum and the Indus, and I was reminded that I was in the cradle of our civilisation. This is where Shiva's tears after the death of his wife Sati are said to have created the temple pond of the Katas Raj temples.

We also crossed the rivers Ravi and Sutlej. Some of the most romantic songs from Punjabi folklore have been written about the Ravi and its banks with the common refrain—Ravi de kinare.

Near Attock Fort I watched the blue Indus waters merge into the murky brown Kabul River.

Lahore was in the grip of the Basant Mela. I did not know about it before, but realised we had arrived at a very special time indeed.

According to one story, the tradition of flying a kite during the mela began when the poet Amir Khusro celebrated his beloved Saint Nizamuddin Auliya's return to health by flying a kite. Whatever the origin, kites covered the sky all day and at night, white kites lit with fairy lights could be spotted as well.

The night was ablaze with lights, the canal running throughout the city was twinkling and sparkling with decorated floats. The terrace of every house was wrapped in lights—the city looked like a fairy land.

There were kite-flying competitions with big money at stake. Noted singers and bands performed on different rooftops and were sponsored by multinationals. Special cuisine was served including Nihari, paaye and halwa puri.

The whole night was spent going from one party to another. We must have gone to five different houses that night.

Young men and women were dancing everywhere, or sitting in each other's laps and disappearing into rooms.

People had upto five meals through the night going from house to house and terrace to terrace.

Everywhere you went it was like a prolonged Eid. Except for the alcohol, which flowed like water. There was too much alcohol—we could not touch it, we settled for chai and sharbat, choices that grew boring as the night carried on. My chai was actually kahwa, a special Kashmiri tea flavoured with elaichi.

Meeta's friend Anwari was our host for the night and was responsible for taking us around. One of the houses we went to was that of Sajjad Gul, a famous TV producer in Pakistan. The term house does not quite capture the essence of Gul's residence, palace would be more appropriate. I am reminded of his hospitality and his very beautiful house whenever I see a show produced by him.

One of the people I met that evening was a fellow Citibank alumnus, Shaukat Aziz. He and I had many common friends. Later, Shaukat went on to become the deputy prime minister of Pakistan.

A few years later, I became friends, on Facebook, with the person who had revived the Basant Mela. He calls me Indira Maa. He is Allama Iqbal's grandson Yousaf Salli or, to give him his given name, Yusuf Salahuddin. Besides the Basant Mela he also organised various musical, artistic and poetic gatherings, and I loved the music he had put on his entertainment and music show Virsa Heritage Revived.

He reminded me later that we had met in Delhi at the Pakistan High Commissioner's place for Eid. I recalled too. A lovely couple, Ghazala and Malik Sahib came to my house for dinner and music programmes and to Suneet's shows. They loved the sarson ka saag and makki ki roti from my house.

He had one of my ghazals sung by the very prominent singer Hina Nasarulla.

Har lamha zindagi ko sajaney lagay hai'n aap
Duniya meri haseen bananey lagay hai'n aap

Har shab merey khyal mei'n aanay lagay hai'n aap
Rasmay wafa bhi khoob nibhaney lagay hai'n aap

Doobey hai'n is taraha say muhabbat ki baihher mei'n
Mainey suna hai khud ko bhulaney lagay hai'n aap

A decade later, I was sad to learn that the Basant Mela had been banned in Lahore because the kite thread had become more and more sharp and was cutting unwary passersby and cable lines alike.

But in 2001, the Basant Mela was celebrated in all its glory and we were out for the better part of the night enjoying the festivities before returning to the Government Guest House which was our camp for the night. It had the most beautiful gardens and flashy cars whizzed in and out.

The next morning, unlike the sleeping city, off we went to play our part as tourists.

I had only ever seen Lahore from the train in 1947 as we passed by on our way to Nainital. For the first time I was actually seeing the city. And it was a revelation. An architectural feat. Like Paris, divided into two by a canal, with the most beautiful buildings on either side. Anwari pointed out Aitchison College, St. Edward's College, College of Architecture and the Medical College. They were all festooned for Basant.

We went to the Lahore Fort, the tombs of Jahangir, Nur Jahan and Anarkali, Shalimar Gardens, Badshahi Mosque, the Hazuri Bagh laid out by Raja Ranjit Singh, the Baradari, Allama Iqbal's mausoleum and the shrine of Data Ganj Baksh. The weather was lovely.

Some of the colonial buildings combined the Gothic and Victorian with the Mughal style. The High Court, Lahore Museum, Aitchison College, General Post Office, Gurudwara Arjan Dera Sahib.

We shopped at the Anarkali bazars past Nicholson Road, where my husband grew up. I bought many parandas from there for my quirky Didi and her friends, they were red, yellow and turquoise with ghungroos and long tassels made of silk thread.

We drove for a while in the famous Hira Mandi, the Red Light Area.

There is a famous play *Jis Lahore Nahi Vekhya O Jamiya I Nahi* and the line is oft repeated in Delhi even now and after seeing Lahore I have to agree with it. If you haven't seen Lahore your birth was not worth it.

On our way back to Islamabad from Lahore, a miracle happened.

Meeta's driver called me Aapa or Baaji like the rest of my friends and took it for granted that I was a Muslim too. He pointed out to me, '*Baaji, woh tussi dekheya?*' He pointed up the hill.

'What,' I asked as I looked around.

'*Yeh Sikhaan da gurudwara hai,* Panja Sahib,' he said.

I got goosebumps all over my arms. I was sixty in the year 2001 and I was six when I had gone to Panja Sahib with Papa. He had put me on his shoulders and given me a bath in that sarovar.

I was trembling.

I told my friends to wait for me and told the driver take me up to it. But I wasn't allowed inside, because I didn't have permission as a non-Pakistani to go inside.

I cried and cried. 'Please let me in. I've come from Delhi and I will never be able to come again.'

Finally, they relented. They wanted my passport details and the driver promised that he would bring it to them. They let me in.

Panja Sahib has the imprint of Guru Nanak Dev-ji's hand on a rock and there is a spring of water that emerges from under this rock. Nobody knows where it comes from. Legend has it that when

Guru Nanak and his companion Bhai Mardana arrived in a place called Hasan Abdul, which is near present-day Rawalpindi, at the foot of a hill, in the shade of a tree, Guru Nanak started to sing a shabad and his companion played the rahab. Devotees started to flock to Guru Nanak.

This annoyed the local saint, Shah Wali Qandhari, who lived on the top of the hill. He decided to cut off access to the spring that flowed from the hilltop, hoping to get his devotees back.

Soon everybody started to feel thirsty, and Guru Nanak asked Bhai Mardana to request Shah Wali Qandhari to release the water. Shah Wali refused Bhai Mardana rudely. Ask with more humility, Guru Nanak said to Bhai Mardana and sent him back again. Once again he was refused. Have faith in God, Guru Nanak is said to have told Bhai Mardana and his devotees, asking them to lift aside a big rock. Pure spring water started to gush forth allowing everybody to quench their thirst.

At the same time the fountain near Shah Wali Qandhari dried up. In a fit of rage, Wali is said to have rolled a huge boulder towards the Guru. The Guru held up his hand and gently stopped the rock, leaving behind an imprint of his hand. When Shah Wali Qandhari saw it, he became a disciple of Guru Nanak.

The gurudwara built on this spot is Panja Sahib. Clear, fresh, spring water still gushes out from somewhere behind the rock and spills over into a large pool. An imprint of a right hand was carved on the rock while it was built in the Mughal style by Maharaja Ranjit Singh (1780–1839).

The gurudwara is beautiful. It is encircled by big darbars and halls where the langar takes place. Hundreds and thousands of people come to pray and eat. It is a beautiful shrine.

I did my mattha tekna and I prayed for everybody in the family and they gave me parshad. I sat there for about half an hour. As I sat and prayed in the holy shrine, my childhood memories came alive. Was it destiny or a miracle that I had come here?

I had a mobile phone, still a rarity in 2001, and called my friends to tell them that I would take some time in case they wanted to go home.

'Don't worry, we are also at a very, beautiful, scenic place. You take your time,' they said. They understood that I was emotional and needed some time to absorb the miracle that had just taken place and the memories it had brought gushing to the surface.

37

Peshawar and the Remnants of My Home

EVENTUALLY I PUT SOME GHOSTS TO REST.

I had decided my pilgrimage to Peshawar would include three places: the house where my grandfather, my mother, Didi and I were born, my school, and the famed Balo-ji ka Ghantaghar.

Peshawar is a valley located in one of the most beautiful parts of the world—in the ancient land of Gandhara and its surroundings. It is a lush location, surrounded by mountains, irrigation canals, rivers and, of course, flowers. There are no such places in the world.

I was travelling to Peshawar after fifty-three years. As we entered I could see the crowded city it had become and yet, I still found the beauty I remembered. There were flowers everywhere, in the traffic islands and the dividers, and lining the routes mustard flowers shown like fields of gold. I could understand why Peshawar's ancient name was Pushpapura, meaning the city of flowers.

Yet, that day my eyes searched not for this natural beauty but for traces of my past. All I saw was a crowded city that I did not recognise. Nothing felt familiar.

Partition had taken place over half a century ago, we had been given house and land in India, I had lived a full life and now called Delhi home. Yet, I had left a life behind, my family had left their lives behind and that would never be settled. Why should roots matter?

Perhaps it is not so much the question of roots as being chopped off from the original tree and having to scrabble to survive elsewhere. Perhaps where we are born is stamped into our genes.

What do you say about the people who came from Peshawar but are now in India? What is their identity? There is no identity left of the people who came because of the partition. I'm a member of small societies, small groups on Facebook about Peshawar, where we meet and talk about Peshawar. Outside of that, what identity do we have? Who knows Peshawar? When I went to renew my passport, the passport officer didn't know where to put my place of birth, since it was Peshawar, but it was not in India now.

I went to meet the Regional Passport Officer, a young and smart Sardar. He solved it by creating a column that said 'Undivided India'. He said, 'There are very few people like you left.' It was true. It's also true that in another ten or fifteen years, there will be no one left. And with the people will go the histories. Everything will be forgotten, and who will be interested in this little story?

But I was alive and I was in Peshawar and I had traced my family back to six ancestors in Peshawar and found only one concrete proud survivor, the clock tower. It was built by my great grandfather, Lala Balmakand Sahib, in 1900, who gifted it to Queen Victoria for her Diamond Jubilee—a fact mentioned in most travel books about Pakistan.

I was carrying one myself—*Footprints* by Dave Winter and Ivan Mannheim. Seeing his name in print was like a magnetic pull, or a password to my missing past.

I had to see it, I had to touch it, and say farewell.

The fabled house of my childhood dreams was there, and yet not there. When we reached Peshawar, I didn't know my house address, but I had a vague idea that it was near Hashtnagari Darwaza (Hasht means eight and Nagar is village; a road goes towards the famous Hashtnagar area from there, hence the name). I knew that there was a hospital nearby, also built by my grandmother, and a masjid adjoining our house.

We passed these landmarks, I saw the masjid, and there was what might have been a haveli beside it. But the façade of the house had totally changed. I couldn't recognise it. I called an aunt and asked her for the house number. But so many years had passed that nobody could remember it. Yet when we stopped there, I knew this was it. I could make out the railings and the façade, but the terrace and its parapets were missing, and the regal front entrance was not there.

We entered the building. A sign proclaimed this was Khan Klub. We went in.

I told the people of Khan Klub that I had been born there, this had been my house. My voice broke. Tears flowed from my eyes.

The people at Khan Klub were kind and cried with me.

They brought their senior owner. He patted me on the head and comforted me.

When I had calmed down a little, he told me the tale of the house and the hands it had changed over the years. Three brothers had been allotted the house, and over time they had divided it. One portion had been razed to the ground, in the middle there was a shopping mall, and one remaining bit of the house had been restored and was Khan Klub.

The owner told me to look through Khan Klub to my heart's content. The first place I went to was my mother's room. I climbed up and I thought I would come to Mummy's door, but it was all changed—the large room of my memory, even its doors were not there now.

The original haveli had a hundred rooms; this remnant had forty. They had been further redesigned and re-apportioned. Large rooms had been divided into many smaller ones. I couldn't connect to the one where I was born.

Yet, the mosque beside the house was there and the downstairs area looked like I remembered, but it was different.

The owner wouldn't let us go till we had lunch. Tiptip, Lotun, my hostess Meeta, Anwari and I sat down to eat. I don't remember what we ate. Perhaps it was kebabs, but I was lost between the past and the present, between disappointment and joy. I must have spoken but I know not what. Our hosts refused to take any money from us. No money was exchanged that day. Only emotions were.

Later, I joined groups that talked about Peshawar's history and learnt from Peshawar-based historian Dr Ali Jan that Jemima Khan and Imran Khan had stayed there and that it had been the base of most foreign journalists during the Afghanistan war.

The war might have been over on paper and 9/11 was yet to take place but the city was still full of foreign journalists, many of whom were going to the frontlines and then retreating to the safety of Peshawar to bathe, rest and eat.

From the haveli, we went up to the Khyber Pass, no man's land. We passed Jamrud Fort, constructed in 1836 by Maharaja Ranjit Singh's general Hari Singh Nalwa, who was the commander of the Sikh Khalsa Army. It reminded me that swathes of Sikh heritage and monuments are littered through the Khyber Pakhtunkhwa area and that the Jamrud Fort was originally called Fatehgarh, to celebrate the Sikh victory over the tribes of the area and the expansion of Maharaja Ranjit Singh's empire beyond the Indus and right up to the Khyber Pass, establishing Sikh rule in Peshawar. How much of my Sikh heritage would I never know?

My thoughts turned to Papa's friend Khan Sahib who lived in Jamrud and had helped Papa safely make his way to India. I thought of the collection of coins I had inherited from my mother that had been dug up in Jamrud, which I still treasured. This was where we had attended Khan Sahib's daughter's wedding; gun shots had been fired in our welcome and the men had danced in all their finery. Papa had been given a special choga to wear and a shamla-wali pagdi had been tied on his head and the children had run around enjoying the vast spread of delicacies.

History is as much about the lives of ordinary people like us who have lived here, as it is about the battles that have been won and lost and the empires that have flourished and fallen.

I was lost in the landscape of my thoughts as the bleak, unforgiving brown of the Hindu Kush rose steeply all around me and we wove our way to the legendary pass through which Alexander the Great and Genghis Khan had made their way and about which Rudyard Kipling had written:

When spring-time flushes the desert grass,
Our kafilas wind through the Khyber Pass.
Lean are the camels but fat the frails,
Light are the purses but heavy the bales,
As the snowbound trade of the North comes down
To the market-square of Peshawur town.

It was on the cover of Sayed Amjad Hussain's book on Peshawar that I first came across this poem by Kipling.

It was spring now as well, as we emerged from the Khyber Pass—the best-known of the Northwest passes into the subcontinental plains of India—to discover that the romance of yore had now been supplanted by something far more familiar. It was full of music shops selling Indian music. Quite anticlimactic. But it gave me a respite from the emotionally charged mood that had befallen me ever since we had entered Peshawar.

We drove back. Once we reached Peshawar, I wanted to go to the Gurudwara, I wanted to go to my school, but it was evening already and not very safe, I was told, even though we were in purdah, wearing burqas. 'You must not wander around in the evening,' we were warned.

But we could stop at the clock tower near the Qissa Khwaani Bazaar, our guide conceded. 'Only for a short while.'

The bazaar was crowded. Surrounding us were stores selling dry fruits and stalls selling food, like burra kebab, seekh kebab, naan and halwa puri.

The storytellers, from whom the market takes its name, were long gone. In another time they would sit in the square around the clock tower, telling stories. Now even the few recordings that had been made cannot be found.

As I stood there the clock tower rose high in front of me. This was the clock around which had revolved the lives of the people in Peshawar for a long time.

I got down from the car. I had never known the person who had built it, I had just heard about him, yet I felt a pull. The pull of blood, I had been feeling it all day.

It was bigger than I imagined. Three storeys high, brick-coloured and located at a fork in the road. It was as crowded as it was mentioned in the travel guide. Electrical poles and wires criss-crossed around it, flags and announcements papered it. My eyes searched and found the marble plaque announcing its maker as Lala Balmakand Ahuja. Banker and General Contractor of Peshawar, it read underneath. An entire city's contractor. This small plaque was the only proof that our family had ever existed here. I wiped my eyes.

I wanted to climb to the top but everybody advised me against it.

'Too dangerous. We cannot stay that long.'

I gave in. My friends took photographs of it. I touched the clock tower and pressed my forehead to it. The tears would not stop. We were there for what felt like only a moment, yet half an hour had passed.

Dusk was falling. It was time to leave.

Ta'assurat

(After seeing the Peshawar Ghanta Ghar, built by my
great grandfather Shri Balmakand Sahib)

Hasrat-e-deed mei'n ek cheez puraani dekhi
Apne ajdaad ke waqto'n ki nishani dekhi
Ek imarat ki zabani jo kahani dekhi

Dida-e-shauq barasne laga lehro'n jaisa
Waqt ke saaz pe bajte huwe ghanto'n jaisa

Kis qadar soz mei'n duba huwa lamha aaya
Kuch buzurgo'n ki dua'o'n ka bhi tohfa aaya
Mere ehsaas mei'n ek aisa sarapa aaya

Jis ne shafqat se barhe pyaar se chooma mujh ko
Aa meri lakht-e-jigar keh ke pukara mujh ko

Aur bhi chehre the kuch mere gharane wale
Naaz karte the bahut jin pe zamane wale
Aaj bhi dekh ke kehte hai'n sab aane wale

Kis qadar paak zamee'n par hai basera tera
Surmai shaam, munawwar hai sawera tera

Driven by a desire I saw something
from the past
I saw a memorial from the times
of my ancestors
I saw the story narrated by that
monument
The desire to see swirled around me
like waves
Like a bell tolling on the instrument
of Time
How steeped in lament and emotions
was that moment
How that gift of my elders' prayers
appeared before me
An image arose in my consciousness
Which kissed me with such love
and tenderness
O part of my heart, it called me
There were other faces, too,
of my family
On whom the world set much store
So say all those who come to see it
Your home is on such a pure land
A serene evening and
radiant morning awaits you

38

Childhood Memories Revisited

After Peshawar, the trip became a little less fraught. I went to Murree. It was an hour's drive from Islamabad and was still the small, beautiful hill station I remembered. I walked up the familiar stretch of its one main Mall Road. New hotels and restaurants had sprung up to the sides but not much else had changed. I stood in front of the hospital where Didi was born and called her.

'I'm standing in front of the hospital where you were born.'

'How was it? Did you go home? How was Mummy's room? Did you see the school? The masjid?' the questions tumbled out.

'Yes, I saw the house. The landmarks were there. The ground floor looked like I remembered, but Mummy's room was not there.' I choked a little. 'It has totally changed, so I can't even be a hundred per cent sure that it was our house.'

I had gone to Peshawar to return to the house of my birth, and yet I had come away only 99 per cent sure that the house I saw was in fact the one I had come to see. What tragedy the Partition had wrought that it had even taken away the certainty of our roots.

Didi too was crying.

'I ate paaye,' I tried to turn the conversation to lighter topics. The soup-like dish of goat or cow trotters and hooves was famous in Pakistan and my hosts had offered to take me so often that I finally had to refuse and say I had had enough.

Didi laughed. 'Of course, how could you not eat your favourite meal?'

I reminded her of the time we had all gone to Murree for our summer holiday and how Didi spent hours browsing for jewellery and trinkets in the bazaar. 'It looks almost the same.'

I could not talk for too long—cell phone calls were still prohibitively expensive.

We went on for lunch and ate at the restaurant Bhurban at 2,000 metres above sea level. People are warm and friendly everywhere. They would say we are one people; you are one of us. They talked about their past connections, of extended families still in Rampur, Lucknow, Aligarh, Allahabad, and how they would like to visit Ajmer Shareef.

Eighty per cent of people I met had made visits to Delhi, Bombay, Jaipur and Hyderabad. They had seen the latest Bollywood films, we sang the same songs and praised common poets. Each one prayed for better relations and easing of visas. We discussed the Schengen countries—how though each country had its own character, they had a common visa; that perhaps the subcontinent could follow their lead.

My last stop was Karachi. It felt so much like Bombay with its beach and the ultra-modern shopping areas but was also different in that it was more spread out and the buildings were beautiful.

Everything in Karachi was absolutely different from what I had seen in Punjab and the North West Frontier Province, from speech to dress, food and language. In Karachi, each family was a fiefdom of its own, the aristocracy with lavish lifestyles. Here was the elite Sind Club where the Basant Ball was in preparation. Every family had children studying in Harvard, Yale or Oxford. There were painters and artists and people of every creative stripe.

Not surprisingly, Zehra-ji lived there. After decades of meeting her in India, at my house, or in London, I could finally meet her at her home. We had tea together and she gave me a tour of her house and her garden. She showed me where she wrote. For me, that was my Mecca.

One of the proudest moments in my life was to share a dais

with her at a mushaira, where we both recited. I owe everything to her. Poetry may have been in my blood, something I got because of my father's genes, but the thought and tone (lahaja) of poetry I learnt from Zehra-ji.

It was also through her that I met a lot of poets, artists and writers from the Urdu literary world, including M.F. Husain and Faiz Ahmad Faiz. Whenever Zehra-ji came to Delhi, she would stay with me for two or three weeks. M.F. Husain would come to my house to meet her and our cook Bahadur would make matar-wale chawal that Husain Sahib liked. He even made a painting for me and wrote 'To Indira' on it.

I used to spend long hours with Zehra-ji and Faiz Sahib in London and received my most memorable compliment from him. One day, when I had not gone over, he asked Zehra-ji, '*Arrey, Zehra, aaj tumhari wo dost nahi aayee jis ke aaney se ghar roshan ho jaata hai?*' I can swoon even today.

In Karachi and everywhere I went, every party, whatever evening we spent, I was always asked to recite. My friends would say that Indira writes and that would immediately lead to requests to hear something from my kalam. They would be so surprised at my Urdu.

I carried back from Pakistan a suitcase full of videotapes of Pakistani dramas, Pakistani music and books. I must have brought about fifty books of poetry. I paid in excess baggage more than I paid on the total trip.

Karachi was also the place of friends. Like Rana Shaikh, former director of PTV. She took one of my ghazals and made it the official soundtrack of her mammoth drama *Partition Ek Safar*. It was a story of a family separated due to partition, with members living in Bangladesh, India and Pakistan. Udit Narayan and Shreya Ghoshal sang the beautifully dramatised song. Rana and her husband visit India whenever possible. Her family is from Delhi.

Samina Peerzada, yet again from the artistic world. In Urdu we would call it mushtarqi duniya, our joint world. A brilliant actress who made and acted in many films alone and along with her actor husband Usmaan Peerzada. She became a household name in India after her role as a mother in *Zindagi Gulzar Hai*, *Durr e Shahwar* and so many more.

Connecting with someone is not necessarily a bond, it is a pure gift and joy to fully know and feel true friendship.

On the eve of my departure, I had the honour of having tea at the governor's residence. His wife was from Bangladesh, and they were known to my friends. So, we were invited.

I saw all the places that are now written about in Partition history. I was surprised to learn about certain communities that I wouldn't have expected to see in Pakistan, but I was told that they were the backbone of the Pakistani middle class: the Pakistani Goans, the Parsis and the Bene Jews. Many of these communities had migrated in the early days of the East India Company. Sindh and Punjab were annexed in 1842 and 1849 and gave rise to business opportunities from breweries to hospitality, shipping and construction. Karachi and even Lahore had churches, synagogues and fire temples.

I was also shown the place where meetings had taken place before the split of India and Pakistan and where Jinnah used to sit.

Apart from the splendour of the governor's mansion and its historical significance, I was enamoured by the sprawling manicured gardens and orchids as far as the eyes could reach.

When I left it was that time of the evening when the sun and the earth are changing guards. When the sun is at an arm's length, almost touchable, hanging amongst trees. Hundreds of pigeons and mynahs were returning home, as was I. They soared together a few times as if in a flypast bidding farewell.

I was leaving the country of my birth and ancestors; I had never come across such love, such warmth and hospitality. Happiness, they say, is the only feeling that multiplies when divided. I touched the ground and boarded my flight.

Khush raho ehle watan, hum tto safar kartey hain.

39

The World of Ghazals

'ARRE BIBI-JI, AAPNE KAMAL KAR DIYA!'

Zia Alvi-ji would say pushing his hair back with his fingers. It was his standard praise when he was happy with the ghazal I had written on his given topics.

When he was unhappy with the ghazal he would say '*Bibi-ji, ye kya likha hai apne?* (Ma'am, what have you written?)' and pull his hair forward on his forehead. The poor young man had to deal with a woman older than his mother. But I had my way most times. My poem was my thought, no harm if it was simply put forth without difficult Urdu words. He just could not understand that my friend circle did not consist of Urdu scholars.

Zia Alvi-ji was my ustad for about eighteen years, starting 2003. I continued my poetry analysis classes for almost twenty years, sometimes discussing poets, something ghazals and nazms, and sometimes the schools of poetry. Poetry was my first love, and nothing could keep me away from it. The ghazal and I were in a never-ending relationship, or continuous practice like people who play bridge or tennis. To me it was my only leisure time. Poetry complemented the peace I found in my house, in my garden, and with my family. It completed me.

In 2004, my first book *Hum-Umr Khayal* was published. I was sixty-four years old. It had sixty-four ghazals.

'Hum-Umr Khayal' translates to thoughts of my age travelling with me.

It was released by the then chief minister of Delhi, Sheila Dixit, who was a great lover of music and poetry, and Ahmad Faraz Sahib, the world-famous poet of our century after Faiz Ahmad Faiz, who was on a visit to India.

~

HUM-UMR KHAYAL AND INDIRA VARMA

Ahmad Faraz

Among the ladies from the subcontinent of India and Pakistan, those who have, over the past few years, been adding their share of pearls to the treasure trove that is Urdu poetry, some have achieved great name and fame while some have remained cloistered behind veils. But gradually, these curtains are becoming more and more gossamer and women writers are gradually making their mark on the Urdu literary horizon.

In India, particularly their participation in mushairas was part of that poetic tradition whose most manifest face is a character by Hadi Ruswa.

Over the years, as more and more women began to write verse, many names came to the fore. Their efforts have been documented and recorded in many works of literary criticism.

The name of Indira Varma-ji is now becoming increasingly prominent in this lineage of women poets. Indira-ji has experimented in both the genres of ghazal and geet. I can't say I am entirely familiar with her geet, but she has stepped forward with her experiments in the ghazal and many of her verses have made a home in our hearts with their heart-tugging quality.

This particular quality of poetry is achieved only when the poet's own personality has the same charm and attractiveness. Indira-ji's charm, which reflects the goddess-like aura of nobility, has seeped into her poetic endeavours too. It is this quality that sets her apart from the other women poets.

~

As I walked up the stage, each ghazal seemed to bring a piece of the past. Some had been written in compelling melancholy, some were like a stretched silence, some revealed a splintered heart full of despair while others gave a glimpse of the new skin that had grown over old wounds.

Every ghazal owed its origin to every chit (pharra) I shared with my friends at Citibank, at Thomas Cook, at ICCR. They were the scribblings in my schoolbooks. They were the couplets I uttered spontaneously at soirees in our house. They were every tear I shed, they were full moons and springtime, births and deaths. They were notebooks that I wrote in for decades, they were even the poetry that I lost to a storm as we were shifting houses on a rainy night, and once to fire, where they were thrown in rage.

But still I wrote.

All over the house, in tapes, in books, on notes, in records, everywhere.

Sometimes a ghazal danced in my blood. I could see it in my mind's eye. When I was able to understand what the words were saying to me, I put them down on paper.

The ghazal never left me even for a day or even for an hour. We were one. My heartbeat was the ghazal.

Maybe that is why I was destined to meet some people involved with ghazals, who wrote the ghazal and sang the ghazal.

The universe helped.

I once shared a stage with Ahmed Faraz Sahib at a mushaira. It was an exhilarating moment, one I still cherish.

I heard Iqbal Bano face to face. What she could do to a ghazal, a thumri, few could. Her thumris need an entire book of appreciation. The bitter sweetness in her voice and the defiance that made her famous, these were but the playing out of the lives of all women. The words she sang were always exciting and beautiful, but it was her tone and the life that she brought to music that resonated with me.

I have a vast collection of her unpublished ghazals which include the sublime 78 rpm record with *Tu lakh chale re gori tham tham ke, payal mein geet hain tham tham ke.* On the flip side was *Ulfat ke nayee Manzil ko chala tu bahein dal k bahon mein, dil torney waley dekh k chal, hum bhi tto parhey hain rahon mein.*

I was fortunate enough to meet Farida Khanum, who called my food sureela and my ghazals meethi. She spent a whole day in the house. I can hum and sing hundreds of her ghazals; my collection of Farida Khanum runs into thousands.

One year, Music Today had arranged to make an album of my ghazals to be sung by Farida Khanum. I was over the moon. Who in the world gets such chances? The studios were booked and the music director had flown in from Mumbai. The ghazals had been selected but for no apparent reason there was trouble at the border and she had to leave for Lahore.

But God also gives compensation if you miss such a mammoth chance. In 2020, Farida Khanum's niece got in touch with me from London. She was compiling an album of Rewaiyati ghazals and wanted to feature three of my works in it. Rewaiyati is the traditional manner of singing the ghazal where a solo singer is accompanied by a person playing the tabla and another on the harmonium. Very few singers do that today. Nowadays everything is so elaborate, done in a studio with a hundred-piece orchestra, which drowns out the meaning of ghazal. After all, the meaning of ghazal is to make love to a woman. And for that you don't need a hundred people standing over your head with musical instruments.

She said Badi Ammi recommended me. That means Farida Khanum recommended me and my ghazals. Miracles—my life is full of them.

Another was listening to Mehdi Hassan all night in Dhaka. When composing a ghazal a metre is chosen to fit the words. I always chose Mehdi Hassan's *Ranjish He Sahi* and *Baat Karni Mujhey Mushkil Kabhi Aisee To Na Thi.*

We appreciated the poetry and the music as we had been taught—waiting for the shair to complete before raising our hand in appreciation or saying wah wah. There was never a thought of whistling or clapping, or saying zindabad zindabad as people do these days. The very idea makes me squirm.

We used to listen to qawwalis at Priya's house or at our friends' Rani and Vinod Kapur's house—the wonderful first couple from Delhi, who started and maintained the baithak style of music, the long-forgotten tradition of past eras—where renowned qawwals like Aziz Warsi used to come. Later we could listen to qawwalis at Roopy and Brijesh's house where the famous qawwals Shankar Shambu sang and we would crawl on our knees to offer them nazrana, we handed it over with both hands, heads lowered in respect.

I grew up on romance with Begum Akhtar, her adaa and her nakhraas. Her diamond nose pin sending lashkaras to the entire hall, enticing the audience. I sat with her on her last performance in Delhi for Doordarshan, the Mallika-e-Ghazal who had her own distinct style of ghazal rendition and inspired almost every legendary ghazal singer after her, and I was treated to her signature effervescent rendition.

For years I had felt my poetry was not mature enough to take officially to the public realm, but when I started reading my father's poetry, it inspired me to think seriously about publishing.

Zehra Nigah, my guru, would come every year and advise me. 'The ghazal is one of the most delicate, most gossamer-like of all genres within Urdu poetry. Yet it is the strongest, the powerful of all mediums. When the few words written with ink on a white page are strung together into a ghazal, they can hold you by the hand and transport you to the seventh heaven,' she wrote in *Shafaq ke Rang*.

Rakhshanda Jalil has translated all my books. She studied with my son Suneet and is like a daughter to me. Her children call me Naani. I love her husband Najmi. Her mother and I are very proud of this brilliant child who is an acclaimed writer, critic, literary historian, and founder of Hindustani Awaaz, an organisation devoted to the popularisation of Hindi–Urdu literature and culture.

In my poetry, there is no exterior love or religion or people. Whatever I feel, I write. A woman has internal seasons. A woman is not affected by the season outside of her. Her spring, summer, rain everything is inside her. She creates her own Basant, her own Diwali and Patjarh. Visaal and Hijr is in her own mind. That makes the ghazal. The poetry is she herself.

In 2007, my second book of poetry, *Shafaq ke Rang* was released by Jagjit Singh.

Jagmohan Singh Dhiman, India's ghazal king, was better known as Jagjit Singh. He started the orchestrated ghazal trend in India.

He was born on 8 February 1941. I was married on 8 February. He died on 10 October 2011. 10 October is my birthday. Coincidences or some sort of karmic connection? He was less than six months younger than me. He called me Behen-ji.

We met a few times over the years. Once, when he was in Delhi he had called to check if I knew a physiotherapist. His wife Chitra and he had a concert that night and Chitra could not move her shoulder. I picked her up from The Oberoi and took her for physiotherapy to Defence Colony and to the care of one Mrs Chakravorty for a few days. I babysat their little son for all the sessions. Chitra emerged feeling much better and they thanked me profusely.

For years there were always special passes for me in Delhi and an acknowledgement of presence. He released my second book and album *Shafaq ke Rang* in Mumbai in 2003. Rekha Bharadwaj and Sudeep Banerji sang for the album. He said very complimentary things about my poetry and about the courage it must have taken to bring out a serious ghazal album amidst the din we have been hearing in the name of music.

The poet Nida Fazli said, 'When I get to hear Khusroo in this era of bombs and guns, it re-establishes my faith in humanity as a human and this album and book gives you that feel.'

Director and composer Vishal Bharadwaj said the unique album stood out for its simplicity and beautiful poetry.

Shafaq ke rang nikalne ke baad aayee hai
Ye shaam dhoop mein chalney ke baad aayee hai
Ye roshni terey kamre mei'n khud nahi aayee
Shama ka jism pighalney ke baad aayee hai

After the colours of dusk have been splayed out
The evening has come after walking in the sun

This light didn't appear in your room on its own
It has come after burning the body of the candle

40

Searching for My Great Grandfather

My journey to Peshawar and the sight of the ghantaghar had left me wanting more. I wanted to know about my family and our heritage.

I reached out to Minnie Maasi and asked her what she knew. From her, I learnt that my great grandfather Balmakand Sahib had not only presented the ghantaghar or clock tower to Queen Victoria in 1900 but also a hospital. He was then given a special entitlement in the form of a chair by the Viceroy and was presented with a watch, and a song was specially sung for him.

Minnie Maasi in turn directed me to my Diljit Mama in Toronto, who was the eldest relative alive. I also sent him the poem I had written after seeing the clock tower.

He wrote back:

> Indira,
>
> I am amazed. Not only you have the soul of a poet, and write beautiful and expressive ghazals, but without any formal training in Urdu, you write in chaste Urdu. Unbelievable.
>
> My information about Balmakand (referred by everyone as Balo) is totally anecdotal. Unfortunately, I have forgotten a lot.
>
> His last name was Ahuja, never used. His father was Khazanchi (Finance Minister) of [sic] King of Afghanistan. The family lived in Kabul. At one stage, the King called him, and said that he

wanted to replace him by an Afghani Muslim. The family moved to Peshawar, with their riches. I believe that he, and later on, his only son, Balmakand, were the richest in Peshawar.

After moving to Peshawar, and after his father's death, he become a prominent citizen. He was the only Indian allowed to live outside the city walls, in fact, just outside Kabuli Darwaza. No Indian was allowed to drive a buggy, with more than two horses. He was allowed to drive a four-horse buggy. For protection, he was given 24-hour guards from the British Indian Army. His house and the grounds fell into neglect after his and his wife's death, and much later the land was leased to two individuals, who built two cinemas on the site. I do not know, what is there now. This site is just outside, and to the left of Kabuli Darwaza.

He used to go to London every year, of course by boat, and spend six months, including the trip. Every time, he would bring beautiful things. I saw many of the things as a child in your grandfather's brother, i.e. Amrik's father's house.

He had four daughters and a son. The son was married at the age of 17. Like any rich man's son, he was spoilt. He used to gamble a lot. Once, he lost heavily, came home to get some money to pay his gambling debt. His older sister was in-charge of the household affairs. She refused to pay. He threatened to commit suicide. She thought it was an empty threat. He took poison, also gave it to his bride. Both died.

Balmakand died soon after, people say of broken heart, but possibly from heart disease, which I, Lakhbir, Amarjit, Harbans and Jaginder inherited. His last child, a daughter (Jaginder and Harbans's mother), was born after his death. His wife died two years after his death.

You know the rest of the story. If not, I shall bring it up to the time, your grandmother and my mother were married in the guardian's family. But that is the history of the family, not Balmakand's. You should send a copy of this email to Minnie. She may be able to correct, or add to, the facts as I remember.

> This should be enough for the time being. If you gather more information, please share with me. I shall be happy to answer any questions you may have.
>
> I used to write poetry in Panjabi, but no way half as good as yours.
>
> Champa also sends her love.
>
> Diljit

Diljit Mama did not just stop there. He forwarded my poem and letter on to a friend with connections to Peshawar who, in turn, sent it onwards and, in the way that the true desires of the heart take wing and find a life of their own, my poem and my desire to learn more about my grandfather reached Sayed Amjad Hussain, a writer, historian, and the then Professor Emeritus, Thoracic and Cardiovascular Surgery at the Medical College of Ohio.

This was the year 2004, and Dr Hussain, who had been born in Peshawar, had an abiding love for the city, its history, culture and heritage, which had found its way into the five books on Peshawar written by him. By the time I would speak to him again almost two decades later he would have written many more and also been responsible for influencing decisions to maintain historic sites.

In his letter to me, he shared an excerpt from his book *Aalam Mein Intikhab, Peshawar* (Peshawar, One and Only), an 816-page book—written with the help of a number of Peshawari writers—which was a mini encyclopaedia of the old walled city and the email also spoke of his time in Peshawar.

> … The Clock Tower was built in 1900 by Lala Balakmand (which I am sure is corruption of the real name Balmakand) as a gift to the citizens of Peshawar. It was called the Cunningham Clock Tower. The clocks were imported from England and this Peshawar landmark has the distinction of sharing the same kind of clock mechanisms that adorn the Big Ben in London.
>
> I grew up in a small alley called Muslim Meena Bazaar (used to be Machi Hatta) just a stone throw from the clock tower. I remember the rhythm of the city being dictated and regulated by the gong of this tower.

> In the Nineties the clocks stopped working and the local government did not bother to fix it. After we drew attention of the provincial government to this 'criminal' neglect, the clocks were fixed. A local paint store donated paint and labour and the tower got a new coat.
>
> The clocks are now working.
>
> The tower still dominated the city skyline.
>
> The clock tower in on the cover of *Yuk Shehre Arzoo* (A City of My Desires) published in 1995. I took the picture from the minaret of Mohabat Khan Mosque located in the street of the goldsmiths (Ander Sheher Bazaar). I could probably dig out the picture and make copies if someone would like to have one.
>
> I enjoyed the poem very much.
>
> Cordially,
>
> Amjad Hussain

I found another lead in the foreword to *Shafaq ke Rang*, written by Mushirul Hasan, historian and former chancellor of Jamia Millia Islamia. Having done his own research he wrote:

> Indira Varma can legitimately claim to have inherited Upper India's rich and vibrant tradition. She has a distinguished ancestry; her great-grandfather Bal Mukund was a prominent citizen of Peshawar. The British honoured him with a knighthood. Like many others of his generation, he was nurtured in Punjab's multi-religious and multi-cultural background, a scene well portrayed in the writings of Prakash Tandon. No wonder, Indira's great-grandfather spoke and wrote in Urdu and Persian and encouraged his children to do the same. Today, the clock tower in Peshawar is a testimony to the respect he commands even in Pakistan. At a time when the old images have been either erased from public memory or removed from public sites, Balmakand's commanding figure overseeing a crowded marketplace survives the vicissitudes of history.

The universe was conspiring to lead me to my roots, to help me find parts of my family though we had been separated by time and space.

Jab dard uthe dard ke pahlu ka pata dey
Aai lazzat-e-be-naam koi naam bata dey

Tasleem muhabbat ki mujhe jo bhi saza dey
Lekin zamana jeene ki paiham na du'a dey

When it arises, pain gives its
own address
O nameless pleasure, give your name
at least
I accept whatever punishment I get
for loving
As long as the world doesn't bless me
with endless living

41

Orphaned Again

DIDI DRESSED IMPECCABLY, SHE LOOKED MORE BEAUTIFUL THAN THE mannequins she put up in her show windows. She could have a nap and wake up with her saree pleats absolutely unruffled. Always colour-coordinated, she would even match her purse, shoes and jewellery to her clothing.

A weight of under 50 kg throughout her life meant that she felt the cold exceedingly, and from childhood would get cramps in her legs and hands. In Nainital, Badi Mummy would rub brandy on her knees every night. In the Delhi winters, Didi resorted to wearing two pairs of woolen socks under her sandals or heels and twin cardigans with her sarees and beautiful shawls, many of which were from Cottage Emporium.

In her small house at Vasant Kunj, Didi and Bhai had a large carpark across the street. Both husband and wife spent afternoons of Delhi's harsh winters parked in their warm car.

Sushil Bhai would sit in the front seat reading the newspaper between snoozes while Didi would settle comfortably in the back seat with a cushion for a pillow and a shawl over her legs.

It was such an innocent and endearing sight.

When not sleeping she would knit or make the most fabulous pickles for the family.

Didi loved good food. Chaat, fruit, shaami kebabs were some of her favourites. As children we loved to eat meethi makki ki roti;

the makki ka aata was kneaded with jaggery water. Despite her love for food, Didi ate so slowly that even eating one banana would take her an entire evening.

She cooked well and ran a delicious kitchen. She made achaars that were Pishori specialties, like the famed paani-wala achaar with raiee, which used seasonal vegetables and were eaten within a week of potting.

Other Pishori achaars she made are names that are now unheard of. Dabwa'n achaar, which consisted of baingan, kachalu and bhain (brinjal, colacasia and lotus stem), lassun ka achaar specially for Suneet, and neebu and green chillies achaar.

The achaars were neatly placed in the glazed pottery martabans and, like wines, had different ages. Some were five years old, some seven years old, some even thirty years old and as precious as a single malt.

Then of course there was the gobi-shalgam-gajar achaar, without which no meal was complete. Didi made kanji with black carrots and sent jars full to the family. She also made sirke-wala pyaaz. Another delicacy she made was the pashlara saag eaten with makki ki roti, a type of saag I haven't seen in Delhi for over fifty years. I don't think anyone would have even heard this name. Only the Pishoris know about it, that too of my generation or older.

Didi was very religious. She was a regular at the Gurudwara near her house and had special paths for her children. She observed all the rituals her mother-in-law wanted her to carry out. Navratras, Ashtami and Gurpurabs.

Each of us sisters maintained the roots of our Sikh religion yet merged into our husband's ways of life and various rites. At Baisakhi we all looked forward to the jalebs Didi always brought to our house. It was a Pishori Sikh tradition.

Some Sikh rituals are unique, though sadly not practiced anymore. Like the jalebs on Baisakhi and the meethey chawal on Basant and Tika. While bearing some similarities to the Rakhi festival, Tika comes two days after Diwali. Here the sister comes to the brother's house and applies tika on the brother's forehead. The tika is made of chawal and kesar. This is supposed to be a very special day for married sisters who come with much fanfare.

The words recited with the tika are beautiful too. The brother says, '*Sooraj lassa'n chhoriya mooli chori hawa, Uthh behen sulakhriyein Veere nu tika la* (The sun has risen and there is beautiful breeze in the turnip fields, get up my beautiful and capable sister and apply the tika on my forehead)'.

The sister replies, '*Sooraj laasa'n chhoriya mooli chhoriya bee behna tika laya, Veera chir jug jee* (Yes, the sun has risen and there are fresh seeds in the turnip fields, Oh dear brother I am applying the tika, may you live long and happy)'. Then follows banter about the give and take of money.

Another ritual that used to take place in our house was the Thumb Swarna. This takes place a day after Diwali. Thumb means pillar, the pillar that the house rests on. It's a ceremony to celebrate and honour the father as the keeper of the house. It has mostly disappeared from popular consciousness, not even our relatives remember its existence.

The ritual is quite simple in itself. At the dehleej or threshold, a diya is lit and when the father enters and crosses the dehleej he blesses the daughters and gives them money.

Mummy would do this ritual for Papa always. In our family, my daughter-in-law Tinu carries this custom forward for Vineet. Rhea and Aria light a diya for Vineet to enter the house and get a lot of Dirhams. Tinu is also a Sikhni. I feel so blessed that every year she reads a letter which I wrote to her on her first Karwachauth on what to do and how.

Didi passed on our traditions to her children and their spouses. Tanuj married Puja Rastogi, who has stood by him like the rock of Gibralter. They studied together at NIFT, worked together at Benetton, fell in love and got married. Tanuj now is a partner in an electronic business of heavy-duty music systems for homes and showrooms with TVs. They have a daughter Mehak who is graduating in acting and is an aspiring artist. Tanuj has inherited the art of storytelling, fun and even his singing skills from Sushil Bhai.

~

GROWING UP, THE COTTAGE EMPORIUM AND INHERITING MY FATHER'S LOVE OF MUSIC

Tanuj Dhand

I am told I was a really cute child. I was born on 15 January 1971. I was my parent's first born and deeply loved. When I see my childhood photos I see this plump child sitting there and I can hardly relate! I did my kindergarten from Playway and am told I was really naughty. I did my schooling from DPS Mathura Road. All of us kids from the family were in DPS. I was not very inclined towards studies. I was more into sports and was the captain of the hockey team.

I started working really early in life from the age of seventeen. I worked with Fascination India and then Walter Johnson. Along with work, I applied at NIFT and got selected. There I met Pooja, who later became my wife. After NIFT we worked together at Benetton. After Benetton, I started my own garments factory. Being alone I couldn't manage to keep it going. After that I joined Chelsea Exports. I was not very happy doing what I was doing.

I had always been very passionate about electronics and I got a proposition from this place I used to visit very often for the same, to join them. It was a big gamble but Pooja and I decided to take it and today I am the managing director at the same company, Sight and Sound India. This was also the year when Mehak was born to us. Pooja and I firmly believe that she got us this positive change and growth in our lives. Papa and Mumma were ecstatic when Mehak was born. Mumma said she looked just like me. Papa and Mumma couldn't have enough of her.

When I was little, Mumma and Papa both went to work at Cottage Industries, so we spent time together only when they came back in the evening. So, childhood was more about time spent with friends, cousins and my sister. But the times when Mumma used to take me to Cottage with her were the best. She used to treat me at Bankura where the cutlets were my favourite. Then she used to take me to Depaul's for cold coffee. Everyone at Cottage knew us and it seemed like an extended family. I also really enjoyed our trips to London as that was the most time that we got to spend with Mumma.

I used to have extended singing sessions with Papa and have inherited my love for singing and music from him. Later, I became really busy with work and today I feel that they went away too soon, and that I couldn't spend enough time with them, but I keep my memories of them really close to my heart.

~

Pooja recalls Sushil Bhai and Didi: 'Papa and I had a more formal relationship but Mumma was the best in-law any girl could have had. She always called me Noo Rani. Like most families, we also thought ours was a crazy lot but Mumma always said, 'They are all Dhands, not us. We both are sane.' Whenever Tanuj and I fought she always took my side. I was blessed to have her. She always encouraged me in everything I decided to do. So elegant, so beautiful. Whenever we were to go out, Mumma's clothes were always ironed and ready and mine, never! She would help me get ready then. Actually, I can't write about a life loved and lived in such few words—I just miss them a lot.'

Their daughter Mehak, 'Meri Jaan' to Didi and 'Buggu' to Sushil Bhai, spent hours in their house where she used to draw with her Dadi and was loved and pampered wholeheartedly. 'Dadu was an amazing singer and I used to spend hours singing with him. He made me believe that I was an even better singer than him. Dadi made me this amazing karele ki kachri and as a child, I was the only girl that absolutely loved eating karelas because Dadi made them so well. I remember Dadi and Dadu used to take me for walks to Vasant Vatika and those are some of the nicest memories I have with them.'

Poppins studied hotel management and was a manager on board Jet Airways. She married Rohit Bajpai, a general manager with Marriott Hotel. A brilliant young man, loved by all.

Sushil Bhai took early retirement and there were plans for him to join my husband or some other big export house as he was an expert, but the time passed and he stayed home, running errands for his family.

Ten years later, in 1999, Didi retired as assistant general manager from Cottage Emporium. She had an enviable career graph given that when she had joined forty years ago she had been a sales assistant, with a salary of 180 rupees a month.

She did not rest after retirement. She joined Petals, a boutique for children's clothing and designed there. She took up many window display assignments, earned money and kept herself busy.

She joined my son Suneet as a manager in his showroom and helped him with customer sales. It was her last assignment.

Didi left us in 2010 after two days of being unwell.

A mystery, negligence, tragedy … it was all of those.

Didi always had a bit of a heart problem, like my mother. But there was no indication that it was anything serious. That morning husband and wife left the house to have a dosa lunch. Sushil Bhai suggested that they show her medical reports, too, to the doctor, since they were out and she was not feeling well. She never returned home.

Later we pieced the day together. The doctor had asked them to stay for the night because they wanted to perform a few tests. She had a massive heart attack that night. The next day when we went to see her, we were told that she had to have a bypass.

'Look after Poppins' were the last words I heard from Didi. They wheeled her away to the operation theatre. We never saw her alive again.

25 April 2010.

The whole family was devastated. We did not know what hit us.

This was the third time Roopy and I were being orphaned. We

had lost another parent who had nurtured us in the most turbulent time of our lives. Who stood out amongst all six of us and earned to feed two younger siblings, a mother and aged grandparents.

We had no father, no brother, no godfather. Didi had been all those to us.

We just fought against the tide with God as our guide. For all three of us our love for each other was the wind beneath our own wings.

Now we were left with things. Didi had passed on Badi Mummy's diamond nose pin to Roopy. I had the box of coins, two sarees from Mummy, Papa's binoculars and two hand-coloured photographs of my great grandfather that had come from London. The remnants of so many lives boiled down to a few things. Even if we were left with dozens and hundreds of the most precious things, nothing could replace or bring alive in even the meanest form the person we had lost.

Sushil Bhai followed soon in February 2014, due to blood cancer which had gone undiscovered.

He was fine till 15 January, Tanuj's birthday. Suddenly, he developed very high fever and intense body pain. He was taken to the hospital. We bid goodbye to him on 1 February, holding Poppin's little finger.

~

THE LIFE AND TIMES

Ruhi Dhand

Like my brother, I studied in Delhi Public School, Mathura Road. I then did a certificate course in hotel management from South Delhi Polytechnic, which I passed with a first-class distinction. This was followed by a certificate course in ticketing, another in anchoring and news presentation as well as some work for Doordarshan. I then moved into aviation hospitality, public relations and training, which led to part-time jobs with the Holiday Inn Hotel, Japan Airlines,

Taurus Air and Cargo Travels, Frankfinn Academy, Ambika Pillai salons, Suneet Varma Designs, Entertainment Design Company, Jet Airways, Kingfisher Academy, Radisson Hotels, and Y and E Style Media.

My longest assignment was a flying career with Jet Airways where I worked for nearly nine years as the manager on board.

Now I am a happy housewife leading a simple life. If I had a choice I would be a farmer, with my hands always in soil, and have long conversations with the vegetables and fruits, my best friends. I love cooking.

Once a year, I still run trainings for a few select clients; my speciality is behaviour and grooming.

I'm happily married to an almost perfect gentleman and a true hotelier, Rohit Bajpai. He's a graduate in hotel management from Dadar College, Mumbai and an ITC-trained professional, who spent twenty years with various hotels and postings in ten different cities around the country. He's also a wine lover who was trained in wine appreciation in South Africa. He's a well-read, and astonishingly intelligent and knowledgeable person. He's called the chalta phirta Google by many.

Currently he is with the Marriott Hotels Group posted in Indore as the general manager for Sheraton Grand Palace.

~

The loss of a family member makes one pull the rest closer, to take stock of who is left before the stories and the people of our childhood completely vanish. It makes us reach out and talk to the people who knew our parents and grandparents, our siblings, from whom we can maybe learn of other relatives and add in some missing pieces to the jigsaw that is everybody's family.

Roopy and I turned to Didi's favourite Minnie Maasi who had been with us in joy and sorrow, whose love and sharing continued till the end. Minnie Maasi had suffered a near fatal accident when she fell between the platform and a moving train. But she was resilient.

After being in the hospital and in plaster for one year she recovered. Minnie Maasi passed away in 2018.

Out of both the families, Badi Mummy's side and Papa's side, just a handful of us are left. This includes my youngest Mama, Amrik Mama-ji's younger brother Surinder Singh, known in the family as Billi Mama-ji and his wonderful wife Dolly Mami-ji. I see them as much as I can; they welcome me with open arms.

Raj Maasi's son, Lt Col MS Paintal Balo Bhapa-ji and his beautiful wife Todo Bhabhi are there as well. I am very close to them. I love them dearly and we still meet as often as we can.

We lost Bholi Didi not long ago. I used to look up to her. Her husband General Bhupinder Singh lives in Chandigarh. Balo Bhapa-ji, Bholi Didi and I were the three cousins playing hopscotch on our last day in Peshawar. With God's grace all the children further have progressed and done well. Amrik Mama-ji's name lives on.

Out of the Hora family, I'm in touch with Tejpal and his wife, Bubbles. Papa would not move a finger without Manno Bua-ji's approval. Her sons held important places in all our wedding cards.

From Badi Mummy's side there is just Rita Maasi left, Minnie Maasi's youngest sister from amongst three sisters and five brothers. The youngest brother Kanwal lives in Dehradun, but I haven't met or seen him in forty years.

And so, life moves on, only families shrink by losses of loved ones one by one.

For Didi

Bahot dino say mere qalam nay kisi ki khatir likha nahi hai
Wo jisko likh kar salam karti, kaha'n gaee wo pata nahi hai.

Juda huye kuch baras huye hai'n laga hai sadiya'n guzar gaee hai'n
Udaas man ye bataye kaisey wo aks kab say dikha nahi hai

Wahi thi duniya mein ek akeli jisey mai kehti thi apni Didi
Wo ehtiraam-o-dua ka rishta kahi bhi mujhko mila nahi hai

Adhoora-pan her jagah hai qayem Khala sa rehta hai her jagah per
Bichhar ke us se wajood mera Jahan mein ab tak laga nahi hai

Ye INDIRA do baras ki muddat mein janey kaisi udaasi chhaaee
Baharein aaeen khiza'n ke jaisi koi haseen gul khila nahi hai

Haa'n Indira in barson mein jaaney kaisi udaasi chhaee
Baharein aaee'n khiza'n ke jaise koee haseen gul khila nahi hai

42

A New Book, A New High

My third attempt to write a book was the hardest. It took ten years of work, and it began in the land of my birth. It became a project that spanned three countries or what had been undivided India.

When I finally returned to Peshawar in 2000, my companions were two close friends from Bangladesh.

On the cross-country drives from Islamabad, Lahore to Peshawar, my friends sang Tagore songs continuously and with marvellous abandon. I could not join them nor understand the words. But it soothed me so much that I found healing at that intensely emotional juncture of my life.

My personal odyssey in Pakistan was to the soundtrack of Tagore gaan. *Gitanajli* was my accompaniment as I searched for my roots.

When I returned to India, I decided to buy some works of Tagore. I reread him. I had read *Gitanjali* and my husband had a huge collection of Tagore but those were his stories not poetry.

I became immersed in Tagore's verse and slowly started translating them. Our family friend Rathikant Basu encouraged me to transcreate them into Urdu nazm, which it turned out nobody had.

The problem was that all of Tagore's poetry had been translated from Bengali to English and Hindi by innumerable poets, each differently. I spent a year not realising I was reading and transcreating the same poetry again and again because of the different versions.

I was lucky that Rathikant Basu and his family were closely connected with Santiniketan.

His sister Supriya Roy had been the librarian at Santiniketan for over thirty years. Through her, he sent me the first hundred translations, then more and yet more. Supriya-ji translated the poems for me from Bangla to English, helping me remain faithful to the spirit of the original. Both Rathikant-ji and Supriya-ji became my literary mentors.

I looked through the English translations from many different sources, finally settling on only those translations that were well read and well known.

The more I read, the more transfixed I was by the sheer beauty of those words that left me enraptured even from the inevitable distance of translation. With my increasing enchantment grew my resolution to translate this poetry into Urdu, a language I have always loved and turned to. With two collections of my own Urdu verses behind me, I was ready for this project—of 'pouring' Tagore's verses in my words.

Rathikant-ji promised to promote and publish my book. He made several trips to Delhi, and even sat with my son Suneet to oversee the cover design and the selection of poems. Later, he met Kumkum Bhattacharya, Director from Visva-Bharati, to consider co-publishing the book. Without him and Supriya-ji this book could never have been possible. The eight-year dream that I had been pestering him about now also became his.

The final impetus was provided by the 150th birth anniversary of Gurudev and the support extended by Visva-Bharati and Santiniketan. They wanted me to transcreate a hundred specific poems within ten months, so that the book could be published under their aegis for the 150th year of celebration.

The task, I must confess, was both daunting and irresistible.

Rakhshanda, who had translated two of my books into English, introduced me to a young professor from Jamia, Rehman Musawwir, to help me and we both burnt the midnight oil and co-authored the book.

It became a voluminous coffee table book called *Romancing Tagore*. The title emerged naturally, organically. After reading so much of his work, it was impossible to miss the romance Tagore saw in the mundane, in everyday life, from heavy monsoon clouds to the fragrance of seasonal flowers, and the chirping of birds or the hum of bees.

Rathikant-ji also considered having the nazms sung. Having been the director general of Doordarshan, the CEO of Star TV, and then running three of his own TV channels, Rathikant-ji had access to the best singers and music directors.

In her introduction to the book, Supriya-ji wrote:

> It may not be out-of-place to mention that Indira Varma and her son, Suneet, have been family friends for many years. My brother, Rathikant and I, have from the beginning given her much encouragement in her interest in Rabindranath. Her passion and intensity for the work of transcreation was so infectious that all the members of our family got involved in the book! The availability of these nazms will be greeted with enthusiasm and we express our gratitude to Indira Varma and her colleague, Rehman Musawwir.
>
> The musical quality of these nazms has moved Rathikant Basu, co-publisher of this book, to arrange an Audio CD which will have music composed by Debojyoti Mishra, but reminiscent of Rabindranath's own compositions.

The award-winning composer Debojyoti Mishra, whose works include *Chokher Bali*, *Raincoat* and *Autograph*, came on board as composer. The classically trained singer and Padma Shri awardee Shubha Mudgal also became part of the project—she was singing Urdu nazms for the first time.

And making this a tri-country oeuvre was the presence of Pakistani singer Najam Shiraz who became part of the project, singing Tagore.

Najam is a popular and prolific pop singer, songwriter, composer and peace activist from Pakistan. It was a historic first-ever rendition of Tagore by a Pakistani singer. I had never met him or heard him before, I must confess.

The feat is that the flavour of the compositions is Tagore yet what is being sung is chaste and beautiful Urdu.

On 9 February 2012, the book was released by the then prime minister Dr Manmohan Singh.

There were thirty of us at the book release by Dr Singh—the book release had been made possible by Ashwani Kumar, my munh-bola bhai and then the minister for law and justice. He was my friend Priya's younger brother. In the audience were my family and friends. Vineet and Tinu who had flown down from Dubai for the occasion, Suneet who had designed every page of the book, my sister Roopy, my brother-in-law Bunty and his wife Poonam, Rakhshanda and her husband Najmi Waziri, my samdhan Sushma-ji and Nimmi-ji. There were my friends Rani and Vinod Kapoor, Priya, Rama, Kamna and Radhika Chopra.

Even though Geetika and Kavi-ji could not make it as Geetika was not well and Suneeta could not come down from Dehradun, my cup of joy runneth over.

I could swear Didi was with me, she moved around the room and my eyes watched her, prim and proper, not a hair out of place. Her mischievous smile intact. Fluttering her eyes, she looked at me and said, 'Well-done, Ina'.

I had not been able to look at the many cameras in the room. My eyes were full of tears for all the people I was missing. Those that fed me, those that reared me, those that loved and believed in me. They were all there with me blessing me from the worlds there were in.

One of my favourite transcreations of a very popular Tagore song.

In the album, sung by Najam Sheraz.

Aami chini go chini tomare

Tum se shanasa dil hua us paar ke sanam
Sagar ke par rahte ho us paar ke sanam

Us paar ke sanam mere us paar ke sanam

Tera nazara karta hun sub'h-e-khizan mein bhi
Har chandni ki raat mein soorat teri dikhi
Deedar dil ke beech mein hota hai har ghadi

Us par ke sanam mere us paar ke sanam

Jab su-e-falak mere kanon ka rukh hua
Naghma tera wahan se sunaee mujhe diya
Phir apni jaan tujh pe sanam kar di hai fida

Us paar ke sanam mere us paar ke sanam

Sare jahan mein ghooma, mili na kahin amaan
Lo aa gaya hun ek naya mulk hai jahan
Mehman ab hua hoon tere dar ka main yahan

Us paar ke sanam mere us paar paar ke sanam

I know you, know you O lady from foreign land
You live across the ocean O lady from foreign land

I have seen you on autumn mornings
I have seen you on Madhavi nights
I have seen you in the middle of (my) heart
O lady from foreign land

I have turned my ears to the sky
And have heard your singing
I have offered my soul to you
O lady from foreign land

After travelling around the world
I have come to a new country
I am a guest at your door
O lady from foreign land

43

The Ties of Words and Music

My last work was a collaboration with Zehra Nigah.

It was a music album titled *Dosti ka Ek Samandar,* which is both apt and does justice to our friendship.

I have had many ustads—Ghulam Haider, Dr Ajmal Ajmali and Zia Alvi-ji, but it is Zehra-ji who influenced me the most even from a distance.

She has encouraged me in my pursuit of the ghazal, and she has often beautified a shair or two by changing a word. We are like family now; she visits me when politics and countries permit. She worries for me and I worry for her.

Emotionally I could relate to her and to her romantic but controlled poetry. So dignified, as if she could influence the flow of the wind and the blooming of the flowers with her soft voice. The stars stay awake for her. She depicts the pain of the streetwalkers as eloquently as she does the despair of the Afghan refugees. Her misgivings about Partition and Bangladesh, her romance with her inner self, her realities, her truths—all are laid bare in her poetry. Each one more beautiful than the previous. Her words reach out and heal me. I savour whatever time I can spend with her.

For the first time ever as a mark of respect to a poet, Javed Akhtar, Farooq Shaikh, Muzaffar Ali and Shahid Mehdi Sahib recited for the album.

I quote a few favourite lines from her collection *Shaam ka Pehla Tara,* which was recited by Farooq Sheikh:

Jab jhonka tez hawao'n ka
Kuch soch ke dhemey guzra tha

Jab tapte suraj ka chehra
Oodi chadar Mei'n lipta tha

An integral part of my inner music family is Radhika Chopra who sang for my first album *Hum-Umr Khayal* and *Dosti ka Ek Samandar*. She is not just a singer, she is also a composer who is known the world over. She sings a lot of my ghazals in her concerts and has made me famous, too. I have a Pishori connection with her as well. Her husband Rakesh's family is from Peshawar and her mother-in-law and my mother were close friends. I believe she embroidered the crib made for me when I was born.

~

In 2017, I decided to leave a little present for my granddaughters, Tarika, Nainika, Rhea and Aria—a book of kirtans.

Besides the ghazal, I always loved the kirtan. It is devoid of noise and jarring music; it is soothing. There is a sense of calm and peace that envelops you, your mind and your house when it is played.

Tinu's daughters Rhea and Aria call them mom's holy songs.

My daughter Geetika listens to the Gurbani, and with her very supportive husband Kavi Seth goes for kar seva and has the ardas every month in her house.

All my children—Vineet, Suneet, and Geetika—as well as their families visit the Darbar Sahib as often as they can. Recently my granddaughter Tarika went alone and did Jora Sewa, which means arranging the visitors' shoes and chappals as per order. For that she got a special ladoo prasad.

That by no means makes us less Hindu. We perform havans regularly in the house and practice the sanskars handed down to us by my husband's Arya Samaj family.

All religions teach us goodness and oneness. It is the oneness that brings peace. They also teach that the power of love overpowers the love of power. If we listen and talk to God from within, if we connect with him then there are no boundaries of culture, gender or religion.

I have visited the most famous and the largest mosque in Damascus with my husband and prayed there. It is the centre of the world, say writers. I found peace there. I have sat and cried in a church in London, praying for my husband's life as he was undergoing open heart surgery in 1983. I have sat in Rakhshanda and Najmi's house at milads and felt the same peace come into me when we all stood up for dua as it did when they stood with me in the Gurudwara during ardas when Didi passed away. I have been to Vaishno Devi many times, and have offered so many mannats. Three generations of my family went to the Ponta Sahib Gurudwara recently and brought me parshad. My devar and devrani are Sai bhagats. All that we are doing in all these places of worship or in all these faiths and prayers is expressing gratitude and seeking peace.

A few years ago, I had translated havan mantras for my granddaughters, this time I tried to briefly tell them about the kirtan aspect in the Gurbani. To introduce them to the thirty-one ragas and the popular shabads sung in that raga, with meanings in English.

My idea was not to elaborate on the scientific or the spiritual methodology behind choosing the thirty-one ragas, since that is a topic knowledgeable Sikh authors and musicologists have spent eons on.

My purpose in compiling this book was just to write on the musical aspect of the kirtan not only for my granddaughters but also for my family and friends.

Our family is so involved with music and poetry. I hope to leave behind for them reams of poetry, my poetry, books, and my vast collection of music collected over the past sixty years.

You may call this book elementary knowledge for beginners, a handy book of ragas in the Granth Sahib or even a kunji as we used to call the précis books that were available before the exams.

To get the raags and the shabads correct, I took the help of the famous Namdhari raagis, Bhai Baljit Singh-ji and Bhai Gurmeet Singh-ji. They gave me handwritten notes of the first line of the 155 shabads I have taken in the book. This was a very time-consuming task and I will always be very grateful to them.

I was introduced to them by my very learned friend Manju Deshbir, who also gave me the first four volumes of the Granth Sahib translated by her very illustrious father, Sardar Pritam Singh-ji Chahal.

Another person who helped was Bhai Harjit Singh-ji who came home and spent hours explaining the difficult words, making it possible for me to first understand myself before I began writing.

With all the help and the encouragement, I hope to tell them what I have gleaned and understood over the years like a story my own children and grandchildren used to hear from me at bedtime. It has been simplified to a great extent, so that young people can understand it. Instead of the topi-wali kahani which I must have narrated a million times over, I am making this also a memory they will visit later on in life.

I would be happy if they refer to it sometimes whereever they are in the world, to spread peace and harmony through music, poetry and the sound and words of the kirtan.

They are already to some extent world citizens and will further spread their wings. Let them carry love and peace as their tradition. Love and peace as their religion. Love and peace as their upbringing.

That is what I wish, not only for them but also this world—love, peace and light.

44

The Pishori Threads

Years passed. I started to toy with the idea of writing my autobiography and the first thing that I wanted to know more about was Peshawar. Three nations with new geographic borders may have been born when India, Pakistan and Bangladesh came into being, but for all the people of Undivided India, it was as though we had cut off our limbs. We left behind our history, our culture, and our spirituality.

I had not spent much time in Peshawar but it had made me the person I am. Our roots had been planted in that soil and even if we had been planted elsewhere, that soil called to me.

I had only ever known Peshawar as our family home, but now I wanted to know more about the city itself, its history and culture, and its impact on India.

I already knew one of its major impacts—that on Bollywood. Some of its biggest legends—the Kapoors, Khannas and Khans—all hailed from Peshawar.

Dewan Basheshwarnath Kapoor had bought a haveli near Dakhi Nalbandi in 1918. Legend has it that it is built at the very spot where Mahmud of Ghazni pitched his tents when he invaded the city a thousand years ago. What is verified is that this haveli was where his son Prithviraj Kapoor, the forbear of Bollywood's first family, and a friend and benefactor to our family, was married and his first three children were born. Only the third, Raj Kapoor, survived.

His distant relative Surinder Kapoor, father to Boney, Anil and Sanjay Kapoor, also hailed from Peshawar as did Vinod Khanna, whose father had a textile business in the city. Amjad Khan's father, Zakarya Khan, better known as Jaywant, also hailed from the city, while from nearby Swabi valley came Madhubala's father, Ataullah Khan.

Two other legends from Peshawar are Dilip Kumar or Yusuf Khan and Shah Rukh Khan. Raj Kapoor, Dilip Kumar and Shah Rukh Khan are even more closely associated—their ancestral homes were all a stone's throw away from the Qissa Khwaani Bazaar. Both Raj Kapoor and Dilip Kumar's havelis were declared heritage sites and are now set to become museums.

It was at the Qissa Khwaani Bazaar that the British had killed over 300 non-violent protestors of the Khudaai Khidmatgar movement led by Khan Abdul Ghaffar Khan, known as the Frontier Gandhi and the only Pakistani to receive a Bharat Ratna. The massacre is history but what is not known is that an eight-year-old Dilip Kumar was caught in the streets where bullets were being fired and saved and sent home by a local policeman.

Shah Rukh Khan's father, Mir Taj Mohammad was born in Peshawar, where the family had a business in Qissa Khwaani Bazaar. He too joined Khan Abdul Ghaffar Khan's movement, but left Peshawar before partition in 1946.

So what was so special about Peshawar? How come this distant town at the entry to India produced so many towering personalities for the Indian film industry?

One theory is that when Indian cinema transitioned to the era of talkies, Urdu speakers came to be in demand and Peshawar, where besides Hindko—a language closely related to Punjabi—Urdu and Pashto were the main languages.

History tends to get clouded by recent events. The Peshawar of old was very different from what it was to become. For starters, it is the only city in the world to have been home to all the major religions of the world. From its earliest recorded mention in Vedic texts, it has been ruled by Hindu, Buddhist, Muslim, Sikh and Christian dispensations. Plurality and acceptance of differences came naturally to Peshawar.

Peshawar is where you find the Panj Tirath, a site of antiquity named for its five pools of water, that some historians believe can be traced back to the five Pandavas from the Mahabharata, and others link it to Buddhist times as the location of the alms bowl of Buddha.

Peshawar is where Kanishka built what was then one of the world's largest stupas and where, in 1909, superintending archaeologist of Peshawar, David Brainerd Spooner, excavating outside the gates of the old city at the Shaji-ki-dheri complex, excavated a relic casket inscribed in Kharoshti, containing three fragments of bone belonging to Buddha; these were presented to Myanmar by the British. This is a city that is home to the Peshawar Museum, which houses the world's best collection of Gandhara art and is considered by many to be the best museum in Pakistan.

Peshawar is where Babur passed through as he began his quest to conquer India and where Ranjit Singh's general Hari Singh Nalwa conquered land beyond the Indus, a territory they bequeathed to the British, who created the Durand Line.

Shakespeare asked: What's in a name? He could have been talking about Peshawar, which by many other names has smelled just as sweet. Pushpapura, or the city of flowers, is said to be its ancient name, before emerging as Kaspatyrus in 520 BC on an Achaemenid Persian map, and then as Purusapura, or the city of man, in AD 518 and Begram. It was Parshawar by the time Babur passed through in 1504 and Peshawar when the British took over. Pesh-awar has been variously translated as 'frontier town' and 'first corner'. Locals refer to it as Peshor in Peshawari dialect, and Pathans call it Pekhawar.

Less than 50 miles from the Khyber Pass on the ancient trading route popularly known as the Silk Road, Peshawar was a bustling city of commerce, the recipient of new products and ideas.

The most famous of Peshawar's markets is the Qissa Khwaani Bazaar where traders from distant lands would gather night after night to listen to or tell stories, sometimes over several sittings. It was dubbed the Piccadilly of Central Asia by Sir Herbert Edwardes, the commissioner of Peshawar, after whom the Edwardes College was named. It was here that the first cinema hall was established and then spread towards the Kabuli Gate and into Saddar. In 1915, Peshawar got its first theatre company, and in 1930 came radio, just a couple of years after the establishment of the Radio Club in Bombay. In the 1980s, cassettes of tales told at the Qissa Khwaani Bazaar were available for sale but have now disappeared as have most of the qehwa khaanas or tea houses where green tea and tales were once exchanged.

Samarkand, Tashkent, Bukhara, Kashgar, Kabul, travellers came to the Qissa Khwaani Bazaar from distant lands of Central Asia, entering through the arched Kabuli Gate, its name a clue to the direction it faced. Under the Sikh rule of Ranjit Singh, Paolo Avitabile became the governor of Peshawar and one of the major works he carried out was rebuilding the city according to European principles, widening streets and building a new bazaar, which, according to Munshi Gopal Das in his book *Tareekh-e-Peshawar*, is the Qissa Khwaani Bazaar.

The bazaars of Peshawar were all known by their trade names—Bazaar Misgaran (bronzeware shops), Batera Bazaar (pet shops) and Namak Mandi (groceries). Imagine the scenes from the bazaar in the nineteenth century, men yelling and beating bowls to attract customers, open stalls with mounds of dried fruits and nuts, bread, meat, boots, shoes, saddles, bales of cloth, hardware, readymade clothes, books, and shops serving food in earthenware that looked like it had been brought from China and on the streets, people from Persia, Afghanistan, India, as well as the tribes from the mountains.

As the bazaar winds on towards Gor Khatri, we return once again to the clock tower, the Cunningham Clock Tower. The mysterious Cunningham is Sir Alfred Frederick Douglas Cunningham who was a commissioner of Peshawar around 1892.

After I started writing the book, I wrote to Dr Hussain again.

Not only had the list of books he had authored grown but so had the titles below his name. He was now Emeritus Professor of Cardiothoracic Surgery, College of Medicine and Life Sciences and Emeritus Professor of Humanities, College of Arts and Letters, University of Toledo. He sent me his book *The Frontier Town of Peshawar: A Brief History*, whose cover is a watercolour of the clock tower.

Around this time, Tinu's friend recommended I join two groups: Pishoris and India Pakistan Heritage Club. I duly applied and was accepted as a member. This turned out to be a boon.

In the Pishoris group, naturally everybody was from Peshawar. Some still lived in Peshawar and some had been displaced due to Partition, to India or to other parts of the world. They welcomed me with open arms.

Some knew my house, they had seen it, they sent me pictures, sent me instances about it, about my family.

I also connected with the travel writer and historian Dr Ali Jan who lives in Peshawar. I could not have asked for more. He was a fount of information about our house in its avatar as Khan Klub, including the fact that Imran and Jemima Khan had stayed there in 1997 soon after their wedding, and that after 9/11 when celebrity journalists from networks like BBC, CNN and CBS swarmed to Peshawar, Khan Klub was filled to capacity. The fall and closure of Khan Klub was also due to its proximity to Afghanistan and its new reputation for being unsafe.

I have never met him, but Dr Ali Jan brought me closer to my family. After the information about Khan Klub he also sent me images from inside the Cunningham Clock Tower and finally, he discovered my Mama Amrik Singh's house in Peshawar.

This was the house that features in one of my last memories of Peshawar, where I had played hopscotch with my cousins Bholi Didi and Balo Bhapa-ji as our parents discussed how and when we would leave Peshawar. He tracked down what had happened to it after our families left and shared with me pictures of the house, the deal of its sale and even its registration date.

Amrik Mama-ji's house is now located at 65 Sir Syed Road (formerly St John's Road). The sale and purchase of the house took place on 16 May 1948. It was attested and approved by Arbab Ahmed Ali Jan, Peshawar's deputy commissioner: controller of evacuees property in the presence of Arbab Nur Muhammad Khan who was buying it and Bachittar Singh who was selling it. Bachittar Singh played the role of vendor as well as attorney for the other members of the family. These included his mother Ksher Devi, and his brothers Amrik Singh, Gurbachan Singh and Surinder Singh, all of whom were my Mamas.

Through Ali I received twenty-nine pictures of my Mama's house. One showed a portrait of a Sikh gentleman on its walls. It had been hanging there since the house had changed hands. I sent it around on my family group and it was identified as the portrait of my great grandfather, Sardar Ganga Singh, who was the father of Sardar Kripal Singh and my Nana-ji Sardar Manmohan Singh. I was seeing the image of my great-grandfather from Papa's side for the first time. It had survived over seventy years, cared for by strangers, and found and sent by a stranger. The kindness of strangers is no small thing, and maybe that is enough to keep the world turning.

~

A BRIEF HISTORY OF PESHAWAR

Dr Ali Jan

Peshawar lies at the entrance to the world-famous Khyber Pass. The fertile vale of Peshawar, which is watered by the Kabul and Swat rivers, is the capital of Khyber Pakhtunkhwa province. This was the centre of the ancient kingdom of Gandhara and is still rich in archaeological remains.

Peshawar is a 'frontier' town, the meeting place of South Asia and Central Asia. It is the oldest living city in this part of Asia, a place where ancient traditions jostle with those of today, and where the bazaar in the Old Walled City has changed little in the last hundred years except to become the neighbour of a modern university, some modern hotels, some international business chains and one of the best museums in Pakistan.

The railway, built by the British, divides Peshawar's Old City from the Cantonment, laid out by the British after 1850, with wide tree-lined streets bordered by gracious administrative buildings and spacious bungalows in large gardens. Clubs, churches, schools, the Mall, Saddar Bazaar and the airport are all part of the British contribution to modern Peshawar. Peshawar University, founded in 1950, and surrounded by University Town, lies to the west on the road to the Khyber Pass. Hayatabad, the newest suburb, is west of the university nearer the Khyber Pass.

An important archaeological dig in the Old City at Gor Khatri has established that Peshawar is one of the earliest living cities in this part of Asia, inhabited continuously from the fourth to the sixth century BC, when it was a province of the Persian Achaemenian Empire. From then onwards it was ruled in turn by the Mauryans, Greeks, Scythians, Kushans, Sassanians, White Huns, Hindu Shahis, Ghaznavids, Ghorids, Suri Afghans, Mughals, Durrani Afghans, Sikhs and the British, before becoming Pakistan in 1947.

Under the name of Gandhara, it was a centre of Buddhism, especially Graeco-Buddhism. Rock edicts of Ashoka still exist in two places; and a stupa excavated outside the Ganj Gate in 1909 was found to contain a casket (now housed in Peshawar Museum) with an inscription of Kanishka, a first-century AD Kushan king whose empire stretched from Afghanistan to Central India with Peshawar as its capital, as well as relics believed to be those of Buddha himself. Buddhism in the region gradually declined by AD 1009. The Mughal emperors always found it difficult to maintain their authority over the Afghan border tribes, who finally established their independence during the reign of Aurangzeb. Peshawar was a favourite residence and winter capital of the Kingdom of Afghanistan founded by Ahmed Shah Durrani. After the end of Sikh rule in 1849 the city passed to the British.

In ancient times, a circular mud wall was erected around the Old City to protect it from invaders and marauders. It was rebuilt during Sikh rule by their governor, Avitabile, who was an Italian mercenary general in Emperor Ranjit Singh's army. He also redesigned the interior of the city on European lines. A total of sixteen gates were also built under his direction, namely, Kabuli, Bajauri, Aasamai, Kutcheri, Rampura, Hashtnagri, Yakatoot, Kohati, Sarasia, Sirki, Thandi-khoi, Barzaqan, Ganj, Ramdas, Dabgari and Lahori Gate. Some gates were named after destinations which they faced; for instance, Kabuli Gate led towards Kabul and Lahori Gate led towards Lahore. Hence, the names trace the historical, cultural and commercial connections of a city located on an ancient caravan route.

~

In the Edwardes College archives, where the older generation of my family had studied, he found a page in the principal's journal which mentioned that Amrik Mama-ji's father Sardar Kripal Singh was made treasurer of the Old College Boys Association. Alongside his name was also that of Mehr Chand Khanna. A close family friend and the Rehabilitation Commissioner who was in-charge of the relocation of the refugees who came from Pakistan.

What I could not manage on my trip to Peshawar, to climb through to the top of the Ghanta Ghar, was made possible by Ali who entered the door at the bottom of the tower, climbed the spiral staircase, past the windowed balconies and right till the top where the clock's machinery rests and you can see the name of the clock manufacturer. It's a London address from 1899.

Ali Jan also did some research on the engravers of the plaque of the clock tower. The plaque is signed off with the name Nathoo Ram & Sons Agra. He discovered that they were an Agra-based contractor firm who worked with the legendary John Marshall who was director-general of the Archaeological Survey of India from 1902 to 1931. Nathoo Ram & Sons worked on such projects like the restoration of the Moti Mahal Mosque in Delhi where they provided marble paving and marble carving work. In our correspondence, and the knowledge that my grandfather's last name was Ahuja, he was able to decipher the font on the clock tower's marble plaque and correct the assumption that the last name read 'Dhuja'.

The clock tower had been my most tangible link to Peshawar and my family's history. I had thought that the half hour I spent in the tower on my only visit would have to make do for a lifetime, but I had been blessed. I was being allowed to see it and explore it and discover more about my family through the eyes of Ali. I have gained more from the book than I have given.

Chand, Suraj, aasman jo hai yahan wo hai wahan
Rang, khushbu, gulsitan jo hai yahan wo hai wahan

Aao dekhein mil ke hum tum roshni ke raastey
Ye chamakti kehkashan jo hai yahan wo hai wahan

Kyon lakeeren kheench di hain is zamin per aap ne
Poochta hai aasman jo hai yahan wo hai wahan

Sarhadon ki bandishein bas dosti mein hain faqat
Warna ye sara jahan jo hai yahan wo hai wahan

Zindagi ki saans jis se chal rahi hai dosto
Wo hawa-e-mehrban jo hai yahan wo hai wahan

Un se keh do dost ban kar ab rahenge hum sabhi
Chahato ka kaarwan jo hai yahan wo hai wahan

Ek jaisi guftgu hai dono janib INDIRA
Pyar ka her ek nishan jo hai yaha wo hai wahan

45

Genes, Family, Life

GENES. I MARVEL AT THIS WORD. HOW SOME LIKES AND DISLIKES, hobbies and habits travel from generation to generation.

Baldev and I, our children and their children are dog lovers. On one of his foreign trips, Baldev brought back two pups—Siberian huskies—from Russia. Aeroflot allowed him to bring them. They caused quite a commotion at the Delhi airport, but Baldev got away with it since he was such a frequent traveller and everybody knew him.

When we took them to the vet, the vet was too scared to touch them. They were like jungle cats and he advised us to keep them outside the house.

But it was not in Baldev's nature to listen to anybody. So, a huge doghouse was built for the dogs on the terrace, and they were each fed fourteen rotis with meat in the morning and then fourteen again at night. My old cook was ready to leave.

I implored Baldev to give them away to a zoo or a family who had a farm. Eventually he agreed and after a fortnight, we gave them to Manju and Vijay Mehta who had a huge house in Friends Colony. Manju incidentally is my half-sister who I still meet and love. The dogs were often seen on their boundary wall having leisurely strolls.

The longest living dog in our family was Baileys, a black Cocker Spaniel. When the grandchildren were young, they would piggyback on her. Baileys created havoc when Baldev passed away. She would not let anyone come near him. It was heartwrenching to see her with Vineet and Suneet when she jumped into the hearse van. I cannot ever forget that scene.

Vineet and Tinu have Imli in Dubai. Tinu's relationship with Imli is unique. She has long conversations with her but will not pet her. Imli goes beserk wagging her tail when Tinu mentions Vineet or Rhea or Aria. It is rare to see such affection. She follows Tinu around and sits gazing at her with deep affection.

Geetika's daughters Tarika and Nainika regularly feed stray dogs. I have four outside my house who come running to Nainika's call and are fed milk and bread daily. They are called Milo, Brownie, Rubble Double and one more such weird name—Bouncy, I think.

Tarika carries dog biscuits in her bag and wants to open a big home for stray dogs. Half her pocket money was spent feeding dogs when she was in school.

Geetika, Kavi-ji and their two children, Tarika and Nainika, also had a Cocker Spaniel whom I named Oreo. He used to eat papaya, in fact, whine for it like a baby. He was with them for ten years and died in Geetika's lap.

My Muffins, a beautiful white Maltese with origins in Singapore, passed away two years ago on Valentine's Day. He was a gift from Geetika and Kavi-ji on my seventieth birthday. He was my most beloved old age companion and understood every word I said in English or Hindi.

We have had many Bozos.

Suneet has two beautiful Dalmatians named Chhote Lal and Ram Dulari.

Suneet is an artist and designer par excellence, but had he missed this vocation of his he would have become a storyteller. A Dastan Go. Chhote Lal and Ram Dulari are the subjects of some of his best stories. He can keep an evening going single-handedly with his yarns, some true some made up with a lot of mirch masala. We listen, holding our sides and crying with laughter. Then his partner looks Suneet in the eye and says, 'It did not happen this way, Suneet did it? You made it up, no?' And the laughter starts again.

Apart from dogs, this is the fifth generation that is crazy about gardening and plants.

Papa brought a green rose from Mussoorie and he did not eat or talk to any one for days when it was trampled on during my wedding.

My mother's daily lament was 'Mere gamle!'

I am crazy about my garden and its flowers are the pride of the family. It is a happy garden, as Tinu says.

Tinu and Vineet's garden is vast. They grow flowers and vegetables and supply the whole family with homegrown and hand-plucked dates every season.

Geetika, Tinu and I have a daily exchange of flower pictures on our family chat. Now Tarika has joined in too.

Nainika grows basil in pots and supplies pesto sauce to the family. Kavi-ji and Geetika live in a sprawling bunglow in Kolkata since Kavi-ji became the chairman of J. Thomas, the tea auctioning company of hundreds of years. They too have a vast garden now.

Yet another craze is cooking.

Geetika has always been a divine chef. Seven years of hands-on service at Taj Hotels have honed her skills. She studied hospitality in England. She has been working with Emirates Airlines for the past twelve years and has been featured in Kolkata newspapers as a home baker. Her Instagram posts are most appetising. She bakes under the name of Geetika's Goodies as a hobby, one that has ramped up during the pandemic.

Her daughters take after her. I have savoured the most delightful desserts with them. I have more sauces in the house than dals and have learnt new names: black bean, chilli garlic, pesto, aglio olio, pasta, pizza sauce, oyster sauce, honey mustard, Caesar dressing, lemon pepper, Thai basil, and sweet and sour. I have countless jars in my fridges. My kitchen is bursting with pastas.

Vineet picked up cooking in Dubai because he loves food. For his fiftieth birthday Tinu gifted him a week's training with a chef in Bangkok. One could never imagine such gifts in our times. He has a tandoor at home in his villa and serves delightful delicacies to his friends and family.

When I talk to him and enquire what he meant, he tells me, 'Today I went to a Mexican Bazaar'; 'Today I went to a Turkish Bazaar, picked up new oils new sauces, new seasoning.' It makes my mouth water to hear his food stories.

But it is Suneet's cooking that has surprised the family. During the pandemic, no one left the house for weeks and months so, Suneet learnt a daily meal on video from Geetika. She became his YouTube. Not only cooking, but he also does the most beautiful food styling and sends amazing pictures on our family group chat.

Tinu has started to cook too now and many a times Rhea makes a meal for her parents.

So, all my children and grandchildren would pass that gol gol roti test in *Bend It Like Beckham*.

All my children are settled.

Vineet and Tinu have lived in Dubai since 1993. Vineet has been hailed as a star banker. Their two lovely girls are world citizens.

Rhea studied in London and Switzerland. She has done her business management in sales and hospitality and works in Dubai. Aria has just graduated from the University of British Columbia in Vancouver and is waiting to spread her wings.

Geetu and Kavi-ji live in Kolkata and have two gorgeous daughters, Tarika and Nainika. Tarika is with Harvard Publishing, Nainika did her master's in psychology from Loughborough University in the UK and is now with Harappa Education.

Sushma-ji lives nearby and Balwant-ji not too far either.

Suneet lives a hundred feet away from me. He is one of the most well-known fashion designers in India. He has given me a beautiful house to live in, a car and a driver, and, above all, protection.

He is like a father or the brother I never had.

As a ritual, when the children come, they all come into my room to read the morning paper together.

We talk, catch-up and then have breakfast together. For me, this is their warmth and love and respect. All my children's friends are welcome to my house and there are jokes about my feeding them garam garam paratha and garam garam anda.

This has trickled down to the grandchildren too. When Tarika and Nainika studied in LSR and Ashoka, I never knew how many people were in my house. All the bedrooms were always occupied.

Both my sons spoil me rotten, both in their own ways. Suneet sings beautifully and when he comes over, we sing all the old songs together, remembering Sushil Bhai and Brijesh Bhai. When Vineet visits me it's poetry time. He loves to hear me recite, he is passionately fond of Urdu ghazals, and we listen to our favourites together. At times I explain the lyrics to him. Bringing more charm to the song. He loves Iqbal Bano, Begum Akhtar, Rafi, Lata, Mukesh.

Just like his father, Vineet buys me every new gadget that comes into the market in Dubai. I love all technology and read so much about it. It fascinates me, especially the new developments in artificial intelligence. I have been using Apple TV for about twenty years, much before anyone heard about it in India. He buys me new phones, new cameras, iPads, laptops, little fun gadgets that become my toys at this age.

I devoted myself to technology once I realised how important it had become to my business. I am hungry to learn and fully participated with the staff instead of just ordering them. I took Photoshop lessons for three months with them. Corel Draw, Team Viewer, Drop Box, Excel and much more.

Suneet gives me the most beautiful clothes, shawls, pashminas, tooshes from all over the world. Perfumes that are so expensive, their price tags would make Didi faint, but I enjoy them which makes him happy. He has given me enough jewellery to distribute it to my four granddaughters on their marriages, most of which I have already passed on through the proper channels of my daughter-in-law and daughter.

He takes me out for Sunday brunches to the Oberoi and though I do not eat much I enjoy the nafasat of the experience and the bond that Suneet and I have. I treasure his words too. In an article for the *Delhi Times* he said, 'Mum was a remarkable, effortless beauty. She would be wearing the simplest of clothes, tiny jewellery, no makeup, and yet have a graceful and elegant aura about her. It was so breathtaking to see her.'

Financially I am well looked after by both.

Tinu brings me enough perfumes to last not the present month or a year but the decade to come. Our relationship is special and strong. We talk often and share a lot. Her love expressed to me on my eightieth birthday video made by my granddaughters was very special. 'You are one absolutely incredible ma-in-law, you really are. Most generous, most helpful, such a warm host and such a good friend. I've loved our chats over the years, so many things to be able to share with you. Wishing you the happiest birthday.'

She sends Rhea and Aria whenever possible. I am very close to my granddaughters and keep in constant touch. These last couple of years have been hard on all of us with the pandemic raging all over the world.

Geetika sends me the most gorgeous saplings and cuttings to make my garden look like a picture postcard. She calls me every morning to check on me. Her daughters Tarika and Nainika are her emissaries. Being in Delhi they baby me to the moon and back.

When the pandemic was at its peak, my oxygen level was checked three times a day and alarm bells started to ring if my temperature climbed to 99 degrees Centigrade. I call them my Naanis.

Nainika even makes me watch films that she feels are very important.

'Naani, you haven't seen *Kung Fu Panda*?!'

Shocking. I sat perforce. I did not understand even a bit of it.

This year, Balwant-ji gave me Hollyhocks that grew over 10 feet tall with large red and white blooms.

I am thoroughly spoilt and pampered.

I wish my mother had lived to see this world of plenty. I wish my grandparents could somehow know we never went hungry ever again but feed many in need. That we have their genes of dignity and have made worthy places for ourselves in this world.

I wish Didi had not gone so soon, Roopy and I just don't feel complete without her. There are so many things I want to tell her; I want to pick up the phone and hear her voice again. I want her to come and eat a kebab and take an hour over it. I want to tell her how much I see her on every page of this book. I want to tell her, 'See we are still three not two. This is our book. This is your book. You educated me, you made me capable of writing this. You were behind all my achievements, my awards, my decoration. So many Baisakhis have come and gone, you never came with the jalebs and yellow meethey chawal.'

I dream so often of us in the Nainital Lake posing for pictures. You skating and winning prizes.

I see you sitting in a wheelchair crying for Suneet, saying you won't go to the hospital without him.

I remember your last words to Roopy and me before they took you inside for surgery: 'Look after Poppins,' you said to us both. We were together even then.

I am past eighty now. I live in a Friends Colony, albeit a New Friends Colony. Life has come a full circle. I grew up in Friends Colony. Got married there, lost Papa and Badi Mummy there. My first child played in the same garden where I did.

I'm at peace.

I wear a beauty mask and sit in my garden dreaming. I visit all the joyful and painful alleys of the past. They give me strength.

So many people have come forward like God's signals to help with this book. A historian from Peshawar, Ali Jan who sent pictures of the clock tower from inside, and of Amrik Mama-ji's house, with my great grandfather's painting still intact.

Six of us overcame the aftermath of the Partition together.

Only the two of us are left now.

I think on a scale of one to ten we have all triumphed.

Umr ki Tanhai

Ek shaam ka mausam banhon mein, ummeed ki subhein laya hai,
Suraj ki shafaq badal ki qaba, mahaul pe aisi chhayee hai
Kuch hijr ke qissey honton par, kuch wasl ke naghmein kano mein
Khamosh fiza ke darpan mein, ek aks ubharta jata hai
Fitrat ke nazarey thehrey hai`n, maazi ka dareecha khulta hai
Kuch khauf ki leherein uthti hain, ek raat ka manzar utra hai
Ehsaas ke sooney aangan mein, aaseb numa kuch saaye bhi
ek rooh larazney lagti hai. Masoom si bachpan ki aankhey
Dariya si rawani lati hain, Tanhai sey bhi dar jati hain
Har wakt guzarta jaata hai, Wo raat gayee, wo baat gayee
Phir subhah huee, phir subhah huee, Phoolon ke katore bhar bhar ke
Shabnam bhi masarrat lati thi, Wo daur gaya, wo umr gayee
Wo shaam gayee, wo raat gayee, Ek umr huee tanhai ki
Likhney ki khuwahish yaadon ki, Reh reh ke jawan ho jaati hai
Ye shaam ka mausam kaisa hai, Jo umr barhai jaata hai
Jeewan ki jitni subhein thin Ye shaam hai kya aakhir sabki?

The Loneliness of Ageing

(A childhood memory of partition)

The season of twilight comes
Bearing mornings of hope in its arms
The sun's rainbow and the clouds garments
Have so spread themselves over everything
And a few anecdotes of separation on our lips
A few songs of union in our ears
In the mirror of the silent world
A reflection appears
And nature's panoramas grow still
A window into the past opens
A few waves of fear rise
A scene from a night appears
In the desolate courtyard of feeling

Some ghost-like shadows appear
And descend into my eyes
The sound of sighs too can be heard
And a spirit begins to quiver
Eyes innocent as childhood
Begin to flow like a river
And I grow fearful of loneliness
And Time passes by
The night passes and with it its talk
It is morning once again, once again
The dew comes bearing joy
Filling the bowls of flowers to the brim
That time is past, that age is gone
That evening is gone, that night is gone
It has been an age of loneliness
The desire to pen down memories
Wells up again and again
Strange is this season of twilight
It keeps extending life
Is this twilight, or the end
Of all the mornings of my life?

Acknowledgements

Shrimati Gulshan Nanda

Shri K.B. Johar

Shri Krishan Murari

Shri Kasturi Lal

Nishat Fatima

The Westland Team

Rakhshanda Jalil

R.S. Baweja

Lavleen Sapra

Bandhula Sagar

Preeti Puri

Tanuj Dhand and Ruhi Bajpai, Uma Didi's son and daughter

Siddharth Mathur, Roopy's son

Ali Jan, travel historian

Amjad Hussain, historian and author